REMAKING AMERICA'S THREE SCHOOL SYSTEMS

Now Separate and Unequal

Milton Schwebel

A SCARECROWEDUCATION BOOK

The Scarecrow Press, Inc.
Lanham, Maryland, and Oxford
2003

A SCARECROWEDUCATION BOOK

Published in the United States of America
by Scarecrow Press, Inc.
A Member of the Rowman & Littlefield Publishing Group
4720 Boston Way, Lanham, Maryland 20706
www.scarecroweducation.com

PO Box 317
Oxford
OX2 9RU, UK

British Library Cataloguing in Publication Information Available

Library of Congress Cataloging-in-Publication Data

Schwebel, Milton.
  Remaking America's three school systems : now separate and unequal /
Milton Schwebel.
    p. cm.
"A ScarecrowEducation book."
Includes bibliographical references (p.) and index.
  ISBN 0-8108-4539-3 (hardcover : alk. paper) — ISBN 0-8108-4542-3
(pbk. : alk. paper)
  1. Educational equalization—United States. 2. School improvement
programs—United States. I. Title.
  LC213.2 .S37 2003

                                                    2002010590

♾™ The paper used in this publication meets the minimum requirements of
American National Standard for Information Sciences—Permanence of Paper
for Printed Library Materials, ANSI/NISO Z39.48-1992.
Manufactured in the United States of America.

To
Bernice, who made everything possible,
Andy and Bob, who filled our lives with light and joy,
And those they brought to us with love:
Carol, Claudia, Davy, Sara, Yikun, Frank, and Henry.

CONTENTS

PREFACE

"**E**nough is enough," my father used to say when his five children's frivolity at the dinner table became too much for him to stomach.

There's nothing frivolous about the half-century debate on the chronic "school crisis," as it has been called, but my reaction to it is the same as my father's.

There's been enough self-deception; enough sweeping the real problems under the rug; enough blaming the victims—the children, especially racial and ethnic minorities, the parents, and the teachers; enough denial about the importance of housing, nutrition, health, and economic security in school success; enough insistence that we need another study to see what works; and enough pretending that we are doing all that we can do to remedy the problems.

Accurate prediction about human behavior is a risky business. I am confident, nonetheless, that at some future time the American people will also declare that enough is enough and will demand an end to the deprivation suffered by millions of children in a grossly unfair and inadequate system of public education. Until that time comes, let them at least know that neither they nor their children are responsible for their plight and that the rules of the education game—who wins and who loses—have been written by those who shape policy in the political and economic spheres.

Recent news reports disclose the unseemly side of corporate behavior through which, underhandedly, rich executives add to their coffers at the expense of their employees and investors. The laws of the land, including those on income and estate taxes, are so biased in favor of the affluent, that grossly unethical methods are not essential to amass wealth and the political power and the influence that accompany it. Either way, legally or not, the poor, and even strata in the middle class, are the losers—losers in income, potential savings, health benefits, and, most assuredly, education.

I wrote this book to make those facts clear and to point to ways of remaking the system of public education.

My thinking was shaped by experiences both in education and in other fields. My undergraduate major, philosophy, at Union College in Schenectady, New York, including a yearlong seminar on social and political philosophy, and courses in international politics, labor economics, and European drama, especially on Ibsen and Shaw, had a profound effect in my early years. Later, I worked as a teacher in urban and rural public schools and in a Catholic school. I was a sales clerk, newspaper reporter, radio news announcer, cottage father for children from broken homes (with my wife as cottage mother ten days after our honeymoon), counselor for youths, employment counselor, labor market analyst, soldier in the U.S. Army in Europe during World War II, director of a college counseling center, psychotherapist, professor, dean, and consultant on education.

I was influenced in my thinking by countless people, including faculty and graduate-student classmates at Columbia University, colleagues and students at New York University's School of Education, Rutgers' Graduate School of Education, Postgraduate Center for Mental Health, University of Southern California, and the University of Hawaii. Among the individuals who helped shape my thinking was Samuel DeWitt Proctor, my late colleague, who was the first Martin Luther King Jr. Professor at Rutgers. Others include Samuel Baskin, Roscoe Brown, Kenneth B. Clark, Cynthia Deutsch, Martin Deutsch, Morton Deutsch, Ralph Dale, Edmund Gordon, Herbert Birch, Howard Gruber, Robert Hoppock, Martin Hamburger, Bernard Katz, Doris Miller, Nathaniel Pallone, Clifford Sager, and Ethel Tobach.

Among others who have influenced my thinking are the following: Gerald Coles, educational psychologist and expert on reading, characterized by a British book reviewer as "the Voltaire of reading specialists," and Maria Coles, whose inspired poetry touches on the lives of immigrants, workers, and women.

Ronald Gross and Bea Gross, who have directed Columbia University's enlivening Seminar on Innovation in Education for many years.

Paul Tractenberg and colleagues at the Education Law Center for their unremitting pursuit of justice for urban children.

Colleagues at the ERIC Clearinghouse on Tests, Measurements and Evaluation, Child Labor Committee, National Organization for Migrant Children, Jean Piaget Society, New York Academy of Science, Rutgers University Council on Children's Literature, the Institute of Arts and Humanities Education, the Union for Experimenting Colleges and Universities, and the International Center for the Enhancement of Learning Potential, particularly Reuven Feuerstein.

Colleagues in the Society for the Study of Peace, Conflict, and Violence of the American Psychological Association, and colleagues in Psychologists for Social Responsibility from whose work I have learned more fully the destructive effects of structural violence—violence that is societally induced. In creating *Peace and Conflict: Journal of Peace Psychology*, which I edited, I am indebted to Morton Deutsch and Richard Wagner, and especially to Michael Wessells.

Educators and psychologists in many countries where I served as consultant or lecturer.

My editors and other staff at Scarecrow Press, who, from the outset, have been helpful and supportive in countless ways: Tom Koerner and Cindy Tursman; Lynn Weber and Amos Guinan; Mary Jo Godwin; Crystal Clifton; and Jessica McCleary.

Mary Anderson of the Lineweaver Elementary School in Tucson, Arizona, and Sara Schwebel, formerly of St. Stephen's and St. Agnes School in Alexandria, Virginia, for sharing curricular material used in this book. Experts in the use of the computer and the Internet: Dianne Kirchner of Rutgers and Robert, David, Yikun, Claudia, and Sara Schwebel.

My colleagues now, and for some years, at the Rutgers Graduate School of Applied and Professional Psychology, including Deans Sandra

Harris and Stanley Messer, through whom I have received support from the Luella Buros Fund, and the founding dean, Donald R. Peterson.

Not least of all, my family—a family of educators and psychologists, with whom I have co-authored books and articles, and from whom, in countless discussions over the years, I have gained insights about learning and teaching, especially on the importance of parental devotion to their children's healthy development and education. So much of this I learned from my wife, a long-experienced teacher and supervisor of student teachers, and from my psychologist/educator sons, Andrew and Robert; from my daughters-in-law, Carol, experienced teacher in urban schools, and Claudia, who was educated in Mexico; from my grandson David, a psychologist and university teacher, and his wife, Yikun, whose pre-college education was in China; and my granddaughter Sara, an experienced private school teacher and doctoral student in American studies; and from my young grandsons, Frank and Henry, former students in private schools, now in urban public schools.

My son Robert, author in his own right, who deserves to be listed as co-author of this book, a title he has refused. His persistent questioning, as my thinking evolved, led me to the insight about the three-tiered system of education. Furthermore, such clarity as the book possesses owes much to his talent as editor.

My three younger sisters and late parents and older brother, who were always sources of love, pride, and support.

As always, I owe so much to my wife, Bernice, for her unconditional support and patience, and all that we have learned together.

Early in life, I discovered that the world was a place of love and friendship and also of hatred and violence, of racism, sexism, and ethnic and religious prejudice. Yet, the evil in the world never dimmed my belief that, given the opportunity, most people are fair-minded and decent. When the cloud of false information is lifted and fellow citizens learn the facts about schooling in America, they will strive to make the educational and societal changes that are needed. To use a musical metaphor, I believe that when the American people learn the score, they will play the right tune.

THE EDUCATIONAL SYSTEMS
WE'VE GOT

Frustration, thy name is education in America! Since World War II, not many weeks have passed without at least one shrill outcry about the state of the nation's schools. "It's a crisis," we are told. Something is seriously wrong and must be fixed.

Periodically, creative minds, funded by government and private foundations, set to work to study the problem or to "fix" the schools. Sometimes the solution is sought within established public schools, sometimes it is sought by escaping those schools. Yet, no matter how determined the effort and how inventive the product, the so-called crisis persists. Because the new solutions take months or years to be tested, by the time their failure is recognized, if not acknowledged, a new "crisis" emerges. At the time of this writing, the proposed solutions are charter schools, a voucher system, and frequent testing to hold schools "accountable" for their performance. These solutions will yield to others in the future, as new crises are proclaimed and, in all probability, the outcomes will be the same—the schools will remain as they were, essentially unchanged, many of them utterly inadequate.

When do crises occur? What is the stimulus to fix the educational system? Crises often follow some kind of unfavorable international comparison, such as when the Soviet Union appeared to have an edge in space in the 1950s, and when the Japanese economy boomed in the 1980s.

They also surface with the release of data unfavorably comparing the performance of American students with those in other nations. Another apparent stimulus to resolving a perceived education crisis is a candidate seeking to become the "education" senator, governor, or president. At times of these proclaimed crises, government and education leaders have scrambled to improve the system. But, like a virus that is immune to every conceivable treatment, the schools over the last half century seem to have been immune to any and all interventions. Blue chip panels have told us nothing we did not know. Patchwork, haphazard changes, even well-fashioned experimental programs, though potentially effective, have not taken us out of the morass that was said to exist.

Crisis management attempts have been doomed to failure because the diagnosis is wrong. Three enormous myths have undermined all such attempts.

The first is the myth that we are faced with an educational crisis. Such a crisis doesn't exist and never did. The reality all along is, in fact, the absence of crisis. What we do have is an ongoing problem of inferior schooling for a large portion of our children. Schoolchildren of the lower socioeconomic classes have been shortchanged during much of the nation's history, and they continue to suffer from that today.

The second myth is that we have only one, unitary educational system that must be upgraded. This is wrong. The reality is that we have three. The first system serves the well to do and privileged, and a few exceptional students from the lower social classes. It is, by any standard, first-rate. This system helps its students learn to learn and to think independently and creatively, even to challenge accepted views, which is the route to invention, discovery, and informed leadership. The two other systems that serve the rest of the population are of lower quality. The second educational system provides basic skills and knowledge and helps its students to learn to learn, but does not encourage independent, creative thinking. It serves that large segment of the population that provides employees for the enormous middle tier of jobs in the country, including those who tend to work in offices, factories, hospitals, and shops where dependability and accuracy in performing routine tasks and the inclination to follow orders are requirements for successful performance. The second system also screens out exceptional students, who are elevated to the first system. The third system, which serves the urban and rural poor, is very much custodial in nature and thoroughly inadequate. It provides mostly rudimentary skills to children who have little reason to envision a bright future. Teaching takes place in settings that are often disruptive and not amenable to learning.

The three school systems could also be named in terms of their societal functions. Referring to the labor market status of graduates (or dropouts) of the respective school systems, the first is the elite leadership school system; the second is the workforce school system; and the third is the marginal school system.

As I define them, school systems include more than the schools the children attend, starting at about age five, and include more than any preschool experience they may have. In particular and of vital importance, school systems include the children's families. Instruction begins at home not at school, and it begins at birth. The quality of "teaching" provided by parent-teachers is crucial to children's performance when they enter school and thereafter. Consequently, any plan to address the nation's serious educational problem (e.g., through the elimination of the third system and the strengthening of the second) must also incorporate and give high priority to the training of parents as parent-teachers.

The third myth is that the educational system is failing to produce students who can meet the needs of our society, as it is now constituted. Actually, those needs are met. When the educational system is judged on the basis of what leaders expect of its performance in maintaining the well functioning of the economy, it is highly effective.

One need only examine the present state of affairs in the United States and compare it with two former competitors whose educational systems we once envied, to recognize the falsity of the claim that the schools are failing to support the economy. Our nation's economy has created incredible affluence. Its unemployment rate was at record low levels at the end of the last century, and even during the recession in the early twenty-first century, it is the lowest among advanced industrial nations; and the United States is recognized as the world's mighty superpower. When the Soviet Union succeeded in sending the first person into space, the outcry was that Soviet children's education in mathematics and the sciences was superior to ours, as if that claim explained their technological success. At an earlier time, the outcry was "Why can Ivan read and Johnny can't?" But when the United States far outpaced the

Soviets by its astronauts' bold and dramatic moon landing and other spectacular explorations in space, no voices were heard declaiming the quality of U.S. education. Likewise, when the Japanese economy was going full speed in the 1980s, their glowing success was attributed to their educational system, which of course was promoted as a model for us. Since the early 1990s when that economy went into a tailspin, no one is on record declaring that Japan's economy is floundering because its educational system had suddenly and seriously declined.

To think that the American economy is suffering, as a result of its educational system, is a myth, further belied by the following comparisons.

- The Gross Domestic Product (GDP) is the market value of all goods and services bought for final use during a year. Divided by the Purchasing Power Parity weight (GDP/PPP) to standardize international dollar prices, the United States in 1999 was the world leader with a per capita GDP/PPP of $33,900, outstripping, in order, Japan at $23,400, followed by Germany, France, and the United Kingdom.[1]
- The consumption of electricity is an indicator of multiple factors, including natural resources, climate, and standard of living. The U.S. per capita consumption in rounded kilowatt hours was 11,800, followed next by Japan's 7,100 hours, France's 6,100, and Germany's 5,600.[2]
- The number of persons per vehicle is a reflection of both need and affluence. For the United States the number in 1996 was 1.3 per vehicle. Italy was next at 1.5, while the figure for Japan was 1.8.[3]
- As a measure of housing conditions in a nation, the number of persons per room is used. In the United States and the United Kingdom, the number is .5 or, in other words, two rooms for every person. A couple living in an apartment with a kitchen, living room, and two bedrooms would be at the .5 level. Germany came next at .6 per room, while for Japan the figure was .7.[4]
- Because of their crucial role in modern society, the availability of computers is another indirect measure of a nation's capacity for growth and progress. In 2000, the number of personal computers per 1,000 people was 511 for the United States, the leader, 306 for the United Kingdom, and 287 for Japan.[5]

- In the ten-year period of 1986–1995, the distribution of Nobel Prizes shows the United States very decidedly in the lead. At least one American physicist won the award in seven of those ten years, and at least one chemist, physiologist (or medical scientist), and economist won the award in their respective fields in eight of the ten years. Between 1986 and 1997, the United States had 65 recipients, Germany 11, the United Kingdom 7, France 6, Italy and Japan, 2 each, and Russia 1.[6]
- The United States has a remarkable record in the number of its people who go on to post-secondary education. In 1993–1994, when 14 percent of Russians, 20 percent of Germans, and 21 percent of Japanese over the age of 25 had post-secondary education, the equivalent figure for the United States was 45 percent. (Information is not available on France, Italy, and the United Kingdom).[7] In the fall of 1997, a record was established in the United States when 67 percent of young people who graduated from high school during the prior year enrolled in a college or university.
- The record is equally impressive for college graduates. In a 1995 comparison of 21 member nations of the Organization for Economic Cooperation and Development (OECD), in only two member countries did more than one-fifth of the population between the ages 25 and 64 complete college: The Netherlands with 21 percent, and the United States with 24 percent.[8] With the passing years, other countries are improving their performance—a good thing for the world—and catching up to the United States, often using our country's education as their model.
- "Quality of life" merits high status in evaluating a nation's accomplishments. The criteria used by the United Nations Human Development project for its index of the "most livable countries" are life expectancy, adult literacy, school enrollment, educational attainment, and gross domestic product. The United States, the leader among large nations, was ranked sixth, Japan ninth, France thirteenth, the United Kingdom fourteenth, and Germany seventeenth.[9]

There are other markers of accomplishment by the United States. This country has over eight thousand nine hundred free public libraries. Its museums, theaters, opera houses, and concert halls are highly regarded worldwide. American cinema and its television productions, sometimes to the regret of cultural nationalists abroad, are consumed globally. The countless regional and local expressions of the arts and humanities bespeak the widespread interest and sophistication of the population. Some one hundred twenty thousand book titles are published annually, catering to the tastes and personal and professional needs of voracious readers. The nation is no less accomplished in the culinary arts, fashion design, and sports. And, for good or ill, it is the unquestioned leader in military power.

The United States could not be the thriving, accomplished society that it is, if it had been suffering for the last half century from the many alleged educational crises in its history, including the present moment. However, it could have been ailing from a chronic problem of gross educational inequity—and it still is.

Although schools are important to a nation's ongoing development, they don't drive a nation's economy. Economic and political forces do that. In fact, those same economic forces, and the powerful leaders behind them, determine how much of the society's resources will be allocated to education and which children will get the lion's share.

The three school systems plus higher education can be called the "educational enterprise." When that enterprise is judged on the basis of its performance in maintaining the well functioning of the economy, it is highly effective. When it is judged on the basis of its capacity to give high-quality education to students in the first school system, it is equally effective. However, so far as its capacity to enhance equality and justice and the full development of all of the children—it is ineffective, the result being that children in the second, and especially in the third school system, are denied a first-rate education.

Why do so many children get inadequate schooling? Not because the affluent and politically powerful want to do injury to children, although that is the outcome. Rather, the economy—which largely drives policy about taxation and the allocation of resources—has no need for a well-educated populace. The hard fact is that the economy operates perfectly well with the leadership provided by the first school system, the responsible workforce provided by the second school system, and the marginal rejects from the third, who swell the ranks of the unskilled service force, welfare rolls, prisons, and the unemployed. To fill the jobs that the Bureau of Labor Statistics forecasts as the largest number in the coming years, one does not require even a high school education, though that would be desirable. About 60 percent require no more than on-the-job training, most of them only short-term training of that kind.[10]

The demands of the economy are usually the driving forces in societal decision-making. As this society functions, with an economy geared primarily to profit, there is no need for change. Whatever contributes to maintaining stability in the political-economic system, such as the schools for future business and political leaders, managers, and professionals, gets abundant support from private and public funds, and this support starts with early education. Whatever contributes little if anything toward that end—schools for the children of welfare recipients, unemployed, immigrants, the poor, homeless, and prisoners—gets very little private and public support. From the perspective of the well functioning *of the economy*, this policy makes perfect sense. From the perspective of the complete development and well functioning *of all the people*, this is a failed, inequitable, and inhumane policy. Later, you will see in greater detail that the history of education shows the tension between these two competing forces, as one or the other prevailed in federal and state decision-making. Mostly, economic motivation has prevailed.

NOTES

1. Borgna Brunner, ed., *Time Almanac 2002* (Boston: Information Please, 2002), 717.

2. *World Development Indicators, 1999* (World Bank, 1999), CD ROM.

3. *World Development Indicators, 1996* (World Bank, 1996), CD ROM.

4. *Britannica Book of the Year, 1996* (Chicago: Encyclopedia Britannica, 1996), 864–865.

5. Brunner, *Time Almanac 2002*, 713.

6. *World Almanac and Book of Facts 1999* (Mahwah, N.J.: Primedia Reference), 198.

7. *Britannica Book of the Year, 1996*, 888.

8. *Britannica Book of the Year, 1996*, 192.

9. Brunner, *Time Almanac 2002*, 714.

10. "Occupations with the Largest Job Growth, 2000–2010," Table 4, in "Occupational Employment Projections to 2010," *Monthly Labor Review* (November 2001). www.bls.gov/emp/emptab4.htm (accessed 15 March 2002). Of the top ten occupations showing projected increases in employment by the year 2010, the only occupation requiring a bachelor's degree (computer software engineer, applications) represents less than 8 percent of the total.

2

WHAT INTERNATIONAL
COMPARISONS REALLY SHOW

Those who see our educational system in current crisis tend to draw on the results of the various international assessments of educational progress. These are tests in reading, mathematics, science, and other subjects. Critics claim that the mediocrity of the educational system in the United States is reflected in results on those tests. Actually, it is the impact of the performance of third system students that brings the U.S. results down.

Furthermore, the test results show that, overall, American students compare favorably with those in other countries. The *trend* of those results and of other comparisons of educational achievement also suggests that rapid progress of a social and educational nature in other advanced nations, unmatched now by the United States, may put this nation in a less favorable position.

Before we examine the results, let us consider a fundamental question about assessment. Assessment is useful if one is uncertain about a person's or a group's abilities. For example, if one has no knowledge about how far and how fast a person can run, it is entirely in order to test that person's running ability and speed. However, it would be ludicrous to subject the winner of the Boston marathon to such a test. So far as the American economic, industrial, cultural, and military prowess is concerned, it is a marathon winner. So far as its prowess in offering high-quality education to most children, it is a loser, and no comparative tests, or tests of any kind, are necessary to establish that fact. In that regard, the international achievement tests serve no useful purpose. Nevertheless, because the interpretation of results has given a distorted picture of the state of American education, we cannot afford to ignore them. Using standardized tests to assess academic achievement is a complex matter. It is one with which Americans should be knowledgeable, especially now that the federal government has mandated the use of accountability testing already common in many states.

As a general rule, students are administered both teacher-made and standardized achievement tests. *Achievement tests* have several valuable features: Compared with teacher-made tests, they are not subject to the potential bias of the classroom teacher. The results reveal whether the given school districts are giving adequate coverage to topics deemed to be important in respective subjects. Next, students are compared with thousands of others of similar grade who were administered the test earlier to help in developing standards for comparison. Further, the tests can be usefully followed up with classroom remedial work in areas of inadequate performance. These are substantial advantages.

Potentially serious flaws, however, can offset these advantages when school districts or states are being compared. The chief one is the assumption that all students who take these tests have had the benefit of equivalent instruction in all the topics covered by the tests. In other words, the curriculum in English for 9th grade students in Hawaii, Arizona, Kansas, and Florida incorporated all the areas included in the tests. That is a questionable assumption. The next is even more questionable, namely, that all the schools equally value the same educational outcomes, so that in the teaching of math, for example, the emphasis they give to memory of principles and skills, as opposed to problem solving, is the same. Obviously, students are advantaged if the test is inclined in the direction favored by the instruction they receive. In addition, the type of test to which students are accustomed has a good deal of bearing on their performance. If they are primarily accustomed to essay tests, they will find themselves on alien soil when confronted with true-false, multiple choice, and other short answer questions. Finally, the pressures created by the use of these tests for comparative purposes among school districts leads some teachers, sometimes encouraged by their administrators, to prepare their students for the tests, a process known as "teaching to the test." Often, this means taking time away from more important learning activities and valuable though usually untested learning, for example in the arts.

Hence, test-score comparisons of acquired knowledge *within* a single nation present us with plenty of problems. Such comparisons *between* nations are further complicated by conditions that jeopardize the validity of the test, leading to compromised results. One condition is the proportion of the population that is given secondary and post-secondary education. In nations that are highly selective in the students who may go on to free, secondary education, those who take the international tests will be that nation's cream of the crop. In the eyes of the world, that nation, compared to one that encourages secondary education for virtually all its students, the United States, for example, will be regarded as superior.

Another condition is the degree of compatibility between test items and the character of instruction (e.g., rote learning versus problem solving). If the tests depend to a large degree on memory, then nations that stress problem solving are at a disadvantage in the comparisons. Put in question form: Can the international tests be designed to tap into the goals and classroom practices of all the various nations? That seems unlikely.

Still another potentially compromising condition is the composition of the student populations in the respective countries, and in particular, whether a significant number of them are immigrant children, or the children of immigrants, whose primary language is not that of the host country in which the tests are given. Such immigrants constitute a significant minority in the United States, where collectively in some states more than a hundred different languages are spoken in homes.

Regrettably, consideration of these potentially compromising factors is all too absent in reports about international assessment programs. Not only is that failing found in the public media, even publications that one expects to be cautious about interpreting the results have seriously distorted their meaning. *The American School Board Journal* headlined a story about a reading assessment study as follows: "Good News: Our 9-Year-Olds Read Well; Bad News: Our 14-Year-Olds Don't."[1] Here is what a close examination of the results reveals about the performance of those fourteen-year-olds. Among 31 nations, they ranked eighth. That is not a poor record, especially considering America's heterogeneous school population. There is something more to be added to highlight the erroneous perception given by the headline. In the words of educational researcher Gerald Bracey, who carefully analyzed the results, "...only one of the seven countries ahead of the United States actually had significantly higher scores." The span in scores between the second highest ranking country and the United States was only 14, out of a possible 600, and by statistical measures, that tiny difference *could occur by chance*. That difference is insignificant, so that it could be said that the performance of children from the United States was, in a sense, tied for second place.

The Third International Mathematics and Science Study generated a variety of test scores, one set being for what was called "the final year of secondary school." In the United States, of course, the final year is the twelfth grade, but not so in many other countries. As Bracey reports, the international average percentage of secondary students who are nineteen years old is 34, compared to 4 percent in the United States.[2] For twenty-year-olds, the international percentage is 20, while for the United States only 2 percent. These differences mean that many more students in other countries have one or two years more education than in the United States, a great advantage in taking these international tests. In Bracey's words, "It remains that the U.S. chose to have 50 percent of its test takers sit for an exam where a quarter of the items covered material that they had not studied."[3] The media, including even *Education Week*, ignored or were unaware of those facts and informed the public that our students performed poorly or scored at the bottom of the heap.

Bracey concludes one article on the international test comparisons this way. "Suffice it to say here that when the data are analyzed with no prior position as to what they say, the nation's schools are seen to be performing at a much higher level than has been presented by many U.S. Department of Education officials or in the popular press."[4]

It should be added that Bracey was one of those who drew on the international test results to support the view that the schools were in crisis until, in analyzing the data in 1990, he came to the conclusion that the so-called crisis in the nation's schools was a manufactured one.

The view that American education is not in crisis is echoed by Diane Ravitch, historian and editor of the *Brookings Papers on Education Policy*.[5]

An objective and critical review of the *test results* shows that, compared with other nations, American students have performed at relatively high levels. An examination of the *media treatment of the test results* reveals a tendency to emphasize, and even create, a negative reading when circumstances do not warrant that.

In 1992, when the International Association for the Evaluation of Educational Achievement released a report on reading that showed that American nine-year-olds ranked very high out of 31 nations, the media were silent about this until a German report was sent to a journalist in the United States. Even then, it received little note, and, when Bracey asked audiences of educators if they had heard of that study of reading achievement, he found a stony silence. Yet, he pointed out that news that was not so complimentary about performance on the mathematics and science tests brought headlines about "F in world competition."

On the reading comparisons for nine-year-olds, the United States ranked second to Finland, a nation with a minuscule problem of second languages compared with the United States. Even in mathematics, while the Japanese scored higher on the whole test, American students performed higher on problem-solving portions of the test, in contrast with test items that called for rote-learned material. Furthermore, in some of the comparisons, sizable numbers of poorly performing American students were non-native speakers of English, had been identified as being limited in English proficiency, and had limited exposure to formal education.

With the passing years, other countries have made marked advances in education, as well as in the populations' standard of living. It is fair to say that those nations were actively improving both the economic and educational benefits of their people at a faster rate than the United States, where the three school systems were in a relatively static state: The first system was still excellent, the second was adequate but limited, while the third was still inadequate. Meanwhile, some of those nations have progressed to such an extent that they have surpassed the United States.

To appreciate the changes in educational performance among leading nations, let us look at some historical background. By the end of World War II, our country became the foremost industrial giant. Productive capacity in England, France, Germany, the Soviet Union, and Japan had been devastated, while in the United States it had been built up in the most technically advanced fashion. Already a model to the world for its universal education, in the United States the schools and colleges in the postwar years virtually burst at their seams with students. At the post-secondary level, this happy development was due in large measure to the provision in the GI Bill of Rights that gave the equivalent of free education to countless veterans who could not otherwise have afforded it. As the most prosperous nation, the United States was in a position to provide those opportunities and to enjoy the economic benefits of a more highly educated population. Many years passed before other countries were in a comparable position. It should be noted that even during those years of American leadership, the three-tier system existed. Without being labeled as such, the third school system was depicted in the 1950s in a very popular novel, later a film, entitled *The Blackboard Jungle*. This portrayed the urban school as an institution out of control.

After the postwar years of leadership in education, a historic shift took place in the performance of American students compared with that of those in other advanced nations, both in test performance and in years of schooling completed. Three factors were at work domestically. First, the schools continued to receive large numbers of *immigrant* children who were not literate in English and were more likely to be handicapped than other children in test-taking in English. The United States had higher proportions of immigrants who were illiterate in the host country's language than other nations in the comparison group, some of which received relatively few immigrants, literate or not. An OECD (1998) study of fourth grade children showed the connection between language of a test and language spoken at home. Children whose language usually spoken at home was the same as that on a mathematics achievement test performed significantly higher than those whose language at home was different.[6]

The second factor in the historic shift involved the *reduction of school dropouts*. Successful efforts in this direction had the effect of increasing the number of high school students, especially in the second and third school systems, who were not adequately prepared for the tests. One motivation for an active dropout reduction program is that school funding is partially based on enrollment. The more children in school, the more funds they receive.

The third factor in the historic shift relates to *African American students*. After World War II, as we have seen, education prospered. Still, we had our "blackboard jungles." Protests about such school conditions in the 1960s and 1970s coincided with demands for other social and political changes, like equality of opportunity for minorities and women, which were important to the well-being of families. The resultant reforms in the schools, and changed attitudes in the nation at large, brought a narrowing in the gap between white and black students, who represented a large portion of the urban school population. Then, "something" happened in the United States, something that led to a slowing in the bridging of the gap between high achievers and low achievers. Let us note that a higher proportion of black than of white children are in the third school system and that school performance by black children lags behind that of whites. Two researchers, Williams and Ceci, found that on the tests of the National Assessment of Educational Progress, the gap between black and white students was narrowed by between one-third and one-half over a fifteen-year period (about 1970–1985), an enormous change.[7] The narrowest gap occurred by the mid-1980s, and since then, the gap has widened. This is the very period during which other nations equaled and began to exceed the United States in test performance and in percentages of high school graduates.

We do not know for certain the reasons for the historic shift in the United States, but we can speculate. Probably the narrowing occurred because the black civil rights movement had led the Kennedy, and particularly the Johnson administrations, to far more liberal and supportive policies toward minority education and well-being than the nation had ever known. Probably the twelve years of the Reagan and Bush presidential administrations, both unfriendly to various forms of affirmative action, both heavily corporate-minded, contributed to the regression.

One of the best indicators of the changed situation after World War II is the percentage of the population that completed at least upper secondary education (high school). As of 1996, American adults in the age group of 55–64 years, who were in high school at a time when the United States was the pioneer in universal public education, represented the highest percentage of graduates, about 78. However, in the same survey, in the age group of 25–34, five countries had percentages higher than that of the United States, and seven others were close behind, all with percentages of 80 or higher. Czechoslovakia and Norway exceeded 90 percent. The United States still leads the large nations such as the United Kingdom, Germany, and France, although that may not be for long.[8]

One way to gauge a nation's priorities is by asking a question raised by the OECD: Compared with funds given to post-secondary education, what percentage is assigned to primary and secondary education? This will tell us how much a country values each level of education compared with other countries. Information in the OECD report about the United States reveals this country's favoritism toward higher education, the province of future leaders and specialists. For the twenty-nine OECD countries, the annual expenditure per student in primary education was 43 percent of that spent on post-secondary education; for the United States, it was only 33 percent. Likewise, OECD expenditure per secondary student was 57 percent of that for post-secondary education, whereas in the United States it was only 42 percent. In other words, at the select level of education (college and university) by which time many students have been winnowed out, the United States provides a disproportionately higher share of budgetary support per student than the average for all the OECD nations.[9] It favors higher education.

This partiality to university education is also evident in what might be called class size or, more particularly, the ratio of students to teaching staff. Compared with the mean of all countries, the United States has a higher ratio of students to teaching staff in early childhood education, in lower and also upper secondary, and in non-university post-secondary education. Only in primary education (where the United States has invested heavily in special and bilingual education) and in university level education is the student-teacher ratio more favorable than that of the average of all countries.[10]

In brief, the American educational enterprise satisfies the needs of the economic system. It cultivates the leaders who control and oversee the maintenance of the system. However, it does not satisfy the educational needs of large numbers of children in the second and third school systems, especially those in the third. Meanwhile, other countries, where the distinction between education for the poor and the more affluent is not so great (just as the gap in income is not so great), are overtaking this country's leadership in mass education. Those countries share some features. Most of them have been influenced by social democratic or eastern European socialist political theory and values. Besides placing high value on education of the population, they provide such benefits as child care for very young children, maternity/paternity leaves, long paid vacations, and national health insurance. All in all, these social supports probably induce feelings of security and reduce stress in parents of schoolchildren.

OBSESSED ABOUT BEING NUMBER ONE

The obsession about being number one may be functional in cut-throat competition among car-rental corporations, in the business world at large, and, of course, in all kinds of sports. There is nothing inherently wrong about that aspiration except that, in this case of international comparisons on achievement tests, at least, it puts the cart before the horse: The curriculum and methods of instruction have become the cart, and the tests, the horse. If tests are used, they should be composed in light of what is taught and how it is taught, including methods of evaluation to which students are accustomed. Teachers should not "teach to the test." Instead, test makers should "test to the teaching."

The quest to be number one and the testing process associated with it deflect attention away from the important questions we should be asking. Are children having learning experiences that maximally help them develop their minds and assimilate basic concepts and skills for further learning? Have the children mastered the ways of thinking and the significant content of the fields of knowledge they are studying? Have they learned to use oral and written language clearly and effectively so that they are able to communicate well with others? Have they come to respect the diverse groups and cultures within their nation and in the world? Those are some of the important issues, not whether a nation ranks first or tenth in international comparisons.

If the American educational enterprise were in the dark about its problems, and if international comparisons were able to shed light on our enterprise's inadequacies, then by all means it would be appropriate to rely on them for that purpose. The fact is that the shortcomings of the second school system and the gross inadequacies of the third school system are glaringly apparent. The international comparisons do not add clarity. Test score comparisons have blurred rather than sharpened our vision of the nation's real educational problems.

NOTES

1. Gerald W. Bracey, "The Third Bracey Report on the Condition of Public Education," *Phi Delta Kappan* (October 1993): 104–117.

2. Gerald W. Bracey, "The TIMSS 'Final Year' Study and Report: A Critique," *Educational Researcher* 29, no. 4 (May 2000): 4–10.

3. Gerald W. Bracey, "The TIMSS 'Final Year' Study and Report: A Critique," 5.

4. Gerald W. Bracey, "International Comparisons and the Condition of American Education," *Educational Researcher* 25, no. 1 (January–February 1996): 5–11, 10.

5. Diane Ravitch, ed., *Brookings Papers on Educational Policy*. (Washington: Brookings Institution Press, 1998), 6.

6. Organization for Economic Cooperation and Development (OECD), *Education at a Glance: OECD Indicators*. (Paris: OECD, 1998): 333.

7. Wendy M. Williams and Stephen J. Ceci, "Are Americans Becoming More or Less Alike? Trends in Race, Class and Ability Differences in Intelligence," *American Psychologist* 32 (1997): 1226–1235.

8. OECD, *Education at a Glance: OECD Indicators*, 333.

9. OECD, *Education at a Glance: OECD Indicators*, 30, centerfold.

10. OECD, *Education at a Glance: OECD Indicators*, 30, centerfold.

③

HOW MUCH IS HIGH-QUALITY UNIVERSAL EDUCATION VALUED?

Everyone thinks chiefly of his own, hardly ever of the public interest.

—Aristotle in *The Great Quotations*

The existence of three school systems and the plight of the second and especially of the third one strongly suggest class differences in education. This goes counter to the claim that the United States values high-quality education for all its children. The only reliable way to assess the validity of that claim is by looking at the record. What political leaders may *say* about education is often hopeful and inspiring, and surely influential in gaining the support of voters. What they *do*, that is, how they vote or rule on the appropriation and distribution of funds to city, suburban, and rural schools is of far greater significance.

Rhetoric does not supply the additional teachers who make smaller classes possible, nor does it provide computers, science laboratory equipment, library books and periodicals, and instruction in the arts. It does not give teachers the opportunity, through workshops and close supervision, to synchronize their attitudes and skills with the needs of seriously deprived children. Rhetoric does not give funds to programs that give poorly educated parents the opportunity to learn to monitor their children's homework and the freedom from economic insecurity and fatigue that they desperately need in order to help with their children's education.

As a reality check, the record of funding the school systems compared with the oft-expressed wish to have all the children given quality schooling, is illuminating. Some history about New Jersey's support for public education in the last quarter century is instructive in this regard. Although each state's school system is unique in some respect, New Jersey's history of funding public education in the second half of this century is similar to that in many other states.

WHAT WE WOULD EXPECT

To start with, one would assume that a nation that sees itself at risk because of its schools' problems would do everything possible to eliminate the sources of that risk. The record shows our nation has done so whenever its economic interests were at risk. For example, when Iraq presumably posed a threat to our oil supply in the Persian Gulf, our government was anything but penurious. Or, when our investments appeared to be threatened, as it seemed in Mexico and in Brazil in the late 1990s, our coffers were opened wide to bolster the threatened economies. The same was done when investors in savings and loan associations in our own country were facing enormous losses.

This was not the case in New Jersey, when the state's supreme court deemed it *essential for the education of its children* that the appropriation should be increased to a desired level. One would expect that political leaders would hasten to satisfy the court's order, and would do it happily in the hope of achieving the desired effect and not merely because of the court's mandate. That would be one's expectation, especially if one believed that high-quality education for all children and academic accomplishment by all were truly valued. New Jersey's history shows that most of its leaders did everything possible to evade the requirement set by the court.

Although New Jersey in 1871 was the last state in the nation to provide free public education, a few years later it made amends for tardiness by amending its constitution in a most noteworthy way. Henceforth, all children aged five to eighteen were guaranteed a "thorough and efficient" public school education. This was not to be just rudimentary education. Rather, the constitution now imposed on the state legislature the duty of providing such education as was necessary to fit children "for the ordinary duties of citizenship...with the view of securing the common rights of all, before tendering peculiar advantages to any."[1]

In 1871, the state of New Jersey was providing all school districts 75 percent of their costs, excluding those for construction and repair. However, by 1881, businessmen and prosperous farmers, no longer willing to pay for the implementation of a thorough and efficient education for all children, got the state legislature to require county governments to bear 90 percent of the costs. So for New Jersey, as in many other states, the action was regression to the former condition: The schools once again had to depend mostly on local support. The consequence in New Jersey, and in the many other states that did the same, was to increase the disparity of the school budget between rich and poor communities.

In the 1970s, almost a century later, those seeking to correct the inequities in school funding turned to the courts, having despaired of achieving a greater degree of equity through the state executive or the legislature. By that time in New Jersey, as the state supreme court discovered, the twenty-nine poorest urban school districts contained the "overwhelming majority" of students with the lowest socioeconomic ranking in the state. Furthermore, 71 percent of all minority students were in those same poorest districts.[2]

In a landmark decision in 1973, the New Jersey Supreme Court declared the state's system of financing the public schools unconstitutional because it failed to provide urban students equal opportunity for a thorough and efficient education.[3] By this action, which called for increased state funding, the state judicial system responded to the needs of urban students. The court made four more decisions, one of which called for evidence of substantive improvements. To prepare students for their future role as citizens and competitors in the labor market, "each pupil shall be offered an equal opportunity to receive an education of such excellence as will meet the constitutional standard [for a thorough and efficient education]."[4]

As it turned out, celebrations on the part of the plaintiffs and their many allies were premature. The state legislature, dominated by representatives from suburban districts, and showing what was to become habitual behavior, dragged its feet.

Pressed by the court, the state legislature enacted the *Public School Elementary and Secondary Education Act* (1975), but *did not fund it* in

1975 or in 1976. Only when the court ordered the schools closed during summer session did the legislature act, and very quickly, thanks to the fact that the court's gun was at its head. The outcome was the introduction of New Jersey's first state income tax.

Still, the resourceful legislature was able to squirm on behalf of its suburban districts. The old system of local funding was retained, despite the court's decision branding it unconstitutional. One of the few major concessions to the court's mandate was the inclusion of equalization aid. Even this violated the spirit, if not the letter of the court's decisions, because this aid went to students in all districts, including those of the wealthy.

One feature of the act passed by the legislature was presumably to achieve equalization, not by larger state expenditures to the urban districts but by placing "caps" (maximum spending levels) on local school expenditures. Another feature was the requirement that all students experience a minimum curriculum of basic skills. Educational researcher Jean Anyon[5] reports on the results of that curriculum approach.

> A basic skills curriculum focused instruction on rote, skill-drill exercises which typically emphasized cognitive skills of recognition and recall. Such a curriculum, utilizing primarily workbooks and worksheets, was relatively inexpensive, and would not require that the state invest in computers, science equipment, or other curriculum materials for urban schools. During the next two decades, the cities, which were closely monitored by the state, did offer a basic skills curriculum to students, while the suburbs continued to offer sophisticated curriculum programs and a range of courses.[6]

Anyon reports that the basic skills curriculum focuses mainly on the cognitive skills of recognition and recall and relies mainly on workbook and other deskwork activities by students. With such instruction methods, she adds, students do not gain experience with computers, science equipment, and other technological resources. They also lack much more: Students in such a curriculum would not be experiencing the questioning and the give and take that opens and stimulates minds, encourages students to think and problem solve, and engages them in the subject matter. These are the skills essential to learning in rigorous programs at the secondary and post-secondary levels.

The kind of thinking that led to the end run around the court's mandate was clearly spelled out by no less a person than the education commissioner. He was quoted as saying in 1976 that there was no point in pouring money into the urban schools because, to be honest about it, urban children, even with years of remediation, would not be able to perform as well as their suburban counterparts. The position of the state government (not surprisingly, the same as the commissioner's), as reported in the courts decision, was unequivocal. "The education [basic skills] currently offered in these poorer urban districts is tailored to the students' present need....[T]hese students simply cannot benefit from the kind of vastly superior course offerings found in the richer districts."[7]

The failure of the legislature's minimum basic skills approach to improve the performance of urban students soon became apparent as reports of the statewide skills tests were issued. In urban centers like Newark, Camden, and Orange, two-thirds to three-quarters of students in various grades failed reading and math tests.[8] The education commissioner's expectations of dismal performance by urban children were fulfilled.

With the passing years, the budgetary inequalities increased as the gap between the richer and poorer districts widened. By 1988, the difference between the two was at a 10:1 ratio, typified by the $1,128,051 per pupil property wealth of children in Princeton compared to that of $111,475 for Trenton students.[9] In other words, the potential source of local school funds based on property taxes was ten times greater in the affluent than in the poor communities.

Once again, plaintiffs went to court and argued the unconstitutionality of the funding system established by the 1975 act. The Education Law Center filed *Abbott v. Burke* on behalf of disadvantaged urban students against the state of New Jersey, Burke being the commissioner of education at the time. This began a long series of *Abbott* decisions into the new century. Note the chronology: The plaintiffs filed suit in 1981. Records for the trial were completed in 1987. The court's decision was announced in 1990. Nine years passed while thousands of urban children attended underfunded schools. And the necessary transformations still had to be debated and acted upon by a recalcitrant legislature, aided and abetted, as it turned out, by a state administration that was as partial to suburban districts and state-taxation controls as most of its predecessors.

In *Abbott v. Burke* (1990), the court decided that the legislature had to amend its 1975 act in such a way as to assure that poor districts would be funded at a par with the wealthy ones. The existing disparities in financing had to be eliminated so that students of the poorer districts could enter the same job market and the same society as those from the wealthier districts. In answer to the state's claim that sophisticated courses in the curriculum are not essential for a thorough and efficient education, the court raised the central question that, in one form or another, had been asked countless times in the last century and before by those championing equal education: "Then why do the wealthier school districts offer them?"

This 1990 landmark decision, which can serve as a textbook to those genuinely interested in working toward a single school system of high quality for all students in the United States, contains the following statement of beliefs:

> We have decided this case on the premise that the children of poorer urban districts are as capable as all others; that their deficiencies stem from their socioeconomic status; and that through effective education and *changes in that socioeconomic status* [emphasis added], they can perform as well as others. Our constitutional mandate does not allow us to consign poorer children permanently to an inferior education on the theory that they cannot afford a better one or that they would not benefit from it.[10]

Action—and reaction—came speedily. Within a month after the court's decision, the newly elected Democratic governor, Jim Florio, and Democratic leadership in the legislature succeeded in enacting legislation that would "reduce expenditure disparities between the state's 30 poorest urban communities and its 108 wealthiest districts, as mandated by the court."[11] The new legislation to implement the court's decision enraged taxpayers. It raised the state income tax, doubling the income tax rate for the wealthiest 20 percent. The intensity of the outcry was unanticipated: "Motorcades converged on the state capitol. The governor's approval rating dropped 19 points, and those who ranked his performance as poor more than doubled from 14% to 32%."[12] This unpopularity, combined with his opponent's promise to reduce taxes, led to his defeat. Shortly after her election as governor, Christie Whitman proceeded to slash taxes and continued, in the old mold, to resist any significant change.

So, as in the past, the opponents of equity for urban children won out and the new legislation was modified before it could take effect. The modified and reduced increases in taxes did little more than offset higher costs. Not surprisingly, in 1994 the court found the modified plan unconstitutional, declaring that the state was responsible for the educational disparity and that only the state could correct it.

The state legislature's response to the 1994 decision finally came in December 1996. What it offered in its *Comprehensive Educational Improvement and Financing Act* was essentially another version of the basic skills curriculum of previous decades. Through this mandated minimum curriculum—and some twisted logic—they implied the urban schools would achieve educational parity with the others. Five months later, the court declared the funding provisions of the new legislation unconstitutional.

With painful consistency, the legislature enacted still another plan to meet the court's requirements. And again, in 1997, the state supreme court found the legislative response unconstitutional, declaring that the legislation had failed to guarantee sufficient funds to provide the help students in the poorer urban school districts needed to achieve the requisite academic standards. The state supreme court ordered judicial relief in connection with parity funding and remanded to the superior court the matters concerning supplemental programs and facility needs. The superior court, in turn, based its own report on the recommendations of expert advisers.[13]

In May 1998, having had the superior court's recommendations, the supreme court issued another decision. By that time, the late chief justice of New Jersey's supreme court, a champion of urban schools, had been replaced by the governor's attorney general. She chose not to recuse herself in this case, despite her prior involvement as attorney general. At issue, besides funding parity and facilities needs, was the demand of the urban school districts that all urban children be given intensive preschool beginning at age three. They were also to be given after-school and summer programs and social and health services. The recommendation of the superior court lent much support to those demands of the plaintiffs. In fact, the superior court went further by proposing that the state spend $312 million to add full-day kindergarten and preschool for children ages three and four, and for summer school and social service programs in urban schools. However, the decision of the state supreme court echoed the views of Governor Whitman's office much more than those of the superior court. It favored some positive changes but lent insufficient budgetary support for some of the most crucial needs.

Theoretically, based on the supreme court's decision, all urban children are to be given intensive preschool beginning at age three, as well as after-school and summer programs and social and health services. The superior court's recommended appropriations for full-day kindergarten and preschool for children ages three and four, for summer school, and social service programs addressed those needs. Those recommendations were entirely consistent with the positions taken by the state supreme court in its previous decisions, under the leadership of the previous chief justice. Now, however, in the words of an editorial in central New Jersey's *Home News Tribune*, under the new chief justice "the [Supreme] Court has reversed the course and bows to the [Governor] Whitman administration's selfish logic that no money is needed in urban districts and that the court should stay out of the debate."[14]

The Governor and Education Commissioner, the editorial continues, "know the GOP constituency is in the predominantly white, middle-class suburbs and that residents of cities, many of whom are poor minorities, don't vote. This administration will offer tokens to urban schools, such as the 'Success For All' early-intervention program. But it won't make financial sacrifices."[15]

Actually, because of the relentless efforts of the Education Law Center and many organized groups in the state, the 1998 supreme court decision, followed by two more decisions, was transformed into a potential victory for urban children in almost 450 schools in 30 school districts. The measures ordered by the court constitute a legal framework that could provide those children with far-reaching benefits, including equitable funding, preschool education, adequate facilities, and reform of teaching and learning through whole-school reform programs.[16] Of course, these must be funded. Already, by 2001, litigation was under way because of the state's failure to provide preschool facilities, and undoubtedly other roadblocks will be put in the way of implementation. Nonetheless, this example of success in New Jersey shows the kind of persistent and tireless ongoing campaign required to overcome some of the many obstacles to quality education for children of poor families.

Up to this point the drama involving the lives of millions of people and the welfare of the entire state unfolded from February 1970, when the plaintiffs first filed suit, to the late 1990s. Little had changed except perhaps the level of frustration on the part of those seeking change. The urban children suffered the consequences of living in disadvantaged communities and attending school in disadvantaged districts. Children in the economically comfortable and wealthy communities enjoyed the benefits of advantaged school districts. The state executive and legislative branches had succeeded in maintaining the status quo.

New Jersey is not unique in this regard. The histories are different in different states, but most have ended up in the same position, maintaining an inequitable system. Recent events in New York State show that it is no exception. In January 2001, a judge of the New York State Supreme Court ruled that New York City schools were "inadequate and seriously underfinanced."[17] The judge charged that the state had failed to meet its constitutional obligation to provide "a sound, basic education" and ordered it to do so. On 25 June 2002, a New York State Appeals Court overturned the judge's ruling, claiming that the state "was obliged to provide no more than a middle-school-level education and to prepare students for nothing more than the lowest-level jobs."[18] In an editorial, the *New York Times* had this to say about the Appeals Court decision: "In a particularly troubling piece of reasoning, the decision suggested that the state would satisfy its constitutional duty if the education provided students would qualify them for jobs as fast-food cooks or bike messengers."[19] The lone dissenter in this four-to-one decision "said in essence that it was blaming the victim."[20]

So much, then, for the claim that the majority of elected leaders of this nation genuinely want all of the people to be well educated. If they could have that without increasing costs, and if the many more graduates would promise to accept life as they would find it, take the jobs that were available, without any trouble-making and new demands, the leaders might be quite accepting of the change. However, such conditions exist only in fantasy.

The attitude of the nation's business and political leaders is not a matter of personal animosity or ill will. It's not as if cartoon-character businessmen, full-bellied and smoking thick cigars as they sit behind long, well-polished mahogany desks, spend their hours thinking about how they can deny a decent education to the poor children in the cities and rural towns. It is, rather, a logical outcome of the operation of a system that places high value on the accumulation of capital. Taxation obviously reduces personal and corporate capital. When it is used to educate one's own children, or a desired elite, the outlay is considered worthwhile. However, there is no reward in this system for reducing one's capital in order to support the education of other people's children, especially when *those* children are not perceived as offering any future profitable return to the taxpayer.

EVERYTHING, AND NOTHING, HAS CHANGED

This attitude of modern-day leaders is not new and not a product of the late twentieth century, or even of the twentieth century itself. As early as the 1820s, mechanics and artisans along the eastern seaboard, stretching from Boston to Washington, having won a measure of political equality, began to strive for educational equality. An 1829 newspaper account reported on the purposes of a new organization, the Association for the Protection of Industry and for the Promotion of National Education (At the time, the word "industry" was equivalent in meaning to "labor").[21]

> *Reasons for the Formation of the Association.* Because industry is at present unprotected, oppressed, despised, and indirectly deprived of its just reward; and because there is in this republic no system of education befitting a republic; none which secures the equal maintenance, protection, and instruction of youth—of the children of the poor man as of the rich; none which is at once free from sectarian and clerical influences, and from aristocratic distinction; none which is calculated to induce in the rising generation those habits of industry, those principles of sound morality, those feelings of brotherly love, together with those solid intellectual acquirements, which are necessary to secure to all the fair exercise of those equal political rights set forth in the institutions of the land.[22]

This was part of a call for public elementary education. Such calls put forth by workers in Philadelphia, Trenton, New York, Boston, and Washington seem so tame and so sound, that even now some people may be surprised at reading the heated opposition to it. When an organization, the Mechanics and other Working Men of the City and County of New York, asked "for the adoption of a general system of instruction at the expense of the State which shall afford the children, however, rich or poor, equal means to obtain useful learning," the *National Gazette* of Philadelphia, reported this demand and characterized it as a gross injustice, "equivalent to the idea of an actual compulsory partition of their substance."[23] The rich would not share their wealth or toil for others.

Education in the United States has changed as much since the 1820s as the nation itself. The struggles of groups like these precursors to labor unions contributed greatly to the success in gaining free elementary and, later, secondary schools. Yet, resistance seems as strong as ever to "a compulsory partition of their substance."

BUT WE NEED THEM!

The general viewpoint expressed in the media and repeated over and over again by America's leaders goes like this: We need the population well educated in this, the information age. If we are to compete in the global economy, our young people must be well schooled in mathematics; the sciences, including computer science; foreign languages; and economics. Their skills must be elevated to qualify them for positions in the knowledge-intensive job categories. Their creative gifts must be developed to the fullest to give this nation an edge. Our future rests on high-quality education.

Let us compare that generally accepted viewpoint with a version of future occupational needs developed by a national agency known for its expertness on occupations. The Bureau of Labor Statistics developed projections of the fastest growing occupations in the period of 1994–2005. At the top of the list are the following: cashiers, janitors and cleaners, retail salespersons, and waiters and waitresses.[24] Of the top ten occupations showing projected increases in employment by the year 2010, the only occupation requiring a bachelor's degree (computer software engineer, applications) represents less than 8 percent of the total. About 60 percent require no more than on-the-job training, most of them only short-term training of that kind.[25]

Those who value the development of human potential would argue that future cashiers, janitors and cleaners, salespersons, and waiters and waitresses deserve the very best education. However, no one would claim that to do their part in the economy and to earn their wages, they need to be instructed in trigonometry, eighteenth-century English literature, French, or biology. Effective performance in those occupations requires no more than high school level (perhaps only ninth-grade level) literacy and numerical skills. Those occupations also require such personal characteristics as dependability in carrying out the functions of the job and agreeableness in relationships with those whom they serve, both of which could be cultivated in a school that values such characteristics. In any event, it would be difficult to justify tax increases to provide students who will enter such occupations with more than that, except on the grounds that instruction beyond that level could enhance their behavior as future parents and citizens, and enrich their lives. These reasons, while very popular in politicians' rhetoric, and used by educators to justify support for schools, are not very convincing arguments in the market place, because in point of fact they do not readily and rapidly convert into profit.

Still, angry parents and fair-minded citizens fight for substantial improvements. Their actions lead to the court battles that have been so prominent the last half century. In response, politicians *say* they support change, but do very little to achieve it.

CONTRADICTIONS AND DELUSIONS

At one and the same time, our nation's leaders speak in contradictory terms. They declare that the educational system is in terrible shape and we must reform it by achieving specified ambitious goals within a specified brief period of time. Yet, the states insist that they cannot afford to provide more teachers, reduce class size, give free medical and dental care to all children in need, and assure them nourishing food and secure housing. And the taxpayers, by the power of their political influence, veto support for more than the minimum the political system proposes. Finally, even if we gave the best possible schooling, our society would be in no position to say to the children that if you take your schoolwork seriously, you can be assured of a secure future in the form of job and income.

The leaders of the nation make grandiose promises. There is no better example than *Goals 2000: Educate America Act*.[26] This legislation had its origins in the National Educational Goals promulgated in February 1990 by President Bush and the National Governors' Association, which at the time was led by then Governor Clinton.

Until the enactment of the education act of 2002, "Goals 2000" was the centerpiece of the nation's efforts to transform education. To quote from the Senate's report on this act, it is "a blueprint for revitalizing education in America. . . . It aims to change America's approach to education reform. Rather than supporting piecemeal improvements, Goals 2000 would stimulate the development and implementation of systemic reform plans."

And the goals themselves—all children start school ready to learn, high achievement by all students in all school subjects, universal adult literacy, drug and crime-free schools, and so on—are nothing short of magnificent. Achieving them would be cause for national celebration.

At the time the president and Congress endorsed them, there was about as much chance of achieving these goals by the year 2000 as there was of eliminating poverty, or to be more fanciful, of establishing a colony on the moon.

This is the stuff of which delusions are made. A delusion is defined as a "fixed misconception." The leaders of this nation seem guided in their decision-making by the fixed misconception that their noble rhetoric, especially when enacted into law, will take on a life of its own and somehow be realized in real life. Set desirable goals, publicize them, grant the states limited funds, and expect the seeds to bear the desired fruit. This "goal delusion" effectively shuts off a penetrating examination of the actual problems.

Among other delusions is the belief that if we try hard enough and experiment rigorously enough we will come up with just the right method of organizing our schools, maintaining both discipline and standards, and teaching our classes. Unfortunately, this outlook characterizes the grand educational plan set forth by President George W. Bush, much of it approved by Congress and signed by the president in January 2002. Test, and test some more, to make the schools accountable and to compel them to function effectively. This get tough policy, with not much of a carrot considering that the federal contribution to education amounts to no more than about 7 percent of the total, will flounder as others have. Meanwhile, federal funds will be increasingly channeled to private and parochial schools, as parents are encouraged to pull their students out of failing public schools and transfer them to the non-public ones. One might think that the assumption that schools themselves are entirely responsible for their outcomes, regardless of level of support and funding, would lead government officials to propose closing all failing schools and establishing private ones. It is not likely that anyone would take that fatuous route. Meanwhile, during the Bush administration, many more children will experience wasted years in inferior second and third systems—with instruction geared all the more to tests.

THE UNITED STATES HAS WHAT IT WANTS

The United States, at least those who govern it whether through policy-making positions or the power of money, has the educational system it wants. At most, this generalization could be modified to read: They have the educational system they are willing to pay for. They don't advertise that fact; instead, they use fig leafs, like blaming teachers or parents or children, as cover.

Regrettably, the use of fig leafs has bad "side effects," because it denies one the opportunity to understand and resolve problems. That is why openness and disclosure offer the best chance of maintaining a dynamic democratic society.

Whatever the future of education may be, whatever the American people may decide to demand, nothing beats frank recognition of the real state of affairs: The nation has three school systems, and they are unequally supported.

NOTES

1. *Robinson v. Cahill,* 62 N.J. 473 (1973), 268.
2. *Abbott v. Burke,* 119 N.J. 287 (1990), 342–343. Jean Anyon, *Ghetto Schooling: A Political Economy of Urban Educational Reform* (New York: Teachers College Press, 1997), 133–134.

3. *Robinson v. Cahill*, 62 N.J. 473 (1973).

4. *Robinson v. Cahill*, 69 N.J. 449 (1976) 459–460. Jean Anyon, *Ghetto Schooling: A Political Economy of Urban Educational Reform* (New York: Teachers College Press, 1997), 136.

5. Anyon, *Ghetto Schooling*, 136.

6. Anyon, *Ghetto Schooling: A Political Economy of Urban Educational Reform*. Dr. Anyon drew information about the curriculum offerings from the following sources: *Abbott v. Burke*, 119 N.J. 287 (1990), 364; Louis R. Centolanza, "The State of the Schools: Consequences of a Curricular Intervention, 1972–1980" (Ed.D. diss., Rutgers University 1986), 540–542; William A. Firestone, Margaret E.Goertz, and Gary Natriello, *The Struggle for Fiscal Reform and Educational Change in New Jersey* (New York: Teachers College Press, 1997).

7. *Abbott v. Burke*, 119 N.J. 287 (1990), 364, quoted in Anyon, *Ghetto Schooling*, 137.

8. Anyon, *Ghetto Schooling*, 138.

9. Margaret E. Goertz, *The Development and Implementation of the Quality Education Act of 1990* (New Brunswick, N.J.: Consortium for Policy Research in Education, Eagleton Institute of Politics, Rutgers University, 1992), 7. William A. Firestone, Margaret E. Goertz, and Gary Natriello, *The Struggle for Fiscal Reform and Educational Change in New Jersey* (New York: Teachers College Press, 1997).

10. Anyon, *Ghetto Schooling*, 141.

11. Firestone et al., *The Struggle for Fiscal Reform and Educational Change*, 2.

12. Firestone et al., *The Struggle for Fiscal Reform*, 2.

13. "Report and Decision of Remand Court," Superior Court of New Jersey, Chancery Division-Mercer County, S. Ct. Docket No. M-622–96, 22 January 1998.

14. "Now, Who Speaks for Urban Children? The Supreme Court Turns Its Back on Poor Districts," *Home News Tribune*, 22 May 1998, 14(A).

15. "Now, Who Speaks for Urban Children? The Supreme Court Turns Its Back on Poor Districts," 14 (A).

16. "Chapter 19A: Implementation of Court Decision in *Abbott v. Burke*," Public Law 1998, c. 45, effective 1 July 1998 (*Annual Appropriations Act*, Fiscal year 1998–1999), New Jersey.

17. Richard Perez-Peña, "Court Reverses Finance Ruling in City Schools," *New York Times*, 26 June 2002, 1(A).

18. Perez-Peña, "Court Reverses Finance Ruling in City Schools," 1(A).

19. Editor, "Blaming the Victim," *New York Times*, 26 June 2002, 22(A).

20. Editor, "Blaming the Victim," 22(A).

21. Rena L. Vassar, *Social History of American Education*, vol. 1, *Colonial Times to 1860* (Chicago: Rand McNally, 1965), 165.

22. Vassar, *Social History of American Education,* vol. 1, 165.

23. Vassar, *Social History of American Education,* vol. 1, 245–247.

24. George T. Silvestri, "Occupational Employment to 2005," *Monthly Labor Review* 118, no. 11 (November 1995): 60–84, 79, Table 3.

25. Bureau of Labor Statistics, www.bls.gov/emp/emptab4.htm (accessed 15 March 2002).

26. National Education Goals Panel, *The National Education Goals Report: Building a Nation of Learners* (Washington, D.C.: National Education Goals Panel, 1994).

4

SOCIAL CLASS DIFFERENCES IN THE PURPOSES OF EDUCATION

In earlier times, when children learned from their parents all that they needed to know, there were no schools. Those were simple days when even literacy was not a necessity of life and such "schooling" that children received was obtained informally. Later, those who wanted to learn skills and trades could seek apprenticeships.

The dizzying changes in the last two centuries, especially the twentieth, have made formal education a necessity to satisfy the needs both of the society and the individual.

SOCIETAL NEEDS FOR EDUCATION

A nation requires some common schooling. This insures that its citizens share a language, a history, and an ideology, even if other languages, histories, and ideologies are common properties of subgroups within the nation. Through a core of knowledge and attitudes, the schools in this country seek to inculcate the concept and feeling of "being American."

Formal education serves the society in other important ways. It socializes children, presumably enabling them to interact and work with others, including others who are different from them in race, sex, religion, and social class.

Through a screening and selection process, the educational system identifies those children whose talents will be highly developed. All children, from birth, have a parent-as-teacher. Some children have two of them, and some have a surrogate parent-as-teacher. Some parents are exceptionally able in that role, and some are dismal failures. Children of advantaged families, usually benefiting from enriched cultural and educational experiences provided by outstanding teachers-as-parent, leap ahead with an extraordinary head start. They are the majority of the group who will do well in school, receive education in the first educational system, and go on to elite forms of higher education and specialized training. Many of them will fill essential positions as political leaders, executives, professionals, scientists, and others. The educational system also identifies those who will occupy the large middle tier of occupations, such as store managers, nurses, medical and dental technicians, and computer programmers, and gives them appropriate training in four-year and two-year colleges. Finally, the educational system provides those whose abilities have been only modestly developed, usually of lower income families, with training appropriate to societal (or market) needs, and to some extent, their own personal needs.

How simple it would be if the needs of society and those of individuals were always congruent. If that were so, then by satisfying the needs of all individuals, societal needs would be automatically satisfied, and vice versa. Unfortunately, the deviations are extreme because, as we will see, societal needs, at least as defined in terms of a profit-geared market economy, are more easily satisfied, and at less cost, than those of the sum of all individuals. The market economy doesn't have emotions. It certainly needs the first and second school systems and can tolerate the third school system, that is, one which produces millions of children who eventually leave school, even as high school graduates, with unfulfilled potential, with personal development far from complete, and without a defined positive vision of a future.

To be more explicit, let us examine the societal needs in our current market economy in terms of the three school systems. From the first system will come the future leaders in industry, commerce, government, education, health, journalism, and the arts—each of them integral to the political-economic structure. Their roles call for the highly developed intelligence and freewheeling creativity that enable them to be pioneers in their respective fields of specialization. They possess the talent to identify fundamental problems and find bold solutions that advance knowledge in their field. Examples include the cardiologist, who, finding that heart surgery is being used excessively and often unnecessarily, develops and tests nonsurgical approaches to the treatment of heart disease; and the legislator, who, recognizing that oppressed minority groups are being harassed or otherwise oppressed, composes a bill to safeguard their rights and wins the support of a majority in her or his legislature. Examples also include the choreographer, who notes that classic dance ignores rich native culture and folklore and composes new work that incorporates them; the school administrator, aware that the school is not adequately satisfying the educational needs of the children, who recognizes the crucial roles of teachers and parents in making significant change and reaches out to them to work cooperatively as they venture into uncharted educational waters. For those children who will eventually elevate themselves to such positions, the society requires that their learning experiences, at home and in school, prepare them for the critical thinking and imaginativeness required of them. Most, but not all of them, will get those experiences in the homes and schools of the first school system. Some will emerge from the second and, against all odds, even the third school system. So far as the political-economic system is concerned, it matters not at all whence they come, only that they be available to carry on the work of maintaining and enhancing the economy, the infrastructure, and the institutions of the nation.

From the second school system, the society needs that very large workforce that performs the important everyday tasks in virtually all fields of occupational activity. Second school system graduates are society's mighty generator; they provide the power to keep our everyday world humming along effectively. Without them, without the occupations they fill, the usual movement of daily life would come to a standstill, as if the nation were confronted with a long-term general strike.

Efficiency and dependability are two of the major qualities needed to carry out their duties, whether they are firefighters, dental hygienists, bus drivers, lab technicians, factory foremen and forewomen, or department store buyers. They may also be persons in a variety of professions who operate strictly by the principles and protocols laid down by others above them in the respective profession's hierarchy. Creativity is often a welcome quality in any field and, within limits, the second school system fosters some creativity. Jobs may also allow for creativity, as when an auto mechanic finds a more efficient way to tune a motor, or a practical nurse develops a more rapid procedure to move a disabled patient in bed. Creativity applied in this delimited fashion is quite acceptable.

From the third school system, the economy's need is for workers in minimum-wage jobs, especially in the service industries. Schools satisfy the economy's need when they offer training that conditions recipients to the passive acceptance of whatever society has to offer them and that develops habits of punctuality and obedience. Those students tend to believe that their low level of school achievement reflects their own inadequacies, their own lack of innate ability. If there is anyone to blame for their failing or marginal performance, the blame is their own. Self-concepts of that kind, combined with training in submissiveness, may hopefully temper the arousal of violent and criminal behavior as responses to the frustration and demeaning nature of a future that holds out to them low paying jobs with little opportunity for advancement.

It is not realistic to expect that all students, or dropouts, from the third school system would be content with their status. To appreciate this, one must try to empathize with the children, especially the teenagers in the third system. Picture living in a slum apartment, the corridors reeking of urine, in insecure surroundings where drug gangs and prostitutes prowl the streets. Add to that dismal home environment the realization that the future holds little if any opportunity to enjoy the fruits of the culture of their land and little realistic hope of escaping to the world seen on television, in the movies, or in posh cars visible on nearby avenues. The harsh realities they endure, in the face of such frustration, explain why teaching and learning are so difficult to accomplish in the third system.

To sum up our discussion of societal needs as they relate to education, we can conclude that at an enormous cost to potential human development, *societal* needs are satisfied through the operation of the three school systems. The cost to students in the second system is that their personal development is insufficiently realized. The cost is far greater to the many third system children whose development is stunted by inferior educational opportunity. The societal cost is also considerable, among other ways, because of the many prisons that must be built and maintained to house so many alumni of the third system. Yet, despite the societal and individual price paid for the conditions of the third and second school systems, we see no serious, committed efforts to change because the educational enterprise, as it currently exists, is acceptable to those that hold power and formulate policy in our nation. Parents will be discontent, and from time to time protests bubble up, giving rise to demonstrations, stormy school board meetings, court cases, and media attention. Then comes talk about "crisis" and the need for "school reform," followed perhaps by appointment of a commission to "study the problem." This last action quiets the opposition for some years. When the commission finally reports, the root issues are not addressed because the educational status quo is more acceptable to those in power than alternatives leading toward a single first-class system. As for the general population, many people are confused because discourse about the schools never gets to the heart of the problems, that is, to the fact that the nation has three school systems, separate and unequal.

INDIVIDUALS' NEEDS FOR EDUCATION

The educational needs of children take on a clearer light when seen in the context of future adulthood. To develop a healthy adult personality, psychologist Abraham Maslow[1] asserted that one must satisfy a hierarchy of needs. The first three sets of needs are basic: The physiological needs (e.g., food, sleep, sex, sensory stimulation); safety needs (e.g., removal of environmental threats, assurance of order and predictability in the environment); belongingness and the love needs (e.g., affection, love, friendship, and membership in groups).

The fourth and fifth needs, esteem and self-actualization, are considered the highest-level needs. They are particularly sensitive to learning and social and emotional development experienced by the individual. Esteem needs are satisfied by recognition of one's abilities and accomplishments, which leads to self-confidence and independence. The self-actualization needs—the highest in the hierarchy—are satisfied when individuals realize their full potential, when they utilize their unique capabilities and thus "actualize" themselves.

Stimulation, communication, and learning, at home and in school, are keys to the satisfaction of the higher needs. To satisfy those needs and

for optimal development in general, children have a variety of requirements that start at birth and continue throughout childhood:

- Opportunities to interact with their physical environment through
  oral and later manual engagement with rattles, blocks, dolls, toys,
  pots, pans, and whatsoever is available to exercise their perceptual
  and motor functions.
- Opportunities to interact with their social environment through
  communication and play with adults and children.
- Opportunities provided by caring adults who talk and sing to them
  and encourage and respond to the children's early articulations; extensive conversation at home that increasingly engages the children's interests; and discussions about all kinds of subjects, with the
  children participating, both by listening and talking, to parents, siblings, other relatives and friends.
- Opportunities for mediated experiences, that is, through the intervention of parents, teachers, and other caregivers, which help the
  children understand and cope with their physical and social environments. The adults do that by the toys they provide, the books
  they read to them, the television programs they watch and help interpret for them, and the trips to farms, museums, zoos, parks, and
  other places of interest.

Adults who provide these opportunities perform their greatest service
when they hold high expectations of the children. Whether these adults
are parents, or other caregivers or teachers, they expect success in all
kinds of activities: in play, reading, writing, later in academic performance, and in other activities that interest the children, including other
intellectual, artistic, or athletic activities.

Opportunities identified above are not equally distributed in the
world, and not even in our democratic society. The sad fact is that the
separation of children by social class and educational opportunity begins
very early. Long before their parents shepherd them to the first day of
kindergarten, even before they take them to preschool, the children are
already in different educational systems.

From the moment of birth, all children are educated at home. They
have a "home curriculum," including, as the jewels of that curriculum,
learning to understand language and to talk. The tutelage varies in qual-

ity as widely as it does in the schools they later attend. It is not simply differences in the vocabulary employed by the parents, their grammar, or the accent of speech—not just in the quality of language to which the children are exposed that differentiates this home education. The differences involve quality and quantity of instruction and learning and the content of the home curriculum.

In some homes, conversation is limited to the essentials of living together. A parent says to the child during the course of a day: "Sit on the potty. Put your toys away. Come to the table." And the child's responses may be: "No. Help me. I'm coming." In such a home, adult communication may also be brief, infrequent, and mostly about matters of direct concern to daily life: "Your mother phoned." "What did she want?" "She got a part-time job." "Where?" "At K-Mart." "Oh."

In other homes, conversation is a key feature of life that goes on during much of the time that family members are together. The parent says to the child: "What a nice painting you did. Do you want to tell me about it?" "It's a giant. He's very strong. He could knock down a tree." "What do you think he will do with all that power?" "He's a good giant. He won't hurt anyone." And so it goes on. This parent is both teaching the child that the painting has meaning and encouraging the narration of a story. While the parent is stimulating the child's thinking, the parent is also conveying to the child that he or she is very much interested in, and cares about, what the child does.

Adults in this family engage each other in conversation that bears the same characteristics. They share their thoughts about much in their experience, including work, recreation, and culture. One parent says: "I read an article about the growing use of tobacco among teenagers. The big question is how to curb it." The other says: "I'm wondering how to take the glamour out of smoking." The discussion goes on for many minutes. Even young children in those families are encouraged to express their views, which are accepted with interest and respect, no matter how naive those expressions may sound to adult ears. To these children, discussion in which everyone participates without fear is just part of life, as natural and expected as eating and sleeping and playing. Playing with words comes to be as pleasurable as playing with toys.

Parents who stimulate the intelligence and language usage of their children are often affluent, well educated themselves, and live in good school districts or use private schools. Children in their homes are fortunate to have a first-system teacher both at home and in school, at least up to the time they go to residential college. At that point many of them enter first-system institutions—the elite colleges and research universities—and go on afterward to attain postgraduate education and start high-level careers.

By contrast, children in homes with little discussion and interaction generally have third-system teachers at home and often in school, right up to the time most of them (not all) go to a low-paying, often boring minimum- or low-wage job—or in the worst cases, into homelessness or illegal activities, frequently drug-related, that lead them to poor health, prison terms, or an early death.

Besides satisfying societal needs, the educational enterprise, to a considerable degree, satisfies the higher needs of students in the first system, does that to a moderate degree for those in the second system, and does little if any of that for those in the third.

Some children are born into circumstances that enable them to have most of their high-level needs fulfilled for growth and development. Most children are not. If hard reality is to be remedied, considerably more than well-meaning school reform is required.

The current road to educational reform is doomed because it is based on three false premises: There is one school system in the country; that system is in crisis; it is failing to serve the society. Actually, there are three, and, taken together, particularly the first and second systems, they have provided the brain and other human resources for the U.S. political-economic system to become the superpower it is.

For so long the leader in mass education, the United States is now being equaled, even exceeded by other countries in the proportion of secondary and tertiary graduates. That is occurring because the United States prefers the status quo, despite its consequences for many children. Political leaders express much alarm about the state of our educational system and talk about reform, but they have been unwilling to eliminate the third system and upgrade the second.

The so-called crisis in our schools is truly a "manufactured" one, as educators David Berliner and Bruce Biddle explain in *The Manufactured Crisis.*[2] They ask why the "manufactured crisis" was invented in the early 1980s and then identify nine factors that contributed to this development. Among them are: "reactionary voices that were given unprecedented legitimacy in the Reagan and Bush administrations...desires to scapegoat educators as a way of diverting attention from America's deepening social problems...[and] self-interest on the part of some government officials."[3]

My interpretation of this recent crisis is different. It applies not just to the current "crisis," but also to all of them since World War II, and in fact to the status of the education of the non-affluent throughout the nation's history. It explains why the current one, now so old, endures with no end in sight. The symptoms of the "crisis," which are primarily the failings of the third school system, are endemic to our political-economic system, which places higher value on the well-being of the profit, free-enterprise system than on universal well-being. Efforts to reform the schools, as we will see, are not enough. Partly that is so because if school reform is to succeed, it must be accompanied by societal changes that improve the quality of life of the parents of the second and third school system children. And partly it is so because there can be no enthusiastic and continuing well-funded support for real school reform until the society, through its political voice and political action, gives higher valuation to optimal human development.

NOTES

1. Abraham Maslow, *Motivation and Personality* (New York: Harper and Row, 2nd ed., 1987).

2. David C. Berliner and Bruce J. Biddle, *The Manufactured Crisis: Myths, Fraud, and the Attack on America's Public Schools* (Reading, Mass.: Perseus Books, 1995).

3. Berliner and Biddle, *The Manufactured Crisis*, 6–7.

5

DIFFERENCES AMONG THE THREE SCHOOL SYSTEMS

The different purposes of the three school systems—the first produces leaders, the second, reliable workers, and the third, a marginalized population—are reflected in the characteristics of the schools. Much that we consider essential to quality education is found in the first system, less in the second system, and least in the third.

So much has been written about the inner city and urban schools that it is hardly necessary to document their sad state. For example, *Savage Inequalities*, Jonathan Kozol's[1] vivid depiction of the dramas of real life, tugged at many a heart as it revealed the nature of the terribly inferior schools available to the urban poor in our nation's cities. Kozol's comparisons of such schools with those of high quality suggested that the children lived in different worlds. Here is an example of what he observed in poor city schools.

> "Keisha, look at me," an adult shouts at a slow reader in a sixth grade class. "Look me in the eye." Keisha has been fighting with her classmate. Over what? As it turns out, over a crayon. The child is terrified and starts to cry. Tears spill out of her eyes and drop onto the pages of her math book. In January the school begins to ration crayons, pencils, writing paper.[2]

Keisha's teacher happens to be a permanent substitute who is not pleased with being in this class. Considering the situation in Chicago at the time, the class is fortunate in having her because even subs are in short supply. "On an average morning in Chicago, 5,700 children in 190 classrooms come to school to find they have no teacher."[3]

Below is a closer look at several categories of differences among the three school systems, with special emphasis on the first and third systems. This closer look will show how little they have in common.

ATTENDANCE

Children cannot benefit from learning experiences in school if they are absent or sick. If they are sick, they are likely to stay at home, and, if they don't, they are not likely to derive much benefit in their weakened or just headachy, sniffling condition.

The higher incidence of asthma in inner cities debilitates children and leads to increased absenteeism. A five-year study, called the National Cooperative Inner-City Asthma Study, investigated why children in the inner cities of New York and six other cities have a higher incidence of asthma than their suburban counterparts. It concluded that cockroach infestation in houses and apartments was responsible. According to the study's director, Dr. David Rosenstreich of the Albert Einstein Medical College, "These children were three times more likely to require hospitalization for their asthma. And the situation has been getting worse each year."[4] To make matters worse, the chemicals used to control roach infestation can exacerbate the situation by triggering allergies and other health problems.

The national General Accounting Office reports that about 10 percent of poor children suffer the effects of dangerous levels of lead poisoning. Toddlers eat the flakes or breathe the dust of lead-based paint, resulting in "reductions in I.Q. and attention span, reading and learning disabilities, hyperactivity and behavioral problems."[5] Screening for lead could lead to actions to alleviate the condition in children's homes, but fewer than one in five children in poor families have been screened. Medicaid does not provide coverage for screening in many states, despite the fact that if schools sponsored the screening it could cost as little as $75 per child.

According to a report of the surgeon general in May 2000, more than a third of children from low-income families have untreatable dental cavities. A toothache is likely to interfere with concentrating on class activities, paying attention to the teacher, and taking a test.[6] Children in the third school system in particular suffer from these conditions and the ensuing absenteeism.

GETTING SAFELY TO SCHOOL

Getting to school is no problem for students in the first school system even if it may be a problem for their parents, at least for those who drive them. Generally speaking, children's travel to and from school in the first system occurs with relative safety, if only because resources are available for whatever protective safeguards may be necessary.

That condition does not always prevail for those in the third system. Schools may be located near drug-infested areas and may see the occasional eruption of gang wars or other violent behavior. In some settings, the circumstances are not unlike those of a no-man's-land during warfare.

A report of one setting, the Jenner Elementary School in Chicago, brings that image to mind.[7] The danger is so great that the principal cannot recall the last time the children were permitted to play on the playground. In the last five years, a seven-year-old boy was shot dead while walking to school holding his mother's hand; a nine-year-old girl, on the way to school, was sexually assaulted and blinded; four times in a two-week period, teachers hurried their children from classrooms to the hallways to protect them from possible stray bullets smashing through school windows; and students looking out classroom windows saw a man shot before their eyes—a victim of gang conflict—as if they were watching one of the many bloody movies or television shows that fill their leisure hours. The pastor of a church in the neighborhood said that even kids in the day care center have to duck down when the shooting starts.

What effect do conditions such as these have on children? A girl in the fourth grade said that she sometimes thinks she will be shot because "sometimes they shoot in my back."[8] An art teacher said "The kids who can't sleep at night because there's shooting" face serious obstacles to learning. "They come to school and they're sleepy and not prepared." This school is not in the most crime-plagued housing project in Chicago, or in an area experiencing an extreme state of gang warfare.

Many thousands of children attend schools in danger zones of one kind or another. In a recent article on education reform that highlights the fact that "Children, teachers, and staff need to be in an environment that is safe, orderly, and drug free," two Department of Education specialists, Gerald Tirozzi and Gabriela Uro, report that "29% of sixth graders, 34% of middle-junior high school students, and 20% of senior high school students said they were worried about becoming victims at school or on the way to and from school."[9]

The report on the Jenner School, previously cited, includes these telling observations:

> The strain has clearly taken its toll on the school and its children, even though many say they are used to the shooting. Despite its dynamic principal and a program to give children extra help each day until 5:30 P.M., Jenner is one of the city's weakest schools, with 80 percent doing math or reading below grade level. The red brick building is so old and there is so little money to pay for repairs that the principal, unable to get it painted, decided that bullet holes made years ago in the wall of the library should at least be covered with spackle.[10]

Take note of the fact that the principal is "dynamic" and shows herself in various ways to be deeply concerned about the children. Note also that a program is available to give the children extra help and, incidentally, to keep them in school until late afternoon. These are positive features in a largely negative environment. Not even the most committed and expert administrators and teachers, however, can sufficiently counteract the conditions of life for children in the third school system to make them equivalent to those for children in the second system, to say nothing of the first.

The major options under consideration at the Jenner School late in 1997 were: Move the children to another school or establish a safety zone; paying parents to be security guards wearing white arm bands and assigned to dangerous corners; and creating white-flagged "safe havens" in churches where children could duck inside when shooting broke out.

The highly publicized outbreak of violence in suburban schools has changed the picture slightly, but violence in the first school system is still a rarity, creating only minimal risk compared to the danger of violence in the third system.

PARENTAL INVOLVEMENT IN THE SCHOOL SYSTEMS

Parents of children at the Jenner School don't want their children transferred to another school. That won't make their neighborhood any safer,
they explain. They want to participate in the safe zone plan.

Although many parents of children of the third system show such interest and participate in the affairs of their children's schools, there are,
nonetheless, very considerable differences in the involvement of parents in
the three systems. Parents in the first system, generally prosperous, upper
middle-class professionals and executives, have the advantages of more
flexible work schedules and also child care help, enabling them more readily to participate in occasional school day activities. Their education, language ability, comfort in the school milieu, and rapport with administrators
and teachers, give them—and the school—other advantages. A *New
Yorker* article, entitled, "Making the Grade: Going to Private School Involves Hard Work For the Parents,"[11] described one father of children in
a first system school. The article recounted his activities in two private
schools, one each for his son and daughter. He serves on the Safety Patrol
(wearing an orange nylon vest, a whistle dangling from his neck, and carrying a walkie-talkie), the Library Committee, and the Fathers Who Cook
Dinner staff. He attends Parents' Night at both schools, Fathers' Dinner,
Parents' Potluck Supper, New Parents' Breakfast, Cultural Awareness for
Everyone night, Parents-and-Partnership Tea, Parents' Visiting Day, plus
many parent-teacher conferences. This sounds like a full time job. When
the headmistress of his daughter's school admonished the parents to "make
sure your children read; make sure they don't get over-scheduled; and,
lastly, stay home more," this man wondered how that was possible when he
had to spend so much time at evening meetings at the schools. He quotes
a mother as saying, "My daughter walks in the door from school, and I'm
rushing off to a Parents-and-Partnership Tea."[12]

This high level of parental participation in first system schools is what
virtually all reform efforts plead for. With this participation, the children go
off for the day to an institution that has come to serve somewhat as a community center for the family. The children *and* the parents are members of
that community, along with faculty and staff. They all "own" it and, in direct and indirect ways, influence and shape its present and future courses.

The real estate section of a newspaper gives testimony to the magnetic power of first school system education. This was highlighted on the first page of the real estate section of the *New York Times*.[13] The title of this feature article conveys the theme: "First the Schoolhouse, Then the Home." For many parents, journalist Margot Slade writes, the school is the preeminent factor in the choice of where they will live. That, she said, is more important than the town, street, or neighborhood, more important than the size or style of the house or apartment. One parent described the choice of school as "the all-encompassing issue," another said "we made the overriding importance of the schools very clear to real estate agents." Rather than lot sizes or real estate taxes, many parents are more interested in teacher-student ratios, the math curriculum, how faculty and administrators greet them, and how teachers teach. Some parents examine performance statistics that bear on the quality of students in the school and other criteria of the good school. They are not content with the choice of a school district; it is the particular school their child will attend that concerns them.

In this *New York Times* article, one parent stated her satisfaction with her real estate choice in terms that fit the description of a first-system education. She and her husband moved from one area to another—as so many parents have done to get the school of their choice for their children—because they had found a school "with a demanding curriculum and an individualized focus on the needs of students." In her words, they had found a "public school that offers a private-school environment."

Some parents who are not affluent, or even financially comfortable, and who are not college educated, search for better educational opportunities for their children. Their limited financial resources, however, do not permit the same mobility that allows their wealthier counterparts to move to other communities or other sections of a metropolitan area. They may also be at another disadvantage. Although they may be treated politely and with respect, they might not receive the same warm, open door welcome. They are not likely to be on the same linguistic and cultural beam as the more affluent and highly educated parents and staff, and might feel some personal discomfort.

TEACHERS IN THE SCHOOL SYSTEMS

According to the United States Department of Education's National Center for Educational Statistics, American classrooms will require two million new teachers over the next decade.[14] The need is—and will be—greatest in the inner cities. The job of meeting the need is a daunting one.

The case of a woman who abandoned plans to study law in favor of teaching illustrates an important aspect of the problem. In an article in the *New York Times*,[15] she is quoted as saying that she initially planned to teach in New York City schools but changed her mind, not because of any personal experience but only because of what she had heard about the conditions in the schools. "I'm concerned about the fact that I will not be adequately prepared to deal with the lack of resources in the schools we hear about."

This reaction helps explain the shocking findings of a recent survey by a nonprofit group, Recruiting New Teachers: It found that "…two-thirds of urban school systems relied on uncertified teachers who had only emergency licenses."[16]

In New York City, 60 percent of the teachers hired in 2000–2001 were uncertified. As of 1 July 2001, more than 3,500 teachers had filed for retirement that year. To contend with the critical shortfall of teachers, the city introduced the New York City Teaching Fellows program through which 1,600 adults in other careers were hired "to fill chronic vacancies in New York City's woebegone schools."[17] The fellows are given five weeks of training as a teacher before the first day of class, as well as in-service training.

A journalist followed the experiences of one teaching fellow during her first year as a teacher and wrote about the final day of school. At the end, the teacher, beloved by the students to whom she gave so much of herself, was dissatisfied with their achievement. She had given the children love; about that she had no doubt, and she wept as they said goodbye. But she was sad because she felt that not enough of them had learned what they should have. She felt, too, that these children were so needy that she could not possibly do enough for them. That feeling of frustration may contribute to the fact that of the 320 teaching fellows who started teaching in September 2000, 40 left teaching before the end of the school year.[18]

While enrollments in teacher education programs are growing, minority groups are underrepresented. Within the teaching profession in its entirety, the representation of minorities is not keeping pace with the changes in the school population. In fact, there is less diversity among teachers today than in the past. In 1996, with many classrooms filled with nonwhite children, Asians, Hispanics, and other minority youth, high proportions of them with limited English, nearly 91 percent of teachers were white, compared with 88 percent white in 1971. Of the remainder, 7 percent were black (compared with 8 percent in 1971), 4 percent Hispanic, and 1 percent each of Asians and Native Americans.

Student teachers, especially those who lived a middle-class childhood, experience a form of culture shock when they confront the reality of the poverty in which some students live. It is one thing to sit on a comfortable chair in the tranquil surroundings of a university library, reading about poverty and oppression; it is quite another to come smack up against it and its consequences in real life. Despite courses in sociology and anthropology in which the problems of poverty were examined, one author of a book for student teachers who grew up in a low-income though not poverty-stricken family experienced a cultural shock as a student teacher. She wrote in her student teacher journal:

> We were returning [to the Bronx] by bus from an all-day trip to a nature park in Staten Island. The fifth graders were tired but happy after a very enjoyable day of walking the nature trails, visiting the museum, and picnicking and playing outdoors. The children surrounding me on the bus in this happy atmosphere of the day were conversing in a friendly and trusting way. One girl said she hated to think that her cousin was coming to visit for the weekend. I asked her why, whether she didn't like her cousin. She liked her all right, but the cousin, a girl her own age, was coming with her whole family. That meant, she said, "Us children will have to sleep on the floor."
>
> Very naively, I asked what was so terrible about that for a few nights? She looked at me, now a little embarrassed, perhaps at my own innocence, and said, "I can't get myself to fall asleep on the floor because I'm afraid of the big rats." Of course, I had read about poverty and rats and malnutrition and brain damage from lead poisoning in hungry little children who eat the peeling paint off the wall, and more, but I had not connected them

with my children, with this girl who I had felt was not much different from me only 10 years before.[19]

It takes dedicated teachers to be willing to work with children so handicapped by societal conditions. To achieve some measure of success in engaging the students in learning, teachers must be formidable enough to work at counteracting the physical, psychological, and social effects of poverty, some of which make children inattentive and unmotivated for learning.

How much easier it is to teach the middle-and upper-middle class students in the first system, students so much closer to the teachers in ways of culture and speech. The following message written by a young teacher in a boarding school summer program testifies to the pleasure teaching in the first system can give.

Just finished my first day teaching. I think I'm going to be working very hard the next 5 weeks! It's fun, though. The kids are absolutely fantastic! Especially the middle schoolers. Looks like I'm really meant to be a middle school teacher. The 7th and 8th graders are so bright, so enthusiastic.[20]

Differences in teacher quality exist even within school districts. For example, district 10, one of thirty-two school districts in New York City, comprises a large part of the Bronx. Riverdale, as Kozol explains, with its affluent and well-educated families, is distinctly different from the rest of the district, which is nonwhite and poor. The principal of Public School 24 in Riverdale has the highest praise for his teachers, whereas the principal of Public School 79 claims that he is compelled to take the "tenth-best" teachers and he thanks God that they are still breathing! The principal of another school in a poor neighborhood said: "These are the kids most in need . . . and they get the worst teachers." To serve them in over crowded classrooms "you need an outstanding teacher. And what do you get? You get the worst."[21]

At the very least, third-system teachers ought to be well rewarded for their effort. They ought to, but they usually don't receive the same salaries as teachers in the first-system suburban public schools.

At the child care level, where the pay is very low, the differential between quality of care varies according to social class, as explained in the following excerpt from an article entitled, "Even Mary Poppins Wouldn't Work for Child-Care Wages Offered in the U.S."

> "Why doesn't the market work in child care?" Hillary Rodham Clinton asked Treasury Secretary Robert Rubin, who's charged with getting business, labor, and community leaders to do something about the shortage of high-quality, low-cost child care.
>
> Actually, the market works just fine. The market says you don't get what you don't pay for. You don't get high-quality child care at low cost.
>
> Some enterprises can be reinvented, downsized, automated, and continuously improved. Child care is done by people.
>
> Offer long hours and low wages for a demanding job, and you'll have a hard time attracting and retaining Mary Poppins. Those who stay in the job will either be ultra-dedicated or unable to qualify for anything else. The average child-care center teacher earns $6.70 an hour, according to a 1996 study. One third earn the minimum wage. Family-care providers earn even less.
>
> Not surprisingly, half the child care workers in America quit each year. If we want better child care, we have to be willing to pay for it.[22]

Children of affluent parents attend preschools that can pay salaries that attract the best of teachers. If the parents choose to keep the children at home, nannies are available to care for them, or the family can afford a stay-at-home parent.

LEARNING EXPERIENCES THAT PROMOTE THINKING

One might say the credo of elite education is "learn and think," or better yet, learn to think. Acquiring information is useful, and acquiring information for its own sake may be both useful and pleasurable, but acquiring information to be used as the raw material for thinking and for its sibling, problem solving, represents the ultimate in educational value.

The fact is that schooling promotes thinking even when that is not a conscious objective. A cleverly designed study in Liberia by two American psychologists, Sylvia Scribner and Michael Cole,[23] demonstrated the impact of education on cognition. They addressed this question: How do these three groups compare in cognitive ability: (1) People who have had only life experience. (2) People who have had life experience and also training that gave them literacy. (3) People who have had life experience, literacy, and also formal education? The researchers found these groupings among the Vai people of Liberia. Those who had literacy but not formal schooling (the second group) had been trained in reading and memorizing the Koran. Using tests derived from native culture—not tests derived from American or other western culture—they found that the people who had had formal schooling were vastly superior in performance on the tests. In other words, formal education made a significant difference, particularly in logical reasoning and verbal explanation. They attributed this advantage to teacher practices that required students to justify a solution or explain an answer, in other words, they attributed it to the "Why?" question—the question that forces one to think.

Another study bears on the question of how to stimulate thoughtful participation by students. Four educators, recognizing the excellence of science education in five schools in Tokyo, looked for the characteristics that accounted for their high quality. They designed a system to observe, record, and analyze the science lessons in ten classrooms in these schools.[24]

According to their analyzed observations, thinking was the most prominent cognitive process in the study of science in these classes. They found, first, that students mastered the knowledge base covered by the science class; next, they learned to apply it. The focus of the course is on what comes *after* knowledge-acquisition, that is, after reading, understanding, memorizing, or, in other terms, after new information and concepts have been assimilated. What comes after that is the use of the knowledge both in problem solving and in further theorizing and knowledge production. Knowledge is deepened, its meaning made more complete, as a result of its application in thinking and problem solving: developing hypotheses, designing methods of testing them, analyzing the findings, and writing a report on the activity. Such an approach contributes to meaningful learning because scientific knowledge employed to answer questions and solve problems is much more likely to be incorporated in long-term memory than that learned in preparation for an exam.

These two studies provide evidence that schooling in general promotes cognitive growth. Consider, then, the benefits children derive from teaching when *its clearly defined goal is the enhancement of students' thinking ability*, and when the activities in class are geared to that goal.

The following examples illustrate the prominence of thinking in quality programs. The first comes from instruction in a fourth grade class in an urban elementary school for gifted and talented children, the second, from an eighth grade class in a nonresidential private school.

Learning Thinking Skills in an Urban Elementary School's Fourth Grade Class for Gifted and Talented Children[25]

An assignment early in the school year called "Apple Project: A Celebration of Choice" presented the students with five groups of activities. They were asked to choose one activity from each group, although they could earn extra credit by taking on additional tasks. The number of activities in each group ranged from four to eight. To complete each of the activities, students must acquire information and then engage in various types of problem solving, such as analyzing, comparing, categorizing, hypothesizing, and synthesizing, depending on the activity chosen. Many of the activities call for them to use their creative and imaginative powers. Following are samples of activities, two from each group:

Design a new apple and explain your design.
Dramatize the life of Johnny Appleseed.
Judge the quality of three kinds of apples in writing.
Record the ingredients found in apple products and explain why the
    ingredients are added to the products.
Debate the value of organically grown apples to those grown otherwise.
Trace the roots of the apple as it came across the Atlantic aboard a
    ship in 1628.
Organize a school campaign to encourage everyone to eat an apple a day.
Illustrate the life cycle of an apple.
Predict how we will grow apples in the year 2080.
Explain: "As American as Apple Pie."

The children are instructed to seek information about the apple tasks in books, encyclopedias, magazines, on the Internet, or from experts.

Their reports are to be written in proper sentences, and checked for accuracy in spelling, grammar, and punctuation. They must display their results on a poster board, prepare a three to five minute presentation for the class and, finally, complete a self-evaluation form.

The evaluation, known as the Apple Project Rubric, contains four rubrics from which the student chooses one. The highest evaluation—Rubric 4—is earned when the student could report the following: chose one task from each group, researched each of them thoroughly, completing all five activities creatively, thoroughly, and neatly composed, creatively displaying the apple project and presenting my report to class in a clear manner on the due date and, finally, completing at least one extra apple task. The lowest evaluation—Rubric 1—is earned when the apple tasks are not researched, fewer than four activities are completed, and these lack creativity, thoroughness, and neatness, and the final apple project is displayed and presented to the class.

In another project, due almost six weeks later, students are given only two rubrics—4 and 3—to choose from, because by that time in the school year (late October), poorer work is not accepted. This project, "The Incredible World Famous Monster Project," requires students to choose a monster, give it a name, select three or more resources to find information about the monster, such as the Internet, encyclopedias, movies or audiotapes, or other books, and take notes on index cards. They then write a personal narrative from the monster's point of view (that is, the student's point of view), describing the monster's appearance, how, when, and where the monster was discovered or invented, and an adventure that the monster experienced, based on the student's imagination or on factual information found in the research stage. The final step in this project is the choice of two of four tasks: a 3-D model of the monster; a crossword puzzle using at least fifteen words and clues; five creative and detailed math word problems; or a tape recording of the personal narrative, done creatively, calling on family and friends for different voices and sound effects. On the due date, students submit the personal narrative, bibliography, index cards, two projects, and the evaluation rubric.

These projects are characteristic of the life of such classes. The prime importance of knowledge acquisition is taken for granted. Equally important is the use of that knowledge: its application in problem solving and the creative processes.

Learning Thinking Skills in a Private School Course on Twentieth Century American Experience[26]

Eighth grade students in this course were asked to engage in various stages of logical thinking. For example, in studying the use of historical documents, they were given assignments such as the following: Read the first and second drafts of President Franklin D. Roosevelt's War Message to Congress and compare the two. They were also asked to answer specific questions such as: What two words did Roosevelt change in paragraph 1 and why? For example, the first line originally read, "Yesterday, December 7, 1941, a date which will live in world history." In the second draft, the last two words, "world history," were replaced by the word "infamy." The answer can come only as a product of their own thought processes because this question is not addressed in any of their readings or in the teacher's lectures. To answer the question, they must characterize the original words and their replacements, then hypothesize and test out rationales for the change. Those rationales would draw on their knowledge base acquired in this course. However, the teacher was stretching their ability to *use that knowledge base, and to use it thoughtfully.*

A test in this course is built around an "Americanization" poster of 1920. The teacher tells the students to imagine that they are historians and they come upon the poster "in a dusty folder in the National Archives." The poster, which shows two brothers and their mother (one brother is already an American citizen; the mother and other brother have just arrived), urges immigrants to learn the "American language" and become an American citizen. The test about the poster asks questions such as: "Describe each of the three figures in the photo. How does the photo (without the caption) serve as a historical source? As an advertising ploy?" Another question asks: "What does the last sentence of the photo caption mean?" That sentence is: "If the people who come to America do not become Americans, this country will soon be like the old country." Answers to these questions depend on already acquired knowledge, which is necessary but not sufficient, because the knowledge alone will not tell them why the photo can serve as a historical source, or why America would become like the old country. Those answers can only be derived from critical thinking.

In this same class, critical thinking was again required in another assignment. After the first sound movie, *The Jazz Singer*, was shown in class, students were given a two-sentence description of the movie and the following assignment.

> Discuss this statement in a polished one- to three-page essay. In your conclusion, state what you believe to be the movie's central message to its 1927 audience. Remember to support all conclusions with specific evidence from the movie. *Make and argue a thesis; do not summarize the plot.*[27] (Emphasis added)

"Make and argue a thesis" translates into "Do your own original, creative thinking!" This is not the implicit slogan in every class in the first school system. Yes, there are teachers in the second and even third system who plan and employ methods that cultivate thought, but far fewer. This is one of the major differences between the first and the other systems. We hark back to the earlier discussion about mediation: The first system teacher, like the first system parent, is more likely to be equipped and to have the time and resources to help students acquire the tools and skills of thinking. For the most part, parents of first system schools expect that their children will have that kind of education and they welcome it. The result is that with each passing grade, the gap between the first system student and those in the second and third systems in thinking and academic problem solving skills widens. These skills also pave the way to a richer and more expansive curriculum.

THE ROLE OF DISCIPLINE IN THE THREE SCHOOL SYSTEMS

The three school systems can be differentiated in respect to another important feature, namely, student discipline. In the context of education, the term "discipline" can be applied to behavior, application, and independent thinking. "Behavior" refers to living by rules of discipline that are necessary for the well functioning of the school and class, and for creating an optimal environment for learning. "Application" refers to attending to and actively participating in classroom learning opportunities and faithful performance of homework assignments. "Independent thinking" refers to mental activity beyond learning, to reflection on what has been learned in a critical way. Thoughtfulness is the roadway to inventiveness and creativity, in the sciences and the arts, and in life itself.

In general terms, recognizing exceptions, students in the first school system are disciplined in all three, in behavior, application, and independent thinking. Those in the second system are disciplined in behavior and application, but not independent thinking. Their tendency, sometimes encouraged by teachers and parents, is to accept, unchallenged, whatever is taught, whatever they read. Some students in the third system, the most disruptive, are non-disciplined in all three. Others conform to the rules of conduct but, because of disruption, find it difficult to apply themselves to assignments and do not have the opportunity to engage in independent thinking about schoolwork.

These differences have implications both for further education and subsequent careers. The first system children acquire lifetime advantages over the other two. Those in the third system lose irreplaceable opportunities. The differences show up, too, on tests of achievement.

ACCOUNTABILITY TESTING AND ITS EFFECT ON TEACHING THINKING

The strong movement within this country to mandate testing of children's learning in public schools could well discourage activities that foster thinking. State assessment programs are already detractors from those activities, as teachers are understandably led to prepare the students for the tests. And those tests focus largely on learned facts, a far cry from measuring quality education, with its emphasis on thinking and problem solving as well as knowledge. The claim is often made that testing is necessary to identify poor performing schools. The fact is that school superintendents know which of their schools are performing poorly, and it is common knowledge among many parents. Furthermore, subjects that are not tested, such as art, music, and physical education, get short shrift when school budgets are formulated.

Another failing of various assessment plans is their willingness to accept the limited learning objective of meeting standards that primarily test the acquisition of knowledge. But isn't that so much more than many acquire under present circumstances? Yes, indeed, it is, and all children should have that as a minimum. But testing is not the way to achieve that goal. Seeing to it that all the necessary resources for that to occur *is* the way. Besides, test preparation and the testing process are costly, in time and money, both of which are better spent on resources for teaching. The solution is not in penalizing the poorest schools by cutting their funding, which is equivalent to penalizing a sick child for not being able to run fast. The solution is in correcting the in-school and at-home conditions that prevent poor and minority children from getting what first system children have.

The deputy commissioner of the New York State Education Department "grudgingly conceded to me that test prep is probably 'the norm' in failing districts," essayist James Traub reported.[28] Teaching to the test may be appropriate when the test is highly demanding, when it calls upon the powers to think and communicate effectively. The fear among educators is that under those circumstances so many students would fail that the outcry would make standards-based testing untenable. That kind of fear has led in most states to postponement of the exit test as a requirement for high school graduation. In Arizona, for example, after 88 percent of tenth graders failed math, 72 percent, writing, and 38 percent, reading, the state postponed the use of the test for graduation purposes from 2001 to later years, finally to 2006. Even at that point, as Traub adds, students who fail will have what the state calls "an equivalent demonstration opportunity," which, in his words, "sounds suspiciously like the kind of two-track system that exit tests are meant to abolish. The whole episode is painful proof of the absurdity of thinking that testing, all by itself, will raise the academic performance of children who have muddled along in school for years."[29] A more comprehensive way of putting this is that children can't get a first-class education by means of third-class resources.

The argument is sometimes used that our schools once served all its students well, including millions of immigrant children in the late ninetheenth and early twentieth centuries, the implication being that if we return to old-fashioned methods of teaching basics, we will improve the schools. That myth of the great performance of early twentieth-century schools was put to rest by Colin Greer.[30] Referring to what he called the "great school legend," he found, to the contrary, that in large measure the schools failed to give those children the education they needed. Instead, what they got was knowledge that they were scholastic failures and socially inferior, knowledge that marked them for marginal places and low income in the workforce. There were exceptions, of course, and those exceptions are usually advanced to support the fanta-sized school system of the past.

Many years ago, I served on a team of teachers and educators evalu-ating a high school in a community in Westchester County, New York, that had both an affluent residential section and a smaller working-class one. To learn what the students thought about their school, I obtained permission from the principal to invite students at random to an open meeting. During the course of the discussion, many of the twenty or so students spoke positively about teachers, curriculum, and extracurricu-lar activities. A few were curiously silent. Then one teenager, (who, I later learned, was a first-generation American) wearing a leather jacket—in the James Dean era, a symbol of rebellion—spoke up with the fervor of one who feels downtrodden and bitterly resentful: "Yeah, they all like it here. They're the teachers' pets. They get elected, they're the team captains, they get the awards. We get nothing!"

Some of the other teenagers protested that anyone could run for of-fice and could work for good grades. They were sincere. They did not understand the roots of difference that generated the bitter complaint of injustice, because their personal lives gave them too few experiences to enable them to empathize with this student.

That disaffected student, now well into middle age, would not be sur-prised by the action of the governor of his state. The New York Board of Regents, distressed by poor performance on high school competency tests, proposed to spend $900 million to help the students. Most of them, in the words of a *New York Times* editorial, are in "poor districts that have the least qualified teachers and the worst facilities. But after welcoming the new standards and pledging to support them, Governor George Pataki submitted a budget proposing only about $270 million and *redirected much of the money toward affluent districts* [emphasis added]."[31]

Overall, the quality of education in the United States is considerably higher than it was a century ago, and the percentage of high school and college graduates vastly greater. Yet, the *gap in quality of education* offered to the different social classes remains essentially unchanged. Today, as in the past, the three school systems are distinct in ways that make life and learning very different for the students. Indeed, the contrast between first and third school system children, in the educational opportunities available to them, especially to learn to think, is stark, and comparable to that between first and third world nations.

NOTES

1. Jonathan Kozol, *Savage Inequalities: Children in America's Schools* (New York: Crown Publishers, 1991).

2. Kozol, *Savage Inequalities*, 63–64.

3. Kozol, *Savage Inequalities*, 52.

4. Jay Romano, "Approaches to Killing Roaches," *New York Times*, 3 August 1997, 3 (Section 9).

5. Richard Rothstein, "Seeing Achievement Gains by an Attack on Poverty," *New York Times*, 7 March 2001, 9 (B).

6. Rothstein, "Seeing Achievement Gains by an Attack on Poverty," 9(B).

7. Pam Belluck, "Gang Gunfire May Chase Chicago Children from Their School," *New York Times*, 17 November 1997, 1 and 21(A).

8. Belluck, "Gang Gunfire May Chase Chicago Children from Their School," 21(A).

9. Gerald N. Tirozzi and Gabriela Uro, "Education Reform in the United States: National Policy in Support of Local Efforts for School Improvement," *American Psychologist* 52, no. 3 (March 1997): 241–249, 245.

10. Belluck, "Gang Gunfire May Chase Chicago Children from Their School," 21(A).

11. James Atlas, "Making the Grade: Going to Private School Involves Hard Work for the Parents," *New Yorker* 73, no. 8 (April 1997): 34–39.

12. Atlas, "Making the Grade," 35.

13. Margot Slade, "First the Schoolhouse, Then the Home," *New York Times*, 8 March 1998, 1 and 4 (Section 11).

14. Somina Sengupta, "A Traditional Career Gains New Class," *New York Times,* 3 August 1997, Section 4A, 48.

15. Sengupta, "A Traditional Career Gains New Class."

16. Sengupta, "A Traditional Career Gains New Class."

17. Abby Goodnough, "'S' is for Satisfactory, not for Satisfied on Teacher's Sentimental Journey," *New York Times*, 1 July 2001, 1, 22 (Metro Section).

18. Goodnough, "'S' is for Satisfactory, not for Satisfied on Teacher's Sentimental Journey," 22.

19. Andrew Schwebel, Bernice Schwebel, Carol Schwebel, and Milton Schwebel, *The Student Teacher's Handbook* (Mahwah, N.J.: Erlbaum, 1996), 129–130.

20. Sara Schwebel, Personal communication, e-mail, 27 June 2001.

21. Kozol, *Savage Inequalities*, 85.

22. Joanne Jacobs, "Even Mary Poppins Wouldn't Work for Child-Care Wages Offered in the U.S," *Arizona Daily Star*, 8 November 1997, 17(A).

23. Sylvia Scribner and Michael Cole, *The Psychology of Literacy* (Cambridge, Mass.: Harvard University Press, 1981).

24. Marcia C. Linn, Catherine Lewis, Ineko Tsuchida, and Nancy Butler Songer, "Beyond Fourth-Grade Science: Why Do U.S. and Japanese Students Diverge?" *Educational Researcher* 29, no. 3 (April 2000): 4–14.

25. Mary Anderson, Assignments for "Apple Project: A Celebration of Choice," and "The Incredible World Famous Monster Project." Fourth grade class for gifted and talented students, Lineweaver Elementary School, Tucson, Arizona.

26. Sara Schwebel, syllabus for the course, "Learning Thinking Skills in a Private School Course on Twentieth Century American Experience," 1999.

27. Schwebel, Syllabus for the course "Learning Thinking Skills in a Private School Course on Twentieth Century American Experience."

28. James Traub, "The Test Mess," *New York Times,* 7 April 2002, Section 6 (Magazine), 46–51, 60, 78, 49.

29. Traub, "The Test Mess," 60, 78.

30. Colin Greer, *The Great School Legend* (New York: Basic Books, 1972).

31. "Realistic School Standards," *New York Times*, 20 March 1999, 20(A).

6

PARENTAL DIFFERENCES IN THE THREE SCHOOL SYSTEMS

One very large cluster of factors contributes mightily to educational opportunity and outcome—parental teaching.

The educational and achievement differences among children of the three systems are due in large measure to the accumulated effects of social class differences prevailing over several or more generations. That is, parents often pass on what they learned. Advantaged parents, over the generations, accumulate a greater fund of knowledge with which to aid and advise their children, as well as practical know-how about contending with the demands and bureaucracies of preschool, school, and college.

Just as surely as the school provides a curriculum, or course of study, so does the home. Parents are teachers. We are our children's first teachers. We teach them from the moment of birth, by both verbal and nonverbal means. To a great extent, it is from us that they acquire language, surely, along with love, the most precious human attribute. We talk to our children as we hold them, feed them, diaper them, read to them, and tuck them into bed. And we respond with language to their smiles and their gurgling communication. They grow up in a language universe, hearing their parents in conversation and hearing countless other humans at home, in supermarkets, and on the playground, who talk to them in "baby" or grown-up language.

At least the *fortunate* children have that much language in their lives in their early weeks, months, and years. Some parents, often poorly educated themselves, unaware that an infant or young child is stimulated by and responsive to language, raise their children in relative silence. To the great detriment of their infants and toddlers, the parents talk very little and hardly interact with them. When told of the importance of such communication, they will be perplexed, "What for? Babies don't understand."

Every child experiences a home curriculum. It is "written" and implemented by the parents even though they are probably unaware that they are instructing their children in important "subjects." Fortunate children have parents who value curiosity and education and set high expectations. Those children are helped to find an appropriate time and place for doing homework, are taught to exercise great care in doing it, and know that they can expect their parents to review and, if necessary, help them revise their written schoolwork. The quality of the home curriculum, at least as it relates to success in school, depends in large measure on the knowledge of the parent-teacher about raising inquisitive, well-behaved children and about the ways to encourage and support success in school.

Because of their paramount importance in what is truly the early education of infants and children, I have defined "school system" to include the parents and the curriculum they offer. The conditions that contribute to a first- second- or third-system education are found to a considerable degree beyond the walls of the school. They are present from the moment of conception and extend all through the child's schooling.

WHAT PARENTS CAN GIVE

Parents can create *the psychological climate* that induces healthy development and learning. They can role model and reinforce *positive social relationships*, use their *time* and *knowledge* efficiently in assisting them with schoolwork and other learning experiences, set high *expectations*, and finally provide *support* to help achieve those expectations. Although what children need from their parents-as-teachers changes over time, from birth through high school, each of the following categories is relevant at every age: psychological climate, social relations, time, knowledge, expectations, and support. What will be evident is that economically advantaged families in general are also advantaged in connection with each of these categories, and third system children are the most deprived.

Psychological Climate

A relationship of trust, generating feelings of security, is the basis for the kind of psychological climate that encourages learning and positive social relations. Parents are most helpful when, from the early years, they create such a relationship so that their children feel that their parents are not nags or hostile critics but, rather, their strongest supporters and most loyal and loving coaches. In that spirit, children and teenagers feel free to come to their parents to discuss their needs and disclose their problems.

Another aspect of psychological climate is enjoyment of life, including excitement and fun. We witness it in the early years when a mother is engaged in happy "conversation" with an exuberant baby boy and, later, when a father and toddler daughter, sitting on the floor, are enjoying a game of rolling a big ball to each other. And on it goes through the years.

We recognize that positive psychological climate when we see it in a school. Enter some good classrooms and note the excitement in the atmosphere. Children and teachers like being there because they feel safe and they enjoy what they are doing. They are happy together. That kind of climate can be found at every educational level, and those of us who were fortunate to have experienced it, remember it well.

Parents who have the interest and inclination to create that kind of psychological climate at home offer their children an ideal setting for learning and development.

Economic insecurity, due, for example, to unemployment or to inadequate income, can undermine the morale of parents, causing personal distress and, often, marital discord, or in the case of single parents, resignation and perhaps depression. In those conditions, parents are hardly able to cultivate the conditions for a "happy-home" psychological climate.

Positive Social Relationships

Children first learn to interact with others at home. Their first social experiences are with their parents. The fortunate ones sense their parents' approval when they show joy in interacting with people, and their encouragement (rather than disapproval) when they show the first signs of independence. Children flourish in that climate.

Until they go to some child care setting or to a preschool, their social experience is centered in the home, with the principal influences being their parents and siblings, and sometimes grandparents or other relatives close by. As to children's interactions outside the home, the parents usually make those choices, such as the choice of playmates.

To a very great degree, their parents are their teachers and organizers of the social environment. Children also observe their parents' social interactions and learn from them how to relate to other people. If fortunate, they learn to respond with openness, friendliness and cooperation, and reasonable trust. They pick up, as if by osmosis, an outlook on life as something to be relished.

Parents who are bitter and do not relish life because they perceive the world as cruel to them are not likely to be able to foster positive social relationships. Authoritarian parents who were raised with the belief that children must be "broken" and made docile are not going to facilitate positive social relationships.

Time

Time available to the parent-as-teacher and the quality of that time are indispensable resources. This means uninterrupted time, devoted exclusively to this child, for whatever educational purpose, at whatever stage of life.

The time demands diminish over the years, as the young child enters first grade, goes on to middle school and then high school. Yet, the need continues to be considerable, even as the use of time spent together changes. Instead of the focus on language (speech and reading) and social behavior (e.g., sharing with other children) with preschool children, the focus shifts in elementary school to developing sound study habits and, with succeeding years, increased self-responsibility in carrying out assignments and doing that at a level of excellence.

A physically and emotionally drained parent is hardly in the condition to sit patiently and read a storybook to a fascinated child intent both on seeing all the illustrations and also on having the story read again and again. That parent is not likely to be able to give supportive and stimulating assistance to a child in need of guidance and help, as he or she begins school, when the need is greatest. Those limitations are all the more salient when the parent, never much of a student, feels insecure in the role of teacher. Hesitant, unsure, fearful of giving "wrong answers," parents in that situation often seek the safe explanation that they are just too busy to help their children with homework. The reality is that some parents—even those capable of giving aid to their children—*are* too busy coping with survival needs.

Knowledge

Well-informed parents know the importance of interacting with their children, beginning on day one. They talk to the baby and respond to the infant's limited communications. For the toddler, they choose dolls, toys, and play items appropriate to the child's age, and select picture books that will stimulate the child.

Parents of school-age children help them cultivate sound study habits, teach them the intricacies of library usage and computer searches and the methods of doing research for school assignments. They make use of community resources to enrich their children's education.

Scientists know little about reliably appraising the newborn's intellect as it relates to future adult intellect. We *do* have reason to believe that stimulating experiences and activities for the infant and child contribute mightily to their mental development. One study showed tremendous growth in the number of brain cells in children during the active years from birth to age six, with 400 billion added to the brain.[1] Another study, and this with mice, showed that even in adults, enhanced living environments, in this case, more toys, more space, and more companions, led to increased production of brain cells and better performance in behavioral tests.[2] Together, these suggest the powerful role of a stimulating environment.

The influence of parents in the mental development and educational achievement of their children is difficult to measure but not so difficult to chronicle. School learning is enhanced by a variety of intellectual activities. Preeminent is language: the ability to comprehend written and spoken language and to express oneself orally and in writing. Children who are masterful in those skills thrive in school. The mental and language skills that are so vital to intellectual development and learning are first learned at home. Children who have the opportunity to master them at home have an enormous advantage over those whose skill acquisition is at a lower level.

Children learn to speak from parents and their older siblings. Interactions between them convey language, knowledge, attitudes, and values. The quality of what parents transmit depends on their ability as parents-teachers. The parallel, of course, is to professional teachers. Not all of *them* are alike; however, all of them are required to meet certain minimal requirements. Not so for parents. Any reproductively potent individual meets the minimal requirement for parenthood. The luck of the draw determines the quality of home education. Some parents of children in the second and third school systems who want the best for their children lack the time and the educational and linguistic resources to do the equivalent in their respective homes.

Consider the advantages of children who have well-educated parents. These parents converse with them in well-structured speech. They encourage their children to respond to them, and the parents listen attentively. Their parents read extensively and discuss what they have read with each other and sometimes with their children. Regularly the children have the pleasure of their parents reading to them, at least until the children can read aloud to their interested parents.

Dinnertime is special. It is the occasion for conversation and discussion as well as for food, so that speech and thought and social interaction come to be associated with happy times. More than that, habits of speech, conversation, reading, and discussion become ingrained, so that in school, when class work calls for thoughtfulness and for oral responses or for cooperative group work, these home-trained children are equipped to participate successfully.

It is obvious that children who do not master first grade reading and number skills are at a disadvantage in second grade. It is not so obvious, but just as real, that children who do not master the skills that the more fortunate ones acquire during their first few years of life, such as knowing the alphabet, reading from left to right and finding meaning in words, are at a disadvantage in first grade. In both instances, the poorer performing children soon recognize that they can't do what their classmates can do. Of course, their teacher knows that too, and often the other children also know it. Under the circumstances, the poorer performing children are doubly disadvantaged: They can't do grade-level work and, when they compare themselves to their classmates, they suffer the effects of feeling inferior as learners.

Consider this analogy, too. When children transfer from one school district to another, they are evaluated to determine appropriate grade placement. A child who has finished third grade but is backward in basic knowledge may be placed in third grade again. When a child enters kindergarten deficient in skills learned in the first years of life, there is no earlier grade in which to place her or him.

One of the most important features of the home curriculum is reading stories to children. The benefits of storybook reading are not just to entertain children and keep them away from television for a time. The crucial point is that reading to children gives them a great boost in their educational development. Reading expert and educational psychologist Gerald Coles says unequivocally:

> There is no question that preschool storybook reading contributes to eventual reading success: significant and positive correlations have repeatedly been found between it and later reading achievement in school. Additionally, storybook reading has been shown to expand oral vocabulary and strengthen an eagerness to read.[3]

Coles refers to studies by others that show that storybook reading gives children an awareness of the structures and rhythms of language. They then mimic what they have heard in their make-believe reading. Children become aware of the connection between the written language (those symbols on the page), and real things, like people and animals and the activities they engage in.[4] Beyond that, they learn various technical attributes of written knowledge, which, to their advantage, they carry with them when they start their formal education.[5]

Parents of first-system children typically possess the following resources that are less available to parents of the third and even of the second: comprehensive knowledge, bibliographic and computer literacy, and familiarity with stimulating learning experiences in the community. Their shelves contain a variety of books, including encyclopedias, and their computers make use of educational software. They live in larger homes with private spaces for quiet studying.

They have the advantage of other resources that are important to school learning: The parents' knowledge about nutrition and health, about rest and recreation and the availability of the best medical and dental services. These are important for their own sake but have special relevance to education because sickness and inadequate nutrition sap a child's strength and capacity to attend to homework and the activities in school, not to mention the ensuing absenteeism.

Expectations

In the first school-system family, the expectation is that their children will learn to speak and read at early ages, and the parents provide the psychological climate, time, and knowledge to support those expectations. When their children go off to school, the parents expect that they will earn high grades at all levels of education, and their foregone conclusion is that the children will go on to a select college or university and a high-status career. There is no doubt about that future. At home, the parents as teachers gear much of their activity with the children for movement in that direction. Some submit applications for admission to first-rate preschools immediately after the birth of the child. Even the handling of their finances includes planning for those futures.

The second school-system parents have aspirations for their children, too. For many, the hope is that the children will do better than they did and will have a more secure future. Some may have aspirations as high as first-system parents, even if they lack the economic support for their realization. However, others may have more modest aspirations. They want their children to be able to speak and read well. Some parents are pleased as long as the children come home with passing report cards and regular promotions. In preparation for a good job, their aspiration for their children may be to graduate from high school and perhaps advance to and graduate from a community college, or even a four-year college.

Parents of the third-system children tend to be the poorest and most stressed. Some of them, too, may have high aspirations, like the first. Some may have more modest aspirations. Sadly, for many, the chief hope of third-system parents is that their children will not drop out, get caught up in drugs and violence and land in jail, or end up dead while still of school age.

Some third-system parents succeed in transcending socially imposed limitations, like poverty. Through high valuation of education and sheer determination, they instill in their children high expectations and devotion to their studies and back them up with a disciplined life. They hope for a college education.

The Yale psychiatrist and pioneer school reformer, James P. Comer,[6] came from a family of that kind. To illustrate the importance of high standards and expectations, and love and support, he tells of his parents' influence in raising a family of educated and successful children. They did this, he points out, despite the handicaps experienced by working class African Americans. His father, who had a sixth-grade education in rural Alabama, was a steel mill laborer. His mother, who at the age of eight decided that education was the road to a better life, but had to leave school early in order to work, was a domestic worker both before the marriage and for twelve years afterward.

These poorly educated parents had a clearly designed child-training program. The mother believed that "the proper balance between order and freedom, pleasure and punishment led to self-discipline, thinking, and development of social skills."[7]

Much of life in the Comer family was infused with warmth, closeness, and trust. Dinner was a special time, when the parents and five children were together and when they were all expected to participate in discussion. The children learned to listen to others and to express themselves clearly. Their parents prepared them for school and beyond and nurtured their interests in learning and their academic aspirations.

Even when parents cannot provide direct assistance with school knowledge, they can, as the Comers did, give their children all the essentials for successful outcomes. They gave them time, relationships of trust, positive psychological climate, high aspirations, and invaluable knowledge about such important behaviors as clear communication, self-motivation, and discipline. Unfortunately, many parents set high expectations for their children but do not or cannot provide the resources or practical help needed to ensure success. Children in these circumstances fall short and, unhappily, feel like failures. Due to the parents' economic stresses and sometimes lack of knowledge about how to help, this more often occurs in poorer, less privileged families.

SOCIAL POLICY AND PARENTING

The parental role is not independent of other influences on the education of children. Its interaction with government policy, and the society's
attitudes reflected by that policy, are complex and vary with the social
class of the parents. For affluent families, unemployment, unemployment insurance, and government-subsidized health insurance are of little if any personal concern. Because children from this social class attend private schools or well-funded public schools, the state and federal
appropriations for education are of little consequence. For parents of
the lower social classes, all of those issues—unemployment, unemployment insurance, subsidized health insurance, and federal and state appropriations for education—are close to life-and-death matters. All of
them, and not just the appropriations for education, are matters that
profoundly affect the education of their children. Most third- and many
second-school system children are in the lower social classes. Their
home education will remain inferior until basic issues of social class are
successfully addressed.

THE SWEDISH EXPERIENCE

Sweden took measures to address the problem of inferior education for
lower-class children. Studies on Sweden's effort to eradicate educational
inequalities are presented in the book *Can Education Be Equalized?
The Swedish Case in Comparative Perspective*, edited by Robert Erikson and Jan Jonsson.[8] This book highlights the role of government intervention in improving the lot of lower-class parents and the quality of
their children's education. It shows that the status and condition of parents are inseparably intertwined with the educational opportunities and
attainments of their children. Although Sweden has a miniscule population compared with the United States, and is different in other respects
as well, the findings reported in this book are relevant to the educational
problems in this country and others.

The contributors to the book examined inequalities in educational opportunity in Sweden over the course of the twentieth century. They
were addressing the following questions: What was the gap in such op-

portunity at intervals during the century? At what point did the gap widen or narrow? What were the effects of the government's concerted efforts to narrow the gap?

They found one period, 1930–1970, during which socioeconomic class-related inequalities of educational opportunity declined. This was a period of governmental policies aimed at reducing social class differences in the nation, especially by reducing income inequalities. The changes were so significant that the authors, Erikson and Jonsson, could assert: "Indeed, poverty in an absolute sense was in practice eradicated in the 1970s." [9] In a later chapter, Erikson reported on the consequence of policy changes across the board in Sweden in the direction of equality.[10] *Since the 1920s, programs that promoted employment, universal health care, and pensions, accompanied by declining economic inequality, ran parallel with increases in educational opportunity.* In other words, Erikson said, "many egalitarian changes 'go together.'"[11] He meant that programs which enhanced the quality of life of the lower social classes also made the parents better equipped as parent-teachers and better able to afford any costs associated with the education of their children, without needing the children to quit school to supplement the family income.

Erikson and Jonsson offer five explanations for class differences in academic performance.

1. Genetic Factors. Genetic factors account for very little in differences between social classes in school performance. While "individual differences in I.Q. are estimated to depend to some 50 percent on such [genetic] factors, . . . estimates of the maximum degree to which class differences . . . may depend upon genetic factors suggest that they can at most account for only a minor degree of the total " relationship between social class and school performance.[12]

2. Home environments. They refer here to "the forms and patterns of interaction between parents and children and other differences in childhood conditions between social classes."[13] The home environments make an enormous difference. In explaining the difference, the researchers, Erikson and Jonsson, refer to the ways in which higher-class parents reinforce their children's academic ability and improve their performance in school. This may include

"verbal training during childhood and practical help with school-work throughout their educational care."[14] Furthermore, the home environment is conducive to expectations about the future, whether high or low. Higher-class parents are confident in the probable success of their children, and this attitude is transmitted to their children in the form of expectations. Unless the expectations are highly unrealistic, the parental attitude also serves as a confidence builder. Economic security is an important factor in the psychological state of parents and in shaping the home environment. That sense of security entails not just income, the researchers point out, but savings and investments as well.

3. Class and cultural bias. This explanation for class differences in performance is based on the theory that "middle class norms pervade the system . . . [and that] teachers tend to reward proper behavior and adjustment to the 'cultural' values prevailing in school."[15] This point of view of Erikson's is supported by another study in Sweden. This one revealed that differences in ability test scores were less correlated with social class differences than were standardized school tests, which, then, were less correlated than teacher grades.[16] In other words, this can be interpreted to mean that the more subjective the assessment (the most subjective being teacher assigned grades) the greater the social class difference. Social class bias favors the favored classes and handicaps the lower classes. Higher-class parents elicit more favorable reactions for their children from schools and teachers, simply by who they are and also by their behavior. Distinctions in lifestyle between classes come into play in school. Presumably, cultural codes are reflected in the values and expectations of the school, its administrators and teachers. Those are the values and expectations of the higher classes, which children in families of those classes absorb almost as readily as mother's milk. They know what to expect in school because the expectations are similar to those inculcated at home. Higher-class parents know the strategies for navigating the system. They teach their children how to interact with and please their teachers; how and when to ask questions and engage in class discussion; how to prepare for and take exams; what class and extracurricular activities to engage in; and when to get help from and perhaps study with

friends. They abide by the rules of the system, whereas, according to Erikson and Jonsson, there is reason to believe that some working-class children in Sweden misbehave in school as a form of protest against such school norms as punctuality and tidiness. No wonder, then, children of the favored classes like going to school more than their counterparts in lower social classes.

4. Health and nutrition. Differences of these kinds "could also account for some of the association between class origin and academic ability."[17]

5. Number of siblings. "Finally, social class differences in sibship size may be another factor of relevance, since there seems to be a (fairly weak) effect of number of siblings on scholastic achievement."[18]

The last four of the five explanations show the powerful effect of the parents on the educational performance of their children. The second (home environment), fourth (health and nutrition), and fifth (number of siblings) explanations are determined by parents. The third (class and cultural bias) is passively determined by them. The social programs introduced in Sweden were intended to strengthen the quality of parental influence in the lower social classes, among other ways by improving the home environment, raising health and nutritional standards, and reducing class bias.

Those programs succeeded in narrowing the gap, but not enough to entirely bridge it. Class differences persisted both in living and working conditions and in inequality of educational opportunity. A greater degree of equality in income was not enough because *class differences in themselves* (the more affluent possessing savings and investments) give educational advantages to those of higher social class status. Also, equality in income did not eradicate inequalities in parental education. In addition, the researchers found class differences, in the form of parental education, are more important to children's school achievement than income. Class differences do this both through specialized knowledge and through expectations about the future.

In his concluding sentence to his study on explaining change in educational inequality, in which he emphasizes the overriding importance of a family's economic security, Erikson says: "This, then, is the hypothesis that our analysis leads up to: Inequality of educational opportunity may decrease with industrialization *if political action is taken to reduce social inequalities*"[19] (emphasis added). His conclusion becomes meaningful when seen in the following light.

- During the period of declining inequality in education, Sweden took the following *political actions* aimed at reducing class inequalities:
    Narrowed the income gap
    Promoted employment opportunity
    Provided universal health care
    Provided universal pensions
    Increased educational opportunity

- When Sweden discontinued the strong *political action* to reduce social and educational inequalities, differentials remained in the following:
    Living conditions
    Working conditions
    Income
    Economic resources
    Educational opportunity

The conclusions we can draw from the Swedish studies are the following. First, improving the economic, and thereby the psychological, security of parents is essential. Second, raising the educational level of the parents—enabling them to be more effective parents-as-teachers, about health and nutrition, as well as school knowledge, and ways of navigating the school—is another essential. Third, counteracting the cultural biases of school personnel is equally important. Fourth, raising the expectations of parents and their children, which means changing their vision of a possible future, is another essential. Finally, changes to reduce educational and social inequality require political action, and that political action must be unending.

For the United States, as in Sweden, political action, it seems, is the major route, perhaps the only route, to working toward equalizations that eradicate class differences at home and in school. Such political action would enable parents, in the second- and third-school systems, to give their children what they need to benefit optimally from their school experiences.

NOTES

1. William R. Shankle, et al., "Postnatal Doubling of Neuron Number in the Developing Human Cerebral Cortex between 15 Months and 6 Years," *Journal of Theoretical Biology* 191, no. 2 (March 1998): 115–140.

2. Henriette von Praag, Gerd Kempermann, and Fred Gage. "Running Increases Cell Proliferation," *Nature Neuroscience* 2, no. 3 (March 1999): 266–270.

3. Gerald Coles, *Reading Lessons: The Debate over Literacy* (New York: Farrar, Straus and Giroux, 1998), 64.

4. Gordon Wells, "Preschool Literacy-Related Activities and Success in School," in *Literacy, Language, and Learning*, ed. David R. Olson, Nancy Torrance, and Angela Hildyard (New York: Cambridge University Press, 1985), 229–255. Cited in Coles, *Reading Lessons: The Debate over Literacy*.

5. Victoria Purcell-Gates, "Lexical and Syntactic Knowledge of Written Narrative Held by Well-Read-to Kindergartners and Second Graders," ERIC Report, 1986, AN: ED056782.

6. James P. Comer, *Waiting for a Miracle* (New York: E. P. Dutton, 1997).

7. Comer, *Waiting for a Miracle*, 22–23.

8. Robert Erikson and Jan O. Jonsson, eds., *Can Education Be Equalized? The Swedish Case in Comparative Perspective*, (Boulder, Colo.: Westview Press, 1996).

9. Robert Erikson and Jan O. Jonsson, "The Swedish Context: Educational Reform and Long-Term Change in Educational Inequality," in *Can Education Be Equalized?*, 65–93, 66.

10. Robert Erikson, "Explaining Change in Education Inequality—Economic Security and School Reforms," in *Can Education Be Equalized?*, 95–112.

11. Erikson, "Explaining Change in Education Inequality—Economic Security and School Reforms," 105.

12. Erikson and Jonsson, "Explaining Class Inequality in Education: The Swedish Test Case," in *Can Education Be Equalized?*, 1–63, 10–11. Information about the I.Q. is taken from Nathan Brody, *Intelligence* (San Diego: Academic Press, 1992).

13. Erikson and Jonsson, "Explaining Class Inequality in Education," 11.

14. Erikson and Jonsson, "Explaining Class Inequality in Education," 11.

15. A. Svensson, *Relative Achievement. School Performance in Relation to Intelligence, Sex and Home Environment* (Stockholm: Almquist and Wiksell, 1971).

16. Erikson and Jonsson, "Explaining Class Inequality in Education," 12.

17. Erikson and Jonsson, "Explaining Class Inequality in Education," 12. Information drawn from J. R. Behrman and P. Taubman, "Birth Order, Schooling, and Earnings," *Journal of Labour Economics* 4 (1986): 121–145.

18. Erikson and Jonsson, "Explaining Class Inequality in Education," 11.

19. Erikson and Jonsson, "Explaining Class Inequality in Education," 109.

7

THE POWER OF
PARENTAL MEDIATION

By the time kindergarten teachers across the country welcome their students at the beginning of each year, the children have been sorted out by circumstances beyond their control. The children had no part in choosing the school district in which they live, the preschool training, if any, that they had, and most significant of all, the adults who parented them. Some have experienced enriched parenting and others, impoverished parenting. For the latter—probably many children in the third school system and some in the second—a policy of "tougher standards" and statewide tests is counterproductive, suggesting that the authors of the policy are out of touch with principles of human development and learning and the role of parenting in the education of children. They seem ignorant of the following, or ignore it.

For children of preschool and school age, it is much too late to correct prenatal and postnatal inequities that put the third school system children at a disadvantage. It is too late to give their mothers the kind of nutritional and medical support they did not have while carrying the fetus, and it is too late to correct the nutritional deficits suffered by the children as a result of parental poverty or ignorance or both. It is late but not too late to provide them with rich cultural experiences at home and elsewhere that contribute to school success. It is very late but not too late for parents to master the language of the school so that what the children hear at school is not foreign to them but rather is like what they hear at home.

There is no conceivable way to duplicate these parental assets for children, especially those from the lower socioeconomic classes, but there are ways to approximate them in some different form, to a far greater degree than is now done. The proposals later in this book are intended to prevent the costly "too-lates" and "lates" cited above. They are meant to provide the "training and support" promised by the ill-fated Goals 2000.

Parent education is not new. It has appropriately encompassed a very broad scope of information, covering the physical and psychological aspects of parenting. For example, the pregnant woman learns about the important role of nutrition in the healthy development of the fetus, the damaging effects of tobacco and alcohol on the fetus, the need for rest and relaxation during pregnancy, and for a loving relation with the expectant father. The future parent learns about the varied aspects of child rearing, from feeding and bathing to physical and mental stimulation.

By 1971, an annotated bibliography on parent education, thirty-nine pages in length, was published.[1] For years before that date, educators and specialists in early childhood development had recognized the need to help parents learn the importance of activities such as stimulating the child's awareness of the physical and social environment, reading and telling stories, and encouraging children to express themselves orally and through writing and drawing.

However, such general parent education was never widespread. School systems did not create a curriculum and offer such studies to parents. For the most part, interested parents sought out such knowledge for themselves, mostly from books, surely the most widely read being *Dr. Spock's Baby and Child Care*.[2]

MENTAL EMPOWERING IN THE RELATIONSHIP

All of the good qualities in the parent-child relationship come together in one of the crucial roles of parenting, when the parent serves as mediator. This means that the parent directly intervenes between the child and an object to get the child to focus on the object. The "object" could be a set of blocks, a picture book, or a relationship with another child. Although children learn a great deal through direct experience with the environment, there is still much that they can learn only when an adult interposes herself between the child and the environment. Mediated learning does not depend on chance. The adult arranges experiences to produce in the child what Reuven Feuerstein, a leading thinker on mediation, calls "appropriate learning sets and habits."[3] Through mediation, parents enable children to acquire the skills of learning and thinking, good study habits, and the social skills that help them succeed in school and afterward.

On the surface, when a parent is reading to a child, let us say a mother to her son, and having him anticipate some of the words in the story, the impact is very apparent. She is reading with enjoyment, he is listening intently and getting joy in correctly knowing some of the words, and they both find the interaction very pleasurable. Repeated experiences of this kind lead him to develop positive feelings about reading.

Beneath the surface, however, something much more profound is occurring. In the role of parent-as-teacher, she is mediating one of the crowning human legacies for her son. Through the actions of reading to him and obtaining his active participation, she is helping him acquire some of the cultural tools that are essential to learning and school achievement and to mental development.

PARENT AS MEDIATOR

Precisely what does the adult do for the child? The American psychologist, James Wertsch, has studied the nature of mediation in the acquisition of cultural tools.[4] These tools enable individuals to have a degree of control and even mastery over their environment or, in other words, to mediate their environment. In order to put this complex process into concrete terms, Wertsch uses, as an example, a pole-vaulter learning to use the pole as a tool necessary to leap over a high bar. Try to imagine vaulting fifteen feet without a pole. Given a pole, imagine vaulting without instruction on holding, running with, planting, and elevating oneself with it. Vaulting is impossible without the pole and without the skills to use it.

"But wait. Couldn't an individual invent this tool for himself?" one might ask. The answer would be, "of course." The same question could be asked about all our cultural tools. However, most of them, like language, developed over millennia. To avoid the need to reinvent the wheel every generation, adults provide opportunity for each new cohort to assimilate the countless cultural tools invented over the long stretch of human existence.

The original concept of mediation comes from the Russian psychologist, L. S. Vygotsky,[5] who was so creative that he has been appropriately characterized "the Mozart of psychology." Like Mozart's, Vygotsky's life was very brief, but his contributions to the psychology of art, education, and mental development were extraordinary.

From him came the profound formulation about the process of mental development: The thoughts in the mind of the child begin as the words of an adult, usually the parent. In the next sequence, the thoughts are heard as utterances of the child, expressed during play, perhaps to a friend or a doll. Finally, they are internalized in the child's mind, becoming the child's thoughts, as if they "belonged" to the child, as they now do. For example, mother says to the child, "A good girl puts her toys back on the shelf after she's finished playing with them." After a number of interactions of that kind between mother and daughter, the child, now playing alone, is heard uttering the same words to her doll. Finally, mother notes with satisfaction that her daughter returns the toys to the shelf without a word of reminder from her, because the little girl instructs herself to do so.

This came about because, through her mother's mediation, the child acquired a tool that helps her organize her universe. To think that these interactions with mother simply "disciplined" the child or taught her "responsibility" (they did both of those) is to underestimate the significance of the child's learning. Through these experiences, she has begun to acquire, that is, to internalize, the cultural tools of order and sequence. Vygotsky described the process in this way: "Every function in the child's cultural development appears twice: first, on the social level, and later, on the individual level; first, between people (*interpsychological*) and then *inside* the child (*intrapsychological*). All the higher functions originate as actual relations between human individuals."[6]

The acquisition of cultural tools is a mighty step forward in a child's development. Israeli psychologist Reuven Feuerstein considers those tools so important that he characterizes children who lack the basic ones for learning as "culturally deprived."[7] When children acquire the tools through mediated learning, they become more able to learn independently. Insufficient mediated learning, in contrast, leads to impaired functioning because the children lack the wherewithal to learn on their own.

To appreciate the crucial role of the mediator we need only imagine a child living alone, magically fed and clothed to survive, while lacking any interaction with another human. The child would be without language or any other cultural legacies that mark us human and differentiate us from the primates that are next on the evolutionary ladder.

And so, after birth, children begin the long process of acquiring their cultural legacy. Parents as mediators of speech put the imprint of dialect on the children and set limits to the initial vocabulary. As mediators of reading, parents initially determine their children's experience with and attitudes toward reading. Outside influences leave their marks too, including relatives, friends, and neighbors, as well as television programs and video games. Nevertheless, during the preschool years and afterward, children who are advantaged by having educated parents are much more likely to have practice in, and learn early in their lives, the important skills discussed below, all of them vitally important to school learning and academic success.

Actively Listening to and Not Simply Hearing a Speaker

That kind of listening calls for attentiveness and participation, in contrast with passive sitting by, with "the loudspeaker" turned up but mostly ignored.

Recognizing the Significant Point in a Paragraph or a Story

Children may know the mechanics of reading and be able to sound out the words with great precision but with little comprehension of the meaning of a passage.

Organizing a Thought and Expressing It Clearly

As the social animals that we are, our existence depends upon communication. In the day-to-day flow of intercourse with adults and siblings, children acquire the necessary communication skills for inter-changes about little and big matters at home and with friends. Family members talk about the food they are eating, about friends and relatives they have been seeing, perhaps about a sporting event they attended. However, the content of school learning calls for a very different quality of thought and expression. The teacher asks a question about a character in a story, or a scientific concept, or a historical event—most of them quite unrelated to the personal lives of the children. These are not the topics of everyday life, the stuff of everyday conversation at home, except in those homes in which some conversation is in fact very much of that sort. In those homes, as in school, the topics are pursued in ways that call for children to organize and express their thoughts clearly, about imper-sonal matters like the theme of a book, so that their auditors—teacher, students, and parents—understand them.

Researching a Topic

One of the great tools for learning is the set of skills involved in draw-ing on resources of knowledge. Children can learn at a young age the value of dictionaries, encyclopedias, atlases, the Internet, and other sources of information. As with other skills, they learn best when they have many opportunities to use these resources, and at first, through the mediation of an adult.

Some of the cultural tools for learning are as apparent as the pole is for vaulting, but many are not. For example, as Wertsch[8] explains, if adults are asked how they multiplied two three-digit numbers, they would answer, "I just multiplied." If they were asked to demonstrate by multiplying 343 × 822, they would proceed to put the numbers in a vertical array as follows:

$$\begin{array}{r} 343 \\ \underline{822} \\ 686 \\ 686 \\ \underline{2744} \\ 281,946 \end{array}$$

Most people, when asked to multiply without use of that structure, would be stymied—unable to multiply. Both the *agents* of action (vaulters or thinkers), and the *tools* of action (poles or multiplication structures) are essential.

LEARNING TO READ

At a very young age, the cultural tools of reading come into play. Reading specialist Gerald Coles expands on the role of phonemes, which are the smallest units of speech.[9] "Phonological awareness" is a major explanation of reading success and failure. Children who are phonologically aware can blend or separate phonemes to identify words. He gives the following examples.

- Blending phonemes: Asking someone to say or identify a word made by blending its phonemes (/b/,/a/,/t/ = bat).
- Segmenting phonemes: Asking what sounds are heard in a word (/b/,/a/,/t/).
- Deleting phonemes: Asking what word would remain if a phoneme were deleted (remove /b/ from bat).[10]

Although learning specialists differ about how phonemes should be incorporated into children's learning experiences—whether by direct or indirect instruction—they do not differ in their view of their importance. In order to be able to read and spell, children must understand that spoken words are composed of sequences of phonemes. They must also identify those phonemes within words, as in the case of "at" in "cat" or "all" in "ball."

Phonological abilities are causally connected to later reading achievement. However, Coles stresses the point that these abilities are not an "independent psychological process," but rather one among other strong influences in the development of reading ability.[11] For example, when phonological awareness training is incorporated with written language, the positive results in reading achievement are increased, and the more the use or practice, the better the results.

Reading educator Eileen Ball discusses the importance of phonological abilities as precursors to learning to read.[12] She says that preschool and kindergarten children who had had thousands of hours of pre-reading activity in print-rich environments come to kindergarten or first grade greatly advantaged. Those literary experiences make them knowledgeable about "the sequential nature of speech." Children who enter school "with a limited number of hours engaged in school-consistent interactions with print, have fewer opportunities to discover how written language maps onto speech. One consequence of this limited interaction with print is that some children will enter school without the prerequisite phoneme awareness knowledge necessary to bootstrap literacy learning."[13]

During those thousands of hours of pre-reading in print-rich environments, the advantaged children acquire much more than phoneme awareness. Stories and reading become part of everyday life and, indeed, a very pleasurable part. The children are "at home" with print and oral language.

In a rational society in which the welfare of children is among its highest values, leaders would set as their goal that all children obtain those preschool experiences during their preschool years—at home and elsewhere. To achieve that goal they must be aware that there is no substitute for parents, or surrogates, who are sufficiently educated to give their children these rich and pleasurable experiences—and who commit all necessary resources to further their education.

Benjamin Franklin's happy recollections of his father's early influence on him and his siblings provide us with a fine example of the parental role as mediator. In particular, he recalls the following about his father.

> At his table, he liked to have, as often as he could, some sensible friend or neighbor to converse with, and always took care to start some ingenious or useful topic for discourse, which might tend to improve the minds of his children. By this means, he turned our attention to what was good, just, and prudent in the conduct of life.[14]

The elder Franklin gave his children the opportunity to acquire the priceless cultural tools of listening (not just hearing, but listening), thinking, speaking, and interacting with others.

PARENT-TEACHER AT HOME

The need for parent training is great. During most of elementary school and all of high school, students are given assignments to be done at home: worksheets, workbooks, essays, book reviews, and readings. In addition, they are expected to prepare for tests and exams at home. For first system children these are all part of a routine that was established for them by their parents. They learned the importance of a quiet environment in an established location in their home. They learned, too, how to manage their time and how to study. They know where, when, and how to study, and they know, too, the resources to call upon when they are stuck and unable to solve a problem, answer a question, or develop a composition. Print, Internet, and human resources are close at hand.

They have other advantages. If they do poorly in school, or even if their grades are not low but below expectations, their parents are likely to use measures more constructive than punishment. They are likely to do that even if the problem takes the form of resistance to studying, an attitude that can raise parental temper to the boiling point. The probability is that the parents will talk with their children to find the reasons for underachievement, or as the case may be, for resistance to learning. If those efforts are not successful, such parents, knowledgeable about psychological resources and sufficiently affluent to pay for it, are likely to seek professional help. In these many ways, the first school system children have enormous opportunities and advantages over other children.

If the second and third system children are to close the gap in opportunity, even a little bit, it must be in part through the training of their parents in the ways of monitoring their schoolwork at home. Besides that, they need to learn how to engage their children in verbal interactions that contribute to school learning. They must also learn to convey their interest in their children's school experiences as well as their aspirations for success.

There are countless ways that parents can perform the teaching role even without reference to the school curriculum. Two educators writing about early childhood education explain that parents need to be made aware of the many opportunities for their children to learn while engaged in activities at home.[15] For example, they use counting skills and spatial relations when setting the dinner table. They learn about what floats and what sinks when they play with toys in the bathtub. And they learn language skills and social graces during dinner conversation.

There is no reason for parents to be aware of these diverse learning opportunities at home, which are simply part of very busy daily routines.

That is why parent educators are needed. And their job is not an easy one because, as several researchers discovered, parents are fearful of looking foolish and being misunderstood by the educator; and they may be embarrassed by their children's performance in school.[16]

WHY THE NEED FOR PARENTING TRAINING?

The art and science of parenting are not taught in school. Knowledge about parenting, for that matter about getting along with one's spouse, is not a requirement for obtaining a marriage license. Ignorance about parenting becomes apparent within days, if not hours, of childbirth. Even in two-parent families, even where the two are highly educated, all too often the new parents are shocked when they discover the exhausting demands of caring for an infant. Nighttime crying, feeding, diaper changing, all of them repeated over and over, night after night erodes the energy and sometimes the morale of the new parents. The early thrill of being a parent loses some of its luster, and the romance in the marriage gets a strong test.

With passing days and nights most parents come to grips with the unexpected demands and manage to regain equilibrium in family life. That early period, after all, lasts only a matter of months. Beyond those stressful months and throughout the years ahead, parents must tend to their children's development; they have much to learn about physical, social, moral, and mental growth. They must learn, for example, that play to children is not recreation as it is for adults; it is one of the richest modes of understanding their environment, the physical environment when they are playing with objects, and the social environment when they are interacting with other children. Some parents do not appreciate the importance of reading, discussing school activities, and helping with homework.

Some evidence of just how unskilled and unprepared some parents are in parenting for educational purposes was revealed in a small study conducted in Florida by Sharon Patterson.[17] In a rural elementary school, a parent survey was undertaken before a parent education program was introduced. The majority of the students in this school came from single parent, low-income homes. The survey revealed that of fifty-three parents, 60 percent did not read to their children, 68 percent did not discuss school activities with their children, while 45 percent did not help with homework.

Why did the parents have such a lack of involvement in their children's schoolwork? The investigator surveyed a representative group of parents and found the following, grouped into three categories:

Knowledge
- The parents did not know how to help their children.
- They did not know the techniques to help their children develop positive attitudes to school and learning.
- Many were unable to help because of their own limited education.

Time
- Single parents, in particular, found it difficult to participate in school functions because of the often-conflicting demands of work and child care.

Alienation
- Parents did not attend school functions because they did not feel welcome in school.
- They had developed negative attitudes toward educators because they felt talked down to.
- Non-English speaking parents felt uncomfortable in school because of their limitations in speaking English.

This study concludes that, to make parent training effective, parents must be given time off from work and child care assistance. They must also be made to feel comfortable and welcome.

Efforts on the part of school people to develop effective relationships with parents are all the more necessary with poor families. Psychologist Bernice Lott studied the kinds of responses low-income parents are likely to receive from school administrators and teachers.[18] She examined many studies that had addressed the issue, and she came up with disheartening findings: School personnel tend to believe that such parents do not value education, care about their children's schooling, encourage successful performance, or are competent to assist their children with homework. Her findings also show that those stereotypes about low-income parents are false. One of her prescriptions for change calls on the schools to take the initiative in creating parent-teacher cooperation. Another requires the schools to provide the families with community social services. A third prescription would make instruction on communicating with such families an important part of teacher training.

As if they had been influenced by Lott's study, three educational researchers, in an article published at the same time as hers, show what happens when these principles are put into effect.[19] In this case, the principles were implemented on migrant worker families and their children, surely one of the most vulnerable groups in the country, faced as it is with severe problems of work, income, and health. Gerardo Lopez and his associates investigated four school districts with large migrant populations that had developed effective parental involvement programs. Their aim was to identify the criteria for these districts' success. They found the main criterion to be "an unwavering commitment to meet the multiple needs of migrant families above all other involvement considerations. In other words, the migrant-impacted schools and districts in this study firmly believed that before any type of substantive involvement could be expected of parents, they first needed to address the social, economic, and physical needs of migrant families."[20] Thereafter, they were able to involve parents in programs aimed at self-improvement and at making them aware of parental rights and responsibilities. Taken together, these efforts on the part of the schools made the parents more effective mediators for their children and contributed to the children's academic achievement.

An ambitious set of studies about parenting tells us more about what some, perhaps many, parents need to learn about their role as mediators. Laurence Steinberg and his associates surveyed twenty thousand students, hundreds of their parents, and dozens of their teachers, and interviewed some over a ten-year period.[21] Here are some of the highlights:

- Although the vast majority of parents want their children to do well in school, only a minority of parents provides the kind of home environment and parenting that facilitates learning.
- Children learn the value their parents place on education by the spoken and unspoken communication of the parents. In some fam-

ilies, the message is unmistakable that parents want, encourage, and strongly reinforce high achievement. In others, where parents may even verbalize their wish for good grades, students get contradictory messages like: "There's a good show on TV? Sure, watch it. You'll do your homework another time." Or, "I just don't have time now to go over the homework with you."

- Parents also communicate through their behavior. "Mom [or Dad], I'm in a class play. Will you come and see it?" The parent pauses and answers: "I wish I could but I'm so busy. Maybe next time." It takes few repetitions for children to learn that school is just not that important, especially if this negative reaction is compounded by a parent not attending functions especially designed for them and not showing much interest in what their children are studying in school and at home.

- The overall style of parenting, according to the Steinberg studies, seems to be of paramount importance. The three types of parenting style are: *Authoritarian*, the controlling, firm, punitive parent, almost more "dictator" than parent; *Permissive*, the overly lenient, accepting, and indulgent parent, almost more "friend" than parent; *Authoritative*, the more balanced, firm but warm and accepting parent, demanding but supportive of the child's increased autonomy, "friendly" but unmistakably in an adult-child type of parent relationship.

The Steinberg studies found the authoritative style of parenting clearly related to adolescents' academic achievement. By the time they reach the secondary level, assisting with homework and encouraging high standards do not have much effect on adolescents' performance. What does count is the effect of growing up in a home with authoritative parenting. For it is there that they develop more mature and autonomous attitudes and habits: They work hard, are self-reliant and persistent, and are aware that how they perform depends on their own effort. If they fall behind, in their class work or for that matter in extracurricular or out of school activities, they know the ways to overcome their current shortcomings. Among those ways is greater effort.

Another benefit of growing up with authoritative parenting is that the parents know the strategies necessary to help their children. They involve themselves in school affairs, participate in school functions, and, if their child is having a problem in school, they arrange to meet with an appropriate person in school to investigate and work toward a solution to the problem. They do not allow things just to happen; they intervene, and jointly with school personnel, they find the means to remedy the situation. In doing so, they are also role models to their children, conveying to them that we do not have to be victims of circumstances, but can intervene on our own behalf. For example, when a child does not understand why an exam answer was marked "incorrect," he or she speaks to the teacher to see if it was a grading error or, if not, to learn from the mistake.

Most of the existing programs of parent education focus on the parental role in helping their children achieve readiness for school. In other words, they are intended to help the less advantaged families be able to offer their children what the advantaged parents were able to do without assistance.

Programs that succeeded in increasing the knowledge of parents or improving the students' academic performance have characteristics such as these:[22] They are voluntary; no parent is compelled to participate. (Unfortunately, that eliminates many parents in greatest need of aid.) They are accessible to the parents, many of whom are of limited means. They are respectful of parents, conveying a positive outlook and not promoting feelings of failure and guilt. They are sensitive to diverse cultures and assign staff whose backgrounds are compatible with those of the parents. Finally, the programs are both intensive and comprehensive, covering all the areas deemed important to achieving school readiness.

THREE PRINCIPLES FOR SUCCESSFUL PARENTING PROGRAMS

Research results show that parent education programs produce impressive results. "Numerous comprehensive reviews of the results of such programs over the years indicate that efforts to help parents become stronger partners in their children's learning can have a significant positive impact on children's cognitive development, school performance, and social functioning."[23] From these studies, three principles with practical implications have been inferred:

- Programs should be structured and they should provide concrete experience, in contrast with teaching generalities about parent–child relationships.
- Programs should be ongoing; they should provide continuing contact for at least as long a period as necessary to assimilate what they have learned and to reinforce it. In other words, one-day workshops won't do the job.
- The combination of group meetings guided by a facilitator and individual sessions with a parent educator seems to be the optimal arrangement. Some parents are unwilling to work with a group until they develop trust and feel respected. Only then can they derive the enormous benefits that the group can give: shared ideas, new ideas, support networks, and the courage to try new strategies with their children.

HOME CONDITIONS ASSOCIATED WITH LEARNING IN SCHOOL

The content of education to train parents as parent-teachers should be rooted in knowledge about home conditions that are associated with successful school learning. Several educators examined research on this matter.[24] Then, building on the research, they identified five processes that seemed to be related to learning. The five processes are described below.

1. *Work Habits of the Family.* Good learners have what might be called well-ordered minds. Their written work is well organized and their ideas are presented clearly. In a parallel way, homes that facilitate learning are also well ordered. Members of the family do not live in chaos, with all of them doing anything they want whenever they want. The family follows a routine, which makes life easier for its members, knowing when it is time to eat, to study, to play, and to sleep. Children have their designated places for study and a designated time for study. Furthermore, and of great importance, their schoolwork has high priority, higher than that of entertainment and play. Recreation is by no means downplayed, but just as adults give priority to their responsibilities on the job and at home, children are taught to do the same about

their studies. Children have responsibilities at home in addition to schoolwork, joining with parents in doing chores appropriate to their age, and doing these tasks, and their school assignments, punctually.

The importance of structure of this kind cannot be overemphasized. Life at the beginning of the twenty-first century is far from that of pastoral days when work was demanding, even backbreaking, but required none of the tight-scheduled flitting around that is so characteristic today. Today, parents commute to work, transport children to school, soccer, dance, or music lessons, and attend meetings at night. Other parents, in less favorable circumstances, work on two jobs, for the sake of survival. Now, also for the sake of survival, some parents need help in time management and in establishing a structured way of life.

Small discussion groups, set up at school or at a home in the neighborhood, can provide a suitable setting for discussions on daily life and how it is organized. Shared ideas that lead in the desired direction can be more easily accepted than proposals given by a professional person on a one-to-one basis. For example, a member of the group proposes to a single mother who must be at work long after school lets out that she and other neighbors are willing to take in the children until she gets home.

2. *Academic Guidance and Support.* Although it is not more important than the other four, this is the "bread and butter" process, the one that most immediately affects children's performance in school. Parents help children understand their assignments, encourage them to carry them out, monitor their performance, and assist them in obtaining and using a variety of resources. Children benefit from ongoing encouragement and from praise for work (homework and home chores) that is well done. Also, they need the help of an adult when they are stumped by a difficult learning problem. Rather than ending up defeated and developing the habit of giving up in frustration or despair, they can learn a powerful lesson when an adult shows them how to overcome the seemingly insuperable problem.

To be of optimal help, parents must be in close communication with teachers so that they can know their children's strengths and weaknesses in their schoolwork. Certainly, in their early years, parents should closely monitor homework and study assignments, checking answer sheets and other paper work. Through those measures, they will teach children the process of careful scrutiny and editing, and in general, of self-assessment.

They will also be teaching them that study should not be the equivalent of mindless reading of passages, or that answering workbook or other questions should not be a thoughtless and mechanical process.

In parent education, some degree of individualized instruction is desirable because parents possess varying levels of knowledge and skills related to school learning. This can be linked to group sessions, such as those on establishing a study routine, useful print resources, or the curriculum in a given grade. Such sessions can also be used to instruct parents in basic knowledge they will need to assist their children, whether in language usage or mathematics. Through this process, parents have a second chance for personal development at the same time as they are empowered to be parent-teachers to their children.

3. *Stimulation to Explore and Discuss Ideas and Events.* Parents can be effective stimulators in this regard without themselves being highly educated. Their role here is to encourage thinking on the part of their children. Dinner, or other mealtimes over the weekend, are good opportunities to set off a flow of discussion on ordinary things like the weather, a popular movie or TV program, friends or classmates. Conversations may include topics of more relevance to school, such as a book, a historical or current event. Dinner conversations can be wide ranging—about science, politics, sports, or a controversial topic such as the use of alcohol or other drugs.

The important learning at home is the kind that helps make children thoughtful rather than impulsive, deep thinkers rather than superficial, creative and inventive rather than regurgitators of half-understood views of others. One step in that direction is in teaching them to be learners, partly by the actions of the parents who continue to be learners, and partly by what parents encourage their children to do as learners. The very questions asked of children can matter very much. The kind that derives a "yes" or "no" response—for example, "Did you have a good day in school?" being less important compared with open-ended questions that compel them to think—for example, "What was the most interesting thing you learned in school today? Why was it interesting to you?"

Family members can watch a television program of interest to all and carry on a discussion about it afterward, with everyone, including the youngest, encouraged to share viewpoints. Some games and hobbies are of educational value, and participation in these should be encouraged as a shared project. The public library can be a joy for children, especially if adult family members also borrow books and read extensively.

To repeat an earlier statement, there are countless ways that parents can perform the teaching role without reference to the school curriculum. They can be helped by being made aware of the many opportunities for their children to learn through activities at home, such as when they practice counting skills while setting the table.[25]

Because parents are role models, it is highly desirable for children to witness their elders reading books, magazines, and newspapers and to hear them discuss their readings. That is precisely what the children should also be engaged in—with their parents and their siblings. Museums, concerts, zoos, and historical sites—all of these contribute to the cultural and intellectual development of the child. With many of these establishments having free or low-cost admission, it is possible for children even in low-income families to enjoy them and afterwards talk about their experiences. In anticipation of the next process, note the emphasis here on talk, talk, talk.

The major task in preparing parent-teachers to perform this role of stimulation and exploration is to overcome several deep-seated beliefs. One is that, since adults know what is best for their children, what good can come from hearing their children's opinions. Another is the fear that opening up a discussion with children, especially adolescents, is like poking into a beehive and is likely to stir up trouble. Overcoming those parental concerns cannot be accomplished by "telling" them what to do. They are most likely to be persuaded by having the experience of give and take in a group discussion among themselves. The dual purpose of such discussion is for them to learn more about conducting discussions at home and to come to learn that openness causes no harm. The educator's task is not an easy one because, as several researchers discovered, parents were fearful of looking foolish and about being misunderstood by the educator.[26]

Successful parent education often enhances the development of the parents themselves. The various experiences they offer the children, such as attendance at concerts and theaters and participation in activities at science museums and art galleries, frequently open new vistas to them, too, and as a result of discussions at home, can benefit all family members.

4. *Language Environment*. Language is basic to learning. The language of school is the language of literature, science, mathematics, history, and the arts. Unlike some communication at home, the language of learning cannot depend on usages like "O.K. . . . What's up?. . . Let's get goin'. . . Well, um . . . Because . . ." and other colloquial expressions; it is more formal. It is clear, precise, and effective. While family members cannot be expected to go about spouting in professorial tones, they can encourage correct language usage by their own practices, and they can stimulate the enlargement of children's vocabularies by using more than commonplace words. Probably there is no better occasion than dinnertime to use effective language in sharing ideas, relating experiences of the day, and communicating feelings. Reading time, introduced during the toddler stage, also provides occasion for discussion and the practice of clear communication. While these experiences are intended to improve children's capacity for learning, they are preparations, too, for enriched lives.

This is a difficult process to introduce to parents of limited education. How we speak is so integral to our identity that the suggestion it needs to be modified can be perceived as an attack on the person. Yet, it need not be intimidating. For example, parents meeting in groups can learn the importance of reading to their children, of using a dictionary for words the children do not understand, and for discussing the story. They learn that discussions in school are similar to the very ones that they as parents, learning about the parent-teacher role, are involved in, where people use complete sentences in their speech and speak clearly. By having discussions at home in which children are encouraged to participate, they will be giving their children practice and at the same time probably will be giving the whole family enjoyable and stimulating experiences.

5. *Academic Aspirations and Expectations*. Early in my career, long before there was research on the effects of adult expectations on children's behavior and school achievement, when I was helping children in an orphanage with their homework, my boss, a sensitive and humane woman, taught me something unforgettable. She said about these children, most of whom had known loss or rejection or both, "They will be what they see reflected in our eyes." Many years later, research on expectations—"on what they see reflected in our eyes"—in publications such as the pioneering book, *Pygmalion in the Classroom,* confirmed the wisdom of a keen observer.[27]

Parents' expectations are communicated in various ways. They do this by the standards they set for study and homework assignments and by their reactions to report cards and test scores. They do it, too, by expressing dissatisfaction with a poorly worded response in a workbook or an essay and satisfaction with high-quality homework, and with a parent-teacher's praise for work well done. Constructive criticism that represents a parent's wish to see their children become strong and effective students is empowering, for it says, "I know you can do better work, and I'm here to help you." The parent is there to assist on a daily basis, if need be, and certainly not just when the report card comes in. High expectations alone, without support, are likely to result in frustration and failure.

Parents show their interest and values about learning by encouraging their children to talk about *their* experiences at school and elsewhere. Adults should listen as thoughtfully and respectfully as they would to an adult's comment. From such exchanges, children see that their parents value their school experience.

Conversation in a single parent home can have the same objective: to initiate a discussion—perhaps starting with the parent's experiences of the day—that goes on to the children's experiences. Children can talk about what they learned, what they liked, whom they ate lunch with, whether they had art or music or physical development, and what they did in those special areas. Through it all, the parent listens intently and asks questions or makes comments to spur the children on to further conversation.

Parents also are influential as children explore future careers, even if only in their fantasies at an early age. In many homes, there is no question but that the children will go on to higher education. That is taken for granted. The children don't have to be told they will be going; it is so much in the atmosphere. When the parents talk about their own college days or, in planning their own futures, they refer to the time "When you go off to college."

For parents to be able to convey to their children the aspirations that they hold for them, the parents themselves must first be conscious of those aspirations. Parents may be so deeply preoccupied with looking for work or may be working such long hours that there is no time or energy or inclination to give much thought to their children's future, not to mention their own. For some, too, their children's futures are delimited by the boundaries of their own present life. A warehouseman who had dropped out of high school and now works on a fatiguing job needs encouragement to think and articulate his views about his children's futures. He may need help in envisioning a future for his children very different from his own present life.

Group discussion may be the method of choice to aid parents in clarifying and perhaps redefining their expectations for their children. To be effective it is probably necessary to attack another problem, namely, the alienation from school of many lower social class and minority group adults. Parents, who as teenagers dropped out of school, or failed to earn a diploma, or were unpopular, are likely still to be carrying the scars of past disappointments. In their own eyes, they don't belong in the world of learning. Their trainers must be well aware of that fact.

To be effective, parent education held in schools must give parents of many third system children the warmest of welcomes and the most sensitive understanding. The past history of the parents would enter discussion only as they themselves introduced it. Otherwise, the focus in a parent education group would be on expectations and aspirations for the children and standards for their children's performance, with encouragement to elevate them in realistic fashion. Besides talking about the present—for example, about what the school expects of their children and how they can help—they could be led to look beyond elementary school, to their children as students in high school, community college, specialized institon (e.g., art, fashion, music), or university. Such discussions are intended for the benefit of their children, however, a secondary benefit may be that of raising the parents' own aspirations.

THE BIG SIX: A PROMISING APPROACH

One of the notable developments in parent education is the Big Six Skills method of problem solving, for use by parents.[28] The Big Six is an approach to help parents and students cope with homework. The job of helping children with their homework seems routine and simple, yet it is a monumental assignment. Besides guiding their children in learning the basic skills of acquiring and using knowledge, the parent, and the child, are confronted, over the years, with homework assignments that encompass a sizeable part of humankind's accumulated legacy of knowledge.

The Big Six method defines separate roles for parents and their children. The parents serve as coaches, and the students as "doers," or more accurately, as "thinkers and doers" to convey the fact that doing is always accompanied by thinking. The six components of this approach are:

1. *Task Definition*. The first step in doing an assignment is in understanding precisely what it calls for. The parent can be most helpful by having the student explain the assignment in her or his own words.

2. *Information Seeking Strategies*. With a clear understanding of what is expected of them, students must now seek out the necessary information. The parent-as-coach can ask the student what sources of information seem appropriate and what use the student could make of them. If the student's list is not comprehensive enough for the information required, the parent can then propose others or help the student obtain other ideas from a peer, teacher, or librarian.

3. *Location and Access*. Now the students must find the needed resources. Parents can be helpful by discouraging their children from depending only on those most immediately available and by encouraging them to think through diverse sources of information from which they could make a selection of the most useful. Here, too, parents may find it desirable to encourage the student to get further advice about accessible sources.

4. *Use of Information*. With the information now available, the student must spend time absorbing and evaluating it and, in the process, deciding what use to make of it, depending on whether this is preparation for class discussion, a one-paragraph or a ten-page paper, or an exam. Students often need help, especially early in their schooling, to develop the habits necessary to carry out the tasks of this step.

5. *Synthesis*. This highly important, but often neglected, step calls for students to make the information "their own." That means that they have assimilated it, made sense of it, and are prepared to use it appropriately for the purpose at hand. Parental help here is not as simple as that of checking the student's preparation for a spelling test. Too often students dutifully do a reading assignment without full

concentration, distracted perhaps by a television program or thoughts of recent experiences. They fail then to capture the meaning of the assignment. The monitoring task is a matter of evaluating whether the student has understood what has been read and studied—understood it sufficiently well to convey it clearly to the parent. In time, it is hoped, students will do that for themselves.

6. *Evaluation*. This involves standards of quality and efficiency. Does the work meet the standards expected by the teacher? Going beyond the Big Six, we should ask, in cases where the parents have higher standards, whether the work meets their standards, as well. Looking toward the future, we also ask whether the project could have been done more efficiently. Parents who initiate and monitor this stage very early in their children's lives lead them to internalize the practices of evaluation. Through mediation, that is, they help the children master the uses of evaluation tools.

We might well use the tool concept for each of the six components above. After all, the ultimate aim of good parenting is to eliminate the need for it altogether, so that the older teenager and the young adult can lead independent lives, making wise decisions by using the Big Six or an equivalent problem-solving approach. They can do that when they have mastered the tools through varied and extensive use of them. As children age and become more adept in their use of the tools in schoolwork, parents are not relegated to the sidelines and are by no means less interested or involved in their children's school experience and achievement. Rather, their interest and involvement take different forms. They want their children to share school experiences with the family, just as adults share their work experiences. They visit the school and the teachers, attend class and school activities, and perhaps volunteer their time, energy, and ideas to the school.

The Big Six is adaptable to helping children at all ages. For example, a three-year-old, seeing smoke come out of a chimney, asks: "Where does the smoke go?" Or a four-year-old asks, "Why don't we live in a castle?" These questions provide wonderful opportunities for parents to initiate the stages of the Big Six, although in elementary form. Parents will, of course, know most of the answers, especially those that come from their very young children. Still, it is a service to those children to go through steps that help them learn to identify and use a variety of sources of information; and very valuable for children to develop the habit of synthesizing new knowledge so that it is meaningful and added to memory.

EVIDENCE OF THE IMPORTANCE OF THE PARENTAL ROLE IN STUDENT ACHIEVEMENT

No matter how obvious a point of view may be, it is always reassuring to have that view further reinforced, especially when reinforcement comes from reliable research.

Research results show that parent education programs produce impressive results. "Numerous comprehensive reviews of the results of such programs over the years indicate that efforts to help parents become stronger partners in their children's learning can have a significant positive impact on children's cognitive development, school performance, and social functioning."[29]

Here are examples of the use of successful parent education programs in three major areas: reading, science, and mathematics. In England, working-class parents engaged in reading activities with their children, aged six to eight years.[30] Teachers sent materials to the parents to read to their children, parents kept a record of the readings, and staff members of the project visited the homes for discussions of strategies the parents could use in helping the children with their reading. It is important to note that such visits provide parents with more than just skills, important as those are. They give them the feeling of partnership with the schools, and, especially for those parents who have had no experience of this kind, the visits give them personal support. The results were very positive: There was more reading at home and improved reading performance in school.

In the United States, a variety of programs have been introduced for greater involvement of parents in their children's studies of math and science. In some programs, such as the Family Math program, parents are encouraged to take special math or science courses together with their children.[31] The advantages that mark such programs as successful are that parents become better prepared to assist their children, parents and children become stronger partners in learning, and teachers and parents become stronger partners in the education of the students.

Especially effective are the studies appraising parent training conducted by Laurence Steinberg and associates Bradford Brown and Sanford M. Dornbusch. As previously noted, twenty thousand students, hundreds of their parents, and dozens of their teachers were surveyed, and some were interviewed over a ten-year period. These studies produced important knowledge about the parental role.[32] Here are some of the highlights that are relevant to differences among the three school systems:

- Although the vast majority of parents want their children to do well in school, only a minority of parents provide the kind of home environment and parenting that facilitates learning. In some cases, as noted before, it is due to lack of opportunity, perhaps because parents are short of time or energy, exhausted by overwork, or distracted by marital or other problems. In other cases, the parents may lack knowledge about how to be effective and spur children in the right direction.[33] Children learn the value their parents place on education by the spoken and unspoken communication of the parents. In some families, the message is unmistakable that parents want, encourage, and strongly reinforce high achievement. Their children have no doubt about that. In others, where parents may even verbalize their wish for good grades, students get contradictory messages like: "There's a good TV program? Sure, watch it. You'll do your homework another time." Or, "You're staying up too late doing your homework." Or, "You will ruin your eyes with all that reading." Or, "How come you have to spend so many hours on homework? Your cousin doesn't." Or, "I'm sorry, I just don't have time now to go over the homework with you."
- As noted earlier, parents also communicate through their behavior. Their communications are negative when they are repeatedly "too busy" to help with homework, attend a school performance, or watch an athletic activity in which the child is involved. They are also negative when they assist the child, but show impatience and annoyance. In the mind of the child, at a subconscious level at least, this kind of parental behavior translates into a sense that school is not that important to the parents. Contrast this with the parent who finds pleasure in a partnership with the child.

PARENT EDUCATION: WILL THIS
COUNTRY PAY FOR WHAT WORKS?

It takes sensitive teaching to develop effective parent-teachers. But first of all, it takes money to create programs for parent education. Despite evidence of their effectiveness in producing higher achieving students, "parental involvement remains minimal to nonexistent in many early childhood environments."[34]

The great divide between, on the one hand, the roles and characteristics of the effective parent mediator and, on the other, the quantity and quality of available training for parents, only indicates the enormity of the problem if the third school system is to be eliminated. It says, too, that a reductionist "solution," like setting more rigorous standards, or statewide tests, or penalizing poorly performing schools, won't do.

"But what about Head Start?" some might ask. "Wasn't that established to give children what they hadn't had a chance to get at home? Why spend money on parent training when the children get what they need in Head Start?"

Considering how little, over the course of its history, the nation has given children of poor and minority groups, Head Start stands out as a welcome intervention. One should not, however, exaggerate its role in coping with educational problems. In that connection, we should consider the very name "Head Start." If the comparison is with other third school system children, then in fact the program does give the children a head start. Those children in the program are given an opportunity— a limited one—to catch up on some of the important learning during the first four years of life. Compared with children in the first system, what they acquire in Head Start barely scratches the surface of the rich curriculum they *did not* experience.

The fact is that "Head Start" is a misnomer. The program should have been called what it really is, "Catch Up." It seeks to give children an opportunity to catch up on what they have been deprived of from birth. Those who are in it do some catching up, which gives them a head start over other children raised in poverty. The catching up is far from sufficient to put them on a par with those raised in more advantaged homes. While Head Start is a positive feature in American education, neither it nor any other program for children can substitute for parent-as-teacher education.

Finally, the great divide between the roles and characteristics of the effective parent mediator and the quantity and quality of available training for parents says that any serious long-term plan to eliminate the third school system and improve the second must recognize that a nationwide program for the training of parents as mediators is an absolute essential. The components of such a program are not just instructional. They include time off from work, child care assistance, and sensitivity to cultural, class, and language differences. They are costly. Will this nation decide that all the children deserve such education?

A nation that says it cannot afford such a program declares that it cannot afford to provide equal educational opportunity.

NOTES

1. Barbara Kremer, *Parent Education: Abstract Bibliography* (Champaign, Ill.: ERIC Clearinghouse on Early Childhood Education, 1971).

2. Benjamin Spock and Michael B. Rothenberg, *Dr. Spock's Baby and Child Care* (New York: E. P. Dutton, 1992).

3. Reuven Feuerstein, *The Dynamic Assessment of Retarded Performers* (Baltimore: University Park Press, 1979).

4. James V. Wertsch, *Mind as Action* (New York: Oxford University Press, 1998).

5. Lev S. Vygotsky, *Mind in Society: The Development of Higher Psychological Processes* (Cambridge, Mass.: Harvard University Press, 1978.)

6. Vygotsky, *Mind in Society*, 57.

7. Reuven Feuerstein and Mildred B. Hoffman, "Mediating Cognitive Processes to the Retarded Performer—Rationale, Goals, and Nature of Intervention," in *Promoting Cognitive Growth over the Life Span*, ed. Milton Schwebel, Charles A. Maher, and Nancy S. Fagley (Hillsdale, N.J.: Lawrence Erlbaum Associates, 1990), 115–136.

8. Wertsch, *Mind as Action*, 28–29.

9. Gerald Coles, *Reading Lessons: The Debate over Literacy* (New York: Hill and Wang, 1998).

10. Coles, *Reading Lessons*, 55.

11. Coles, *Reading Lessons*, 56.

12. Eileen W. Ball, "Phonological Awareness: What's Important and to Whom?" *Reading and Writing* 5, no. 2 (June 1993): 141–159.

13. Ball, "Phonological Awareness," 150.

14. Benjamin Franklin, *Memoirs of the Life and Writings of Benjamin Franklin* (London: J. M. Dent and Sons, 1908), 13.

15. Ariel Anderson and Andrea B. Smith, "Community Building with Parents," *Kappa Delta Pi Record* 35, no. 4 (Summer 1999): 158–161.

16. Margaret Finders and Cynthia Lewis, "Why Some Parents Don't Come to School," *Educational Leadership* 51, no. 8 (May 1994): 50–54.

17. Sharon Patterson, *Increasing Parental Involvement in Grades One, Four, and Five in a Rural Elementary School* (Ph.D. diss., Nova Southern University, 1994).

18. Bernice Lott, "Low-Income Parents and the Public Schools," *Journal of Social Issues* 57, no. 2 (Summer 2001): 247–259.

19. Gerardo R. Lopez, Jay D. Scribner, and Kanya Mahitivanichcha, "Redefining Parental Involvement: Lessons from High-Performing Migrant-Impacted Schools," *American Educational Research Journal* 38, no. 2 (Summer 2001): 253–288.

20. Lopez et al., "Redefining Parental Involvement," 261.

21. Laurence Steinberg with Bradford Brown and Sanford M. Dornbusch, *Beyond the Classroom: Why School Reform Has Failed and What Parents Need to Do* (New York: Simon and Schuster, 1996). See also Laurence Steinberg, "Standards Outside the Classroom," in *Brookings Papers on Educational Policy*, ed. Diane Ravitch (Washington, D.C: Brookings Institution Press, 1998), 319–357.

22. Elizabeth Stief, *The Role of Parent Education in Achieving School Readiness* (Washington, D.C.: National Governors' Association, 1993).

23. Thomas Kellaghan et al., *The Home Environment and School Learning: Promoting Parental Involvement in the Education of Children* (San Francisco: Jossey-Bass, 1993), 119.

24. Kellaghan et al., *The Home Environment and School Learning*, 119.

25. Anderson and Smith, "Community Building with Parents," 158.

26. Finders and Lewis, "Why Some Parents Don't Come to School," 161.

27. Robert Rosenthal and Lenore Jacobson, *Pygmalion in the Classroom: Teacher Expectation and Pupils' Intellectual Development* (New York: Holt, Rinehart and Winston, 1968).

28. Michael Eisenberg and Robert Berkowitz, *Helping with Homework: A Parent's Guide to Information Problem-Solving,"* ERIC monograph.

29. Kellaghan et al., *The Home Environment and School Learning*, 119.

30. John Hewison, "The Long-Term Effectiveness of Parental Involvement in Reading: A Follow-Up of the Haringey Project," *British Journal of Educational Psychology* 58 (1988), 184–190.

31. Karen Ostlund and Kathy Fite, "Change and Children," *Science and Children* 25, no. 4 (January 1988): 20–24.

32. Steinberg et al., *Beyond the Classroom: Why School Reform Has Failed and What Parents Need to Do.*

33. Kathleen V. Hoover-Dempsey et al., "Parental Involvement in Homework," *Educational Psychologist* 36, no. 3 (Summer 2001): 195–209. This review of studies about parental involvement in homework found negative as well as pos-

itive links between such involvement and student achievement. The relationship between involvement and achievement is complex, bringing into play parental expectations, the child's current performance, and the quality of classroom instruction, among others. With homework, parental emphasis only on achievement is undesirable. Parents can be particularly helpful by inspiring positive attitudes about homework and positive perceptions of personal competence.

34. Finders and Lewis, "Why Some Parents Don't Come to School," 161.

8

TYPES OF SCHOOL REFORM: STANDARDS-BASED AND MARKET-BASED

American education has been "reforming" from its beginning; however, the current wave of reform is now only about two decades old. The impetus for the current reform came from the 1983 report of the Commission on Excellence in Education entitled *A Nation at Risk*,[1] although reforms in some states predated that report. To understand the direction of the reform movement, both at the state and national levels, it is important to know that it was not driven by concern for the welfare of American children. The state of the economy was the driving force. Business and political leaders expressed concern about Japan's thriving economy and feared that we were losing our competitiveness. Rather than looking internally, for example, at the auto industry's failure to be more than cosmetically inventive, they attributed the seeming backwardness to the state of education. This behavior harks back to a similar reaction after the Soviet Union put a man in space in 1957. Our failure to be first was blamed on deficiencies in the nation's educational system.

The reform movement in the states was also prompted by economic concerns. As Harvard educator Richard Elmore said: "The stated purpose of many early state reforms—notably in states like South Carolina—was to improve the competitive position of states in the national and international economy."[2] Still another economic factor was reflected in the behavior of the states. The social movements during the period of

1965–1980 led to considerable increases in the state share of educational expenditures. This was due largely, as Elmore explains, to litigation aimed at correcting inequities in funding the schools. The states wanted accountability for the increased allocation of funds, which, we should note, went to second and especially third school systems. Up until the period of the 1970s and 1980s, educators and politicians held that education was a local concern. But now, as parents and others demanded a fairer shake for their children in the distribution of resources, the states decided that it was necessary to determine if they were getting enough benefits from the spending to justify the extra appropriations. In brief, then, business interests were the major motivator, combined at the same time with the attitude that since poorer school districts were getting more state money—without changing much else in the lives of their students—they were going to have to show positive results.

FOUR TYPES OF REFORM

During the current period, four types of reform have risen to center stage. The relevant question to pose is the following: In what way does each of these types address the problems stemming from a three-tiered system of education? That is, did the reforms lead to improvement in education in the second and third school tiers? Are there more mediated learning opportunities, given by parents and teachers, which enable children and teenagers to acquire the cultural tools and skills essential to academic success. Does each type of reform provide them with those opportunities?

The four types are standards-based reform, market-based reform, equity-based reform, and community-based reform. The first two are described in this chapter, the last two in the next, followed in each case by comments related to the three school systems.

STANDARDS-BASED REFORM

The term "standards-based reforms" refers to establishing community consensus on standards of achievement and implementing programs to

insure that the standards are met. In the public media, this type of reform is referred to as toughening up demands on students, assigning
more homework, and setting higher requirements for graduation. For
education policy makers, the issue is not whether the standards are demanding but that they are uniform, put in print for all to share, and subject to evaluation. Hence, another and an indispensable aim of policy
makers is to evaluate the success of the educational system by determining the extent to which schools are meeting those standards.

To evaluate programs, state officials need to develop appropriate
methods of assessment linked to the new standards. These two are in-
separable, at least if the people of the state are to know whether the
standards-based reform is working in the interests of the children.

According to a 1995 report, forty-nine states were already engaged in
one or another kind of standards-based reform.[3] Besides the states, many
school districts were working at implementing such reform, including
those in Chicago, New York, Philadelphia, Pittsburgh, and San Diego.[4]

The sound of it, "standards-based reform," suggests a simple activity:
Just define and set out the standards for all to see. Although it seems easy,
it actually starts with a necessarily long and drawn out process of achieving a degree of consensus on the standards. Consensus means that the
various components of the populace and the power structure—policy
makers, administrators, teachers, parents, tax payers, state and municipal
political leaders, clergy, lobbyists representing the spectrum of ideology
from the center to left and right—find enough of the standards-based reform acceptable to enable the state and the school districts to fund and
implement agreed-upon changes.

Furthermore, we are talking about standards both in the early grades
and in all the subject areas. What levels of reading and mathematics
must children achieve to be allowed to enter junior and then senior
high schools? What concepts and skills should students be expected to
master in science, mathematics, history, English, foreign language, the
arts, and so on, in order to receive a high school diploma? Next, although this occurs infrequently, methods of implementation are addressed. How shall the classes be taught? To put the latter question in
a form that implies outcomes, should discussion of thought-provoking
questions constitute a portion of class time for the purpose of encouraging critical thinking? Or, instead, should that time be devoted to an

even greater stress on accepted knowledge, as that is defined and pre-sented by the textbooks and the teachers?

There is more. How shall student accomplishment be measured? Should it be by the "tried and true" objective tests, such as multiple choice? Or should evaluation take forms closer to real life by including performance assessments, where, for example, students are asked to de-velop a scientific experiment or to answer a question by composing a paragraph. Another kind of performance assessment takes the form of the portfolio: Over an extended period of time, a student's work in a given classroom is evaluated and placed in a portfolio, which would give a better sense of the student's understanding of the subject and of her or his development over this time period than a traditional exam.

Although most states use national tests—which may not match their curriculum—Maryland and Virginia have each created tests of their own, given in grades three, five, and eight. Virginia also tests high school students, and Maryland will soon do the same. The differences in the philosophy underlying these two states' testing programs are very marked. The Virginia Standards of Learning exams, employing multi-ple-choice questions, emphasize factual material, whereas the Maryland School Performance Assessment Program demands elaborate responses and assesses the processes utilized in solving problems. Observers claim that the test differences reflect differences in the focus of teaching in the two states, with Virginia teachers emphasizing factual knowledge, and Maryland teachers, problem solving.[5] It should be added that most states use multiple-choice tests and concentrate on factual information.

The news media give frequent accounts of conflict over instructional methods: Phonics or whole-word? Teach for facts or for personal devel-opment? Anyone who expects quick agreement on any of these contro-versial issues is in for a surprise. So it is not unexpected that the process of change has been a slow one. Nor is it surprising, in the struggles be-tween those wanting far-reaching innovations and those wanting to re-tain the status quo, that the standards-based reforms have moved so much to the middle—perhaps with the exception of Maryland—that the following could be said.

This more moderate stance may help the standards move forward politi-cally. But questions remain about whether such balancing advances the instructional goals of reform, i.e., *rigorous, demanding curricula that stimulate students' abilities to think critically and problem-solve* [italics added for emphasis]. Will standards policies that explicitly incorporate both new and old goals make sense in the classroom? Will they send mixed signals, and simply reinforce the status quo of past, unsuccessful programs?[6]

Comments on Standards-Based Reform

Ironically, even in the attempts to reform schools through standards-based efforts, the necessary compromises to win support for the new approaches deprive students of what their age-cohort in private and leading public schools get on a daily basis. In fact, while such debates go on—about how high to set standards and whether critical thinking is an issue or not—affluent parents who insist on schools that provide "rigorous, demanding curricula that stimulate students' abilities to think critically and to problem-solve," send their children to select private or affluent suburban schools. Or less affluent parents succeed in getting their children admitted to schools for gifted and talented students, or identify exceptional teachers within their school district. Or the parents are assertive enough and have the necessary skills to collaborate in establishing a charter school that seems to offer their children the kind of education they value.

There is something of the absurd in the standards-based reform movement. To use an analogy, it is as if the following occurred: In the high jump, the children are performing poorly; they are unable to exceed one foot. Therefore, we must raise standards. Henceforth, the rod will be placed at two feet. A rational approach calls for remedying the causes for the poor performance in jumping, whether these are related to health, nutrition, family circumstances, motivation, or instruction or, more likely, a combination of these. Through such action, in the future the bar could be raised far higher.

One does not need tests to know that these children have learned too little of the curriculum; nor does one need years of research to know why they are performing poorly. However, instead of remedying the causes of poor educational performance, by eliminating the third system, the standards-based reform movement has created a Frankenstein. Statewide tests have become the measure of student learning and, intended or not, of teacher effectiveness. Test performance inevitably casts a shadow over the classroom, compelling teachers to concentrate on the content of the test rather than on the course of instruction.

Standards-based reform has other negative effects. The emphasis on so-called basics tends to ignore music, art, health, physical development, and sometimes even the social sciences. The arts, in particular, have been the victims of the "get tough" policy, and at a great cost. A recent analysis of 62 studies of the arts, including dance, drama, music, and the visual arts, shows that students exposed to them have higher academic achievement than students who concentrate only on academic subjects. The coordinator of the research, James Catterall of the University of California, said: "Notions that the arts are frivolous add-ons to a serious curriculum couldn't be further from the truth."[7]

Another potential outcome can be disastrous: By "beefing up" standards, evaluating students and schools, and publicizing the results—without first providing the enormous assistance such students and schools require, including certified and experienced teachers and parent training—this movement may be responsible for promoting failure. As students from the lower social classes, many of them from minority groups, continue to fall short in their performance, this movement may also be responsible for reinforcing racist and class-based stereotypes.

A nationwide fourth grade reading test, the National Assessment of Educational Progress, showed a widening of the gap between good and poor readers between 1992 and 2000. The high scorers were mostly white and female. The low scorers were mostly black or Hispanic male students. The discouraging results after a decade of effort to raise the achievement level in reading led to finger-pointing, especially at teachers and the colleges and universities that train them. Oddly enough, news accounts did not report any blame placed on circumstances that led to the following: 34 percent of the poor readers watched television more than six hours a day (compared with only 6 percent of the high scorers); 57 percent of the poor readers (compared with only 7 percent of the high scorers) said that they had friends who make fun of people who try hard in school. Further, the poor readers were likely to have changed schools in the prior two years, whereas the high scorers had not.[8] The poor readers, in other words, tended to come from the third school system.

MARKET-BASED REFORM

The assumption underlying the market-based reform movement has been transferred bodily from market-based economics: Competition and the incentive of earnings will stimulate effective new change and provide incentives for new thinking in education, just as they do in industry. Underlying the assumption drawn from economics is another one: Public institutions, such as public schools, whose prime purpose is unrelated to financial profit, are governed nevertheless by the market economy's laws of competition.

Three major forms of major market-based reform are: *charter* schools, which provide greater freedom for innovation than usually prevails in the public schools; *voucher* system, which provides public money to pay tuition at any public or private school; and *privatization,* which permits a public school system to pay a private corporation to operate its schools. The first two—charter schools and the voucher system—are forms of escape from what parents consider unsatisfactory and overcrowded public schools. Privatization is a form of escape by a school system that has given up on its own efforts at improving performance in its schools.

It is too early to give a definitive appraisal of these three. However, such reports as are available on privatization are not at all encouraging. The high hopes and expectations were not realized. Because they had been initiated with much fanfare, the failures were all the more of a setback. Comparison of privatized schools with other public schools is difficult because, as Henry Levin, who heads the National Center for the Study of Privatization in Education at Teachers College, said, the privatized schools "typically seek students that are not costly to educate. That's not cheating. They are playing by the rules of the game. They want to do a good job, but they also want to make a profit."[9]

The aim of privatization, first and foremost, is profit. Companies that venture into education do so with the support of investors who expect to profit from their investments. According to two studies concerning several schools of the for-profit Edison Schools, "the test scores of Edison students improved no more than those of demographically similar students at schools not managed by Edison."[10] Even in the case of one particular Edison-operated school that appeared to show significant gains in test scores, questions have been raised about changes in the composition of the student body during the comparison period. Some critics claim that Edison counseled parents of under-performing students to transfer them to other schools. True or not, demographic changes occurred during the conversion from a regular public school to a privatized charter one, leaving the claimed gains in this one elementary school to be questionable. Still, successes in some schools should not be dismissed. They may be explained in this way: The for-profit enterprises claim that they can improve outcomes at no greater cost than the school system would have spent. However, to realize positive results at the outset, they have invested more heavily on some projects, which may account for some of their successes.

School administrators, teachers, parents, and school board members may differ widely about a variety of important issues, even about the purposes of education. So far as their overall objective is concerned, however, their overriding objective is the education of children. Among those associated with for-profit schools, the overriding objective is profit. To maintain contracts with public school districts and gain additional ones, they must, of course, show some progress in improving academic performance. That fact would tend to motivate a system of tightly linking teaching to testing. Despite that linkage, at this point the evidence about their performance suggests that privatization does not appear to be the answer to the nation's education problems. Some cities, like Baltimore and Hartford, have fired private companies, and in Albany, "after months of dismal performance," New York State's "most heralded effort," a charter school, terminated its relationship with a private company. In an editorial from which the quotes above and the following were taken, the *New York Times* said "there is nothing magical about privatization . . . . rebuilding failing schools requires the same grit, determination, and patience no matter who undertakes the job."[11]

In school districts that institute the *voucher* plan, public funds follow students admitted to private schools, or to public schools other than their own. Parents are in the position, then, to select schools that they regard as more satisfactory for their children's needs.

In states or cities that authorize their establishment, *charter* schools may be organized and operated by individuals (e.g., parents and/or teachers), businesses, and nongovernmental organizations. These schools have several advantages: A set amount of money is allocated per student, usually grants are available to pay for start-up costs, and the schools are exempt from many state regulations.

Why have these two developments attracted considerable attention? Recent reports about education in the state of Arizona and in particular in the city of Tucson provide us with at least a partial answer to that question.

On four days during the week of 5 January 1998, the *Arizona Daily Star* published reports that bear on the question. On 5 January, it carried a half-page chart with data on *private* elementary and secondary schools in Tucson. About 60 percent of the schools reported a ratio of one faculty member to 15 or fewer students. About 80 percent reported one faculty member to 20 or fewer students. The chart was accompanied by an article entitled "Mighty Asset: School Volunteers."[12] Not only were most of these private schools characterized by favorable class size. They were, as well, enriched by the contributions of the time and talent of many parents and of others, including retired teachers. The students doubly benefited: There were excellent faculty to student ratios, plus the parents, themselves, were more deeply involved in their children's educational experience.

The next day, the *Arizona Daily Star* presented a table on the *charter* schools in the Tucson area.[13] Fifteen schools were already in operation and thirteen new ones were expected to be operational in the 1998–99 school year. The chart gave projected faculty-student ratios for 1998–99 for all but one of the 28 schools. Of the twenty-seven, 55 percent reported ratios of fifteen students or less to a faculty member and 90 percent projected a ratio of twenty or fewer per faculty member.

A few days later, Monica Mendoza's front page article in the *Arizona Daily Star* carried this headline: "State Schools Get a 'D'; It's Unfair, Officials Say."[14] The article explained that *Education Week*, a national education magazine, had graded states in a variety of instructional areas that are presumably indicative of educational quality, and Arizona had not fared well in quality of teaching, school climate, and in the adequacy, allocation, and equity of resources. According to Mendoza, state officials complained that the report did not reflect recently instituted standards. She also pointed out that Arizona's neighbors, including California, did not fare well on the survey.

Neither of these explanations by officials is likely to alleviate the dissatisfaction of parents who find in the survey corroboration of their own observations of crowded and unsafe schools. No wonder, then, that some of them are seeking to escape, and no one is justified in criticizing them for wanting better schooling for their children.

But what of the rest, the vast majority of students in urban and poor rural and even some suburban schools? In effect, that question is raised in an editorial in the *Arizona Daily Star* (10 January 1998). The editor was particularly concerned by the

huge differences in student performance between Arizona schools in high-poverty neighborhoods and those in other neighborhoods. . . .
[I]t is clear that Arizona's greatest efforts to improve the quality of education must start in high-poverty areas. Twenty- or 30-point differences in performance on reading, math, and science tests are shocking. . . .
[T]he findings remind us that for all the official interest in developing educational alternatives, such as charter schools, the greatest efforts must be made in trying to improve the current public schools.
These schools are, after all, where the students are—and where they are failing.[15]

The *Arizona Daily Star*'s editorial contains two excerpts from the *Education Week* report, both of them consistent with the views in this book.

In poor neighborhoods, the deck is stacked against children from the moment they are born. The odds are higher they will have lower-than-normal birth weights, lack access to regular medical care, live in a household headed by a single mother, become victim of crime, have a parent who never finished high school, become pregnant before reaching adulthood and drop out of school.[16]

The editorial goes on to show that children in concentrated poverty areas can learn; they have demonstrated that in the few schools that are really good ones. "But it takes a much larger commitment than this state—and most others—have been willing to make."[17]

Because "the deck is stacked against" their children, inner-city parents, particularly African Americans and Latinos are heavily in favor of the use of vouchers for use in public, private, or parochial schools, according to Brent Staples.[18] Anything is better than what they have, they seem to be saying. Their preference is understandable and, considering the circumstances, justified.

From the perspective of a parent, a voucher for a child may be a viable and highly desirable solution. For those in government, however, who are essentially satisfied with the status quo, it is a fine device to defuse the issues of fifth-rate education in the third school system.

As Staples points out, the voucher strategy of dealing with the horrendous problems in the schools is no more than "tinkering at the margins."[19] He estimates that even if vouchers were available on a large scale—that is, governments at one level or another were willing to come up with vast sums for the tuition—not even 10 percent of the children could be placed in private or parochial schools.

Some preliminary evaluations of charter schools are available. Because the Philadelphia school system was a pioneer in introducing charter schools, by 1994–1995 it was possible to conduct an assessment of its accomplishments. More than seven years after converting twenty-two high schools into small charter schools, educational researchers Christman and Macpherson[20] made a thoroughgoing assessment of five schools. Results were drawn from a number of sources, especially from interviews with more than 300 students and observations in 122 classes. The findings were disappointing: Students played a passive role in their classes; students felt that teachers did not respect them and were not concerned about their interests; the investigators found that the academic standards were low.

Christman and Macpherson concluded that the effects of reform were "preliminary." In light of the following words, their conclusion seems charitable:

> [T]he majority of students were disaffected by uninspired classes, insecure in buildings that were noisy and dilapidated, and offended by teachers who "don't teach" and school policies that punish or humiliate them. . . .Only a small minority of students were in charters that offered real connection and caring along with rigorous course work.[21]

Other early reports are also pessimistic. One of the nation's leading thinkers about education, Seymour Sarason, recognizes that there are too few facts to establish the state of those schools. However, early reports from many quarters leave him "pessimistic" about the possibility that they will succeed.[22]

It would be premature to conclude from the appraisal of the charter schools in Philadelphia that the teachers were at fault. One must know the already conditioned behavior of the students who entered those charter schools. One must also know what kind of preparation the teachers received before and after shifting from a big comprehensive high school to a small charter school. If teacher behavior and student behavior were the same as before, no reason on earth justified the expectation of improvement.

It would also be premature to conclude on the basis of early reports that charter schools cannot be effective. In that connection, it's worth recognizing that even in the worst urban school districts, an occasional school in a disadvantaged section of the community stands out for its excellence. Usually it turns out to have an exceptional principal who inspires and attracts devoted teachers and harnesses the interest and commitment of the parents. Charter schools strive for that mix of outstanding principal, devoted teachers, and committed parents.

Comments on Market-Based Reform

In Sarason's many books, from his early landmark book, *The Culture of the School and the Problem of Change* (1969), to *The Predictable Failure of Educational Reform* (1990) and *Charter Schools: Another Flawed Educational Reform?* (1998), he has stressed essential needs. These include the following: (a) unconditional support on the part of the educational leadership; (b) a majority of well-educated parents who have time and energy to devote to the school; (c) a majority of the children in the school who possess the prerequisites for learning, that is, a solid background for the grade level they are entering.

It is noteworthy that these are the characteristics of the first school system. Because parents and teachers are often involved in establishing charter schools and have a clear notion of the kind of school they want, the chances are favorable that they can approximate such a mix.

Granted that, theoretically at least, charter schools have the *potential* for giving the children an education that approximates that of private and suburban public schools, what are the implications for the rest of the children? Presumably, the charter schools would serve as models for the school district. But big city school districts, like Philadelphia, or even smaller ones, cannot simply mandate a restructuring and expect a miracle. Restructuring by fiat does not modify parent, teacher, administrator, and student attitudes and behavior. It does not alter the work status, income, energy, and available time of parents of low income. It does not change the status, sophistication, or maturity of the teenaged single mom living on a below-poverty-level income. Aggressive, undisciplined students are no easier to discipline and teach. Teachers do not automatically transform their teaching styles to accommodate to new circumstances. District board of education members and influential, tax-minded civic leaders become no more giving to children of parents who have no political clout and don't even vote.

The voucher system has similar shortcomings so far as the rest of the children are concerned. If 5 percent of the schools in a city attract parents to send their children there on a voucher plan, what do we do with the rest of the children? The usual response is that competition will force the other 95 percent of schools to become more effective. This expectation presupposes that the shortcomings in those 95 percent of schools are due primarily to a lack of will, interest, or direction.

A cautionary note about school choice is in order here. A study on parental decision-making about school and its effects in terms of achievement and equity led Dan Goldhaber, an educational researcher, to say the following: "These findings should send a note of caution regarding the equity and demographic consequences of choice given that unfettered school choice would likely lead to increased racial and economic segregation."[23]

We have yet to hear the last word on privatization, the voucher system, and charter schools. That can come only after a large sample of each of them has been in operation a more substantial period of time. On the basis of the evidence now available and the inherent limitations of these approaches for the population of students at large, it is reasonable to conclude that market-based reform cannot significantly alter the state of education in our country.

NOTES

1. United States National Commission on Excellence in Education, *A Nation at Risk: The Imperative for Educational Reform: A Report to the Nation and the Secretary of Education, United States Department of Education*, by the National Commission on Excellence in Education (Washington D.C.: The Commission, 1983).

2. Richard F. Elmore, "The Origins and Problems of Education Reform in the United States," in *Who Chooses? Who Loses? Culture, Institutions, and the Unequal Effects of School Choice*, ed. Bruce Fuller and Richard F. Elmore, with Gary Oldfield (New York: Free Press, 1996), 293–303.

3. Matt Gandal, *Making Standards Matter: A Fifty State Progress Report on Efforts to Raise Academic Standards* (Washington, D.C.: American Federation of Teachers, Educational Issues Department, 1995).

4. Diane Massell, Michael Kirst, and Margaret Hoppe, *Persistence and Change: Standards-Based Reform in Nine States* (Philadelphia: Consortium for Policy Research in Education, University of Pennsylvania, 1997).

5. Victoris Benning, "MSPAP, SOL Ideals as Different as Their Acronyms," *Washington Post*, 14 May 2000, 1 and 9(C).

6. Benning, "MSPAP, SOL Ideals as Different as Their Acronyms," 9(C).

7. Tamara Henry, "Study: Arts Education Has Academic Effect," *USA Today*, 20 May 2002, 6(D).

8. Kate Zernike, "Gap between Best and Worst Widens on U.S. Reading Test," *New York Times*, 7 April 2001, 1 and 9(A).

9. Edward Wyatt, "Investors See Room for Profit in the Demand for Education," *New York Times*, 4 November 1999, 1 and 27(A).

10. Edward Wyatt, "Higher Scores Aren't Cure-All, School Run for Profit Learns," *New York Times*, 13 March 2001, 1(A) and 4(B).

11. "Privatization and Failing Schools," *New York Times*, 30 June 2000, 24(A).

12. Ann Brown, "Mighty Asset: School Volunteers," *Arizona Daily Star*, 5 January 1998, 1(D).

13. Sarah Tully Tapia, "Tucson Charter Schools Allow Choice," *Arizona Daily Star*, 6 January 1998, 1(C).

14. Monica Mendoza, "State Schools get a 'D'; It's Unfair, Officials Say," *Arizona Daily Star*, 9 January 1998, 1 and 3(A).

15. "Dismal Grades for Schools," *Arizona Daily Star*, 10 January 1998, 12(A).

16. "Dismal Grades for Schools," 12(A).

17. "Dismal Grades for Schools," 12(A).

18. Brent Staples, "Schoolyard Brawl," *New York Times*, 4 January 1998, 49(A). Also, Lynn Olson, "New Study Finds Low Achievement in City Schools," *Education Week* (10 December 1997): 35–36.

19. Olson, "New Study Finds Low Achievement in City Schools," 35–36.

20. Jolley B. Christman and Pat Macpherson, *The Five School Study: Restructuring Philadelphia's Comprehensive High Schools* (Philadelphia: Research for Action, 1996).

21. Christman and Macpherson, *The Five School Study*, 12.

22. Seymour Sarason, *Charter Schools: Another Flawed Educational Reform?* (New York: Teachers College Press, 1998), 100.

23. Dan D. Goldhaber, "School Choice: An Examination of the Empirical Evidence on Achievement, Parental Decision Making, and Equity," *Educational Researcher* 28, no. 8 (November 1999): 16–25.

9

TYPES OF SCHOOL REFORM: EQUITY-BASED AND COMMUNITY-BASED

To continue the examination of the four types of reform, with special reference to implications for the three school systems, we turn to the next two, equity-based and community-based reform.

EQUITY-BASED REFORM

This type of reform seeks to overcome the inequalities in the nation's educational enterprise. What follows, after setting a historical backdrop to equity issues, are three forms of equity-based reform, pertaining respectively to race, gender, and income level or class.

The defeat of fascism in World War II saw the rise of liberation and social justice movements in much of the world. In the United States, African Americans, Hispanic Americans, Native Americans, women, the physically and mentally disadvantaged, and those of nonconventional sexual orientation energized political life as they sought equal treatment and opportunity. They elevated the level of discourse on moral issues, more than a century and a half after the nation was established on the principle that "all men are created equal." At the time, of course, that meant all *white men of property*, a small proportion of the population. Now, millions were declaring that *all* men and *all* women, of whatever color and ethnic group, mental or physical state, or sexual orientation were equal. They demanded the rights and prerogatives of equals, and they made it unmistakably clear through demonstrations, sit-downs, use of the judiciary, and the vote that they would accept no less.

Their voices were heard in Washington and the respective state capitals. Legislation was passed, and funding was increased for many purposes, not least of all for education. The Supreme Court and lower courts also responded, issuing decisions favorable to the causes of the various liberation movements, including that for girls and women.

Not unexpectedly, those demands, and especially the legislation and judicial decisions that were responsive to them, were a threat to the stability of the old order of things. If those demands were to continue to be met, then people of wealth and power who had been enjoying a disproportionate share of the gross national product would have to accommodate themselves to something less. They were not happy with that prospect.

During the debates at the time, as in the past when the wealthy needed justification for their status, some professionals came to their rescue. They presented what they called scientific evidence that those who were poor were also intellectually inferior to those in the higher social rungs. These are familiar arguments, used all too widely even to this day. Biologist and writer Barbara Kingsolver put it this way.

> The explosive publication in 1994 of a book called *The Bell Curve* was an attempt to prove, yet again, the intellectual superiority of Caucasians. Written just in time to catch a new current of racism, the book drips with statistics and academic language, but its emotional heart seems bent on justifying the subordinate status of people of color in the U.S. . . . The authors proved one thing, without a doubt: the privileged have not yet tired of hearing how righteously they came by their place at the table.[1]

In that context of presumed class distinctions, the issue before the nation during the debates can be reduced to this question: How should wealth be distributed? An answer in general terms came from John Rawls, a Harvard philosopher, in his book, *A Theory of Justice*. He conceived of justice as fairness. To achieve fairness he proposed two principles. The first principle emphasizes equality: equal rights and benefits for all. The second principle addresses the issue of social and economic inequalities. These "are just only if they result in compensating benefits for everyone, and in particular for the least advantaged members of society."[2] He clarifies this second principle further: "It may be expedient but it is not just that some should have less in order that others may prosper. But there is no injustice in the greater benefits earned by a few provided that the situation of persons not so fortunate is thereby improved."[3]

The second principle seems reasonable and well within the scope of justice. In practice, what is problematic is determining the degree of improvement required for the less fortunate. For example, the implementation of trickle-down economic theory in the 1980s in Britain and the United States (known as Thatcherism and Reaganomics, respectively) was claimed to serve all the people. A few, the wealthy, would receive their benefits quite directly, and the many, indirectly, through a trickle-down effect. Critics at the time had serious doubts that justice was served. Since that economic theory still influences the policies and practices of those governments, this issue is more than theoretical.

The thesis put forth at the time was that if the wealthy were given more incentives (which could often be accomplished only by reducing taxes and, thereby, reducing social services to the needy, among others), everyone would benefit. The popular metaphor employed in those years was "Rising tides lift all boats." Undoubtedly, the rising tides invoked by tax reductions and deregulations of various kinds, such as those intended to protect the environment, or workers' safety, raised many a bright and shiny oceangoing yacht for happy voyages, but left millions of people, many children among them, to fend for themselves in leaky row boats. Rising tides were no comfort to those sinking into poverty. That metaphor is appropriate for the third school system, which has been a sinking operation for decades.

Equity-Based Reform: Race

In one fashion or another black Americans have struggled to educate themselves and be educated since they were brought to America as slaves. In modern times, the Supreme Court decision of *Brown v. Board of Education* in 1954 represents a turning point in that struggle. The court's decision by itself would not have sufficed to yield the achieved gains, especially by middle-class African Americans. It took the civil rights movement to raise the consciousness of millions of black and white Americans. They came to understand that they did not have to stand by passively and accept the inequities of the system, including the educational system. That understanding set off a stream of actions, in the streets, in election campaigns, and in the polling booths. Those actions had an impact on government policies. They led to more equitable practices in schools, in government, and in the business world. While the middle class has profited from the changes, millions of lower-class blacks have not. The children of families in that class are enrolled in the third school system.

The problems of educating children in the third school system are compounded for black children, especially if the composition of the school is largely lower-class black, which means that many of their families have an income below the poverty level. They must deal, as sociologist John Ogbu points out, with two sources of barriers to equal access to education.[4] The first is in the sense conveyed by society, experienced by parents and children alike, that they're not worth something better than what they are given. Classes are overcrowded, plaster is falling from the ceilings, science laboratories are inadequate, treatment by the system at large adversely affects their education.

The second source of barriers to equal access is in self-perceptions and coping responses to circumstances. The result, as Ogbu puts it, is a "low-effort syndrome in black academic striving."[5] Many people, of all races, have sometimes found themselves in a situation that leads them to resignation: "What's the use. I might as well give up." If that occurs a few times in one's life and about inconsequential skills ("I just can't do figure skating"), it matters little. But when children resign themselves to hopelessness and give up any serious effort at school learning, they are surrendering much that is good and worthwhile in life. The school experience of some of those children leads to a pernicious outcome that has come to be known as "learned helplessness," a useful label given it by psychologist Martin Seligman.[6] This develops when individuals, faced with repeated experiences of failure, which are interpreted as due to their inherent inadequacies, feel overpowered. They become passive and apathetic and resign themselves to failure. They have been taught to feel helpless.

Lest anyone blame the teachers in such schools, we should note that the administrators and teachers, as educator Jean Anyon, reporting on ghetto schools, points out, have internalized and are subject to the values and biases of the dominant culture.[7] This is not surprising, considering that long ago two distinguished social psychologists, Muzafer Sherif and Hadley Cantril, established the principle that minority groups in the United States assimilate the conceptions of them held by the majority.[8] In other words, X-group's self-concept is derived from the majority group's concept of X. To many of the black teachers observed by Anyon, the children are "lazy" or "bad" or "stupid." Being as human as anyone else, administrators, and teachers, too, are the victims of the culture's racist attitudes and practices. Today, in many social circles, these attitudes do not produce the ugly racist outpourings of the past; they are more cerebral and very much at subconscious levels. Nevertheless, they are destructive, and not just because of the effect on the children. They are also destructive in not leaving room for the kind of thinking that might yield different understandings about why the children behave as they do and what might be done that would produce favorable results.

We should note that much that is being said about the circumstances of schooling for blacks, and the barriers to access, apply to others as well. Many children in the burgeoning population of Hispanic Americans and also Native Americans are confronted with these same barriers.

Just how those barriers play themselves out in classrooms is dramatically evident in reports by Anyon and Jonathan Kozol in their respective books about ghetto schools. Anyon's studies in the Newark schools, especially in one of them, which she calls the Marcy Elementary School, yielded unexpected insights. At one point during her observations in that school, she notes in her records that she is taken aback to discover that in *this* school she had come to accept very poor education as "good." In an affluent district, had she observed what she considered "good" in the Marcy School's classrooms, she would have regarded it as "a crisis or breakdown of the system." To her dismay, Dr. Anyon realized that she had become part of the system. She had come to regard the educationally unacceptable as acceptable.

The stark contrast with a first system school is apparent in her notations after visiting her daughter's third-grade classroom on the very next day. Most of the parents are professionals. Only 40 percent of the students are minority, and only 10 percent of them are from low-income families. This New York City public school, considered a model, starts with at least two advantages: the educational level of the parents and the socioeconomic status of most of the children's families. Here is what Dr. Anyon wrote:

> After being in Marcy yesterday where chaos filled the halls, and teachers tried angrily and in vain to get the children to go back in their rooms, I went into my daughter's class today.
>   The contrast was overwhelming. The kids were sitting, doing various activities, all over the room. . . . The children were reading . . . and working with manipulables of various kinds. Materials, books, and supplies were everywhere, and in abundance. . . . The children were working easily, absorbed. . . . Chatter filled the air, and smiles: and—most importantly— they seemed involved and interested in what they were doing. They seemed happy to be there![9]

Marveling at how good life was in her daughter's class she realized how far she had gone toward accepting "the starkness of Marcy's bare and vacant rooms, the angry, wounded-looking children, and the resentful, hostile teachers—as acceptable."

Anger and resentment are normal and understandable reactions of parents, children, and teachers, and of all members of an oppressed group, who feel trapped in intolerable circumstances. They have no power to change those circumstances. Like a vicious cycle, their powerlessness generates rage and resignation.

Changing Attitudes through Struggle

Where do those negative attitudes come from, and how can they be countered? The self-deprecating attitudes of students and the biases of their teachers exist in part because psychology is essentially an ahistorical science that tends to draw conclusions from analyses of a highly circumscribed data set, such as IQ test results. To comprehend the consciousness and behavior of black children and determine their capacity for learning, it is not enough to examine the children in the context of the family and community. One must view them in historical context, because the experiences of prior generations, grandparents for example, are not abruptly erased from family consciousness even at the deaths of those most affected by oppression or genocide. As an example, the Jewish experience in Germany under Hitler lasted only thirteen years. Yet, today, children, grandchildren, and great-grandchildren still show the effects of that infamous period. And for Jews, for the most part, their physical abuse and degradation, at least in the West, ended after those thirteen years. For blacks, slavery lasted more than two centuries; oppression continued long afterward, even to this day. Some parents and many grandparents of black children were required to sit in the back of public buses in the south, drink from separate water fountains, and use rest rooms designated for them. In the South, they were addressed as "boy" or "girl." Anyone seeking to understand the behavior of black children, who does not have that background in mind, is engaged in superficial analysis.

Early in the twentieth century, many immigrants of peasant background suffered the effects of superficial analyses. Educators and psychologists, paying no attention to the immigrants' peasant backgrounds, illiteracy, and unfamiliarity with Western culture, classified them as intellectually inferior and conveyed that false belief to the general public. One of the leading purveyors of such notions was Carl Brigham, Princeton professor and a founder of the Educational Test Service. He reviewed World War I soldiers' scores on the army mental tests and, ignoring background, education, and literacy, concluded that most immigrants to the United States were intellectually inferior.[10]

To measure the success of equity-based reforms we cannot ignore historical and current social-political-economic contexts. The Supreme Court *did* act against segregation. The law says that even separate but equal is not equal and not constitutional. So, on a de jure basis, segregation does not exist. On a de facto basis, it is widespread, more widespread in the North than it was before *Brown v. Board of Education*.

Nonetheless, a far higher proportion of oppressed minorities in the United States—black, Hispanic American, Native American—have graduated from high school, college, and university and have gone on into business, government, and the professions than prior to that landmark case. The significant change has come about not because of desegregation of the schools, which has been limited. Rather, it is due to the struggles of those people, allied with some members of the mainstream population, that the nation has come closer to the proposition in the Declaration of Independence that all people are created equal. Those struggles did yield legislation, linked with funds dedicated to the needs of children in poor families, including such programs as Head Start and the Elementary and Secondary Education Act of 1965.

People struggled. The nation, through its government—now compelled to give greater recognition to the promise of its Declaration of Independence and the rights granted by the Constitution—opened the door to new opportunities, opened it considerably wider, although not all the way. That liberalized government policy voiced the dreams of those who had struggled. It helped to reinforce the conviction that they were, in fact, in every important respect the equals of the majority.

No single action could have generated the gains that have been made the last half-century. So far as we know now, they are all of one piece. People had to organize and campaign for equity. Advances came through advocacy, demonstration, organization, insistence, sit-ins, teach-ins, electioneering, long and tiresome meetings, street smarts, political smarts, legal suits, legislation-writing, lobbying, new educational programs, parent organizations, and student and youth organizations. In the course of it all, the consciousness of many people changed.

For many individuals, being a member of their minority group was now more of a source of pride than of shame. As to a change in consciousness of the majority, two recent books come to very different conclusions. If sociologist Alan Wolfe's *One Nation, After All* is to be trusted, then middle-class Americans, many of them clearly conservative, respect the values and way of life of other people. If journalist David Shipler's *A Country of Strangers: Blacks and Whites in America* is to be trusted, then the blatant bigotry of the past has been replaced by a camouflaged, often silent form of prejudice, perhaps no more than an occasional thought, or the discomfort of some whites at being in social settings with blacks.[11] We can speculate that perhaps the ages of those in the majority group make a difference. Perhaps with the passing years, Wolfe's assessment will be more valid than it may be now, and more valid than Shipler's. At least, the younger generations of Americans seem to have incorporated the Declaration of Independence's proposition on equality: Whereas older generations were not interested in films with largely black actors, young people, attuned to black music, may soon be flocking to them as much as to others, as if skin color has no bearing on a film's popularity.[12]

Whether or not there are perceptible changes in the racial attitudes of whites, the fact remains that in the schools of America, and especially in the third school system, the effects of centuries of racism persist and *are* quite perceptible. In an illuminating article, "Invisibility Syndrome: A Clinical Model of the Effects of Racism on African American Males," two psychologists, Anderson J. Franklin and Nancy Boyd-Franklin, explain why their model—"perceived prejudice and discrimination" affect the behavior and well-being of individuals—is applicable to African Americans generally but is "particularly salient for males."[13] They report that "African American men have one of the lowest life expectancies in the general population due to homicide . . . cardiovascular disorders, hypertension, diabetes, and substance abuse. . . . Approximately 30 percent of young black men are involved with the judicial system. . . . Many lack marketable skills and functional literacy; the ability to gain employment, sustain upward mobility, and contribute to the family remains problematic for many African American men. . . ."[14]

The results of these conditions can be overpowering. Repeated racial slights and the sense that the larger society does not value their abilities or character create "the subjective experience of invisibility among African Americans."[15]

Comments about Equity-Based Reform: Race

We can conclude that equity-based educational reform concerned with race, linked with the struggles of the times and the other changes that those struggles wrought, contributed to positive changes in the education and careers of blacks and other minorities, and elevated many to middle-class status. They did not yield hoped-for effects in the large mass of minority children in our urban centers. For too many of them, school—mostly in the third school system—is still irrelevant, and the experiences of those who are African American, perhaps others as well, only contribute to or reinforce the sense of invisibility.

Equity-Based Reform: Gender

It took almost a century and a half after the Declaration of Independence's insistence on equality before women were given the right to vote.

That was the only form of equality promised by the Nineteenth Amendment to the U.S. Constitution. The amendment did not demand equality of educational, recreational, or career opportunity. For those forms of equality, new struggles, beyond that of women's suffrage, were required.

Those struggles reaped their benefits in legislation. First, Title VII of the 1964 Civil Rights Act gave women legal safeguards: The act prohibited discrimination in employment on the basis of race, national origin, religion, and *sex*. Still, not until 1972, as Pamela Keating explains, did anti-discrimination legislation specifically cover educational policies and programs. Title IX of the Education Amendments of 1972 amended the Civil Rights Act and prohibited sex discrimination in higher education and all federally aided school programs. Targets of Title IX were a variety of discriminatory practices so well established as to seem inherent in the national system of education. These practices include boys' interscholastic athletic programs (e.g., basketball) that were more developed and better funded than those for girls; vocational courses that were segregated by sex (e.g., carpentry shop for boys, home economics for girls); the absence of school services for pregnant students; and, at a more subtle level, but highly destructive, gender bias in how the two sexes are represented in curricular materials.[16]

Other legislation followed. The Women's Education Equity Act, passed by Congress in 1974, provides funds for programs to achieve educational equity and also for the development of model programs. Then, in 1976, Congress required more insistently than before that federally funded vocational education programs must eliminate sex bias and stereotyping.

This impressive record of legislation was meant to assure girls and women equal access to educational and career opportunities. The reservations that follow are in no way meant to belittle or deprecate that record. Nevertheless, it must be said that deeply ingrained habits of thought and behavior are not automatically transformed by legislative acts. That sad fact is as true about efforts to achieve equal access and opportunity for oppressed minorities as for girls and women.

So far as gender is concerned, Keating points to the fact that while some women have taken on nontraditional employment roles, for the most part they are concentrated in "low-paying, low-status occupations: secretaries, nurses, and elementary school teachers. For most women, opportunity is little more than an extension of the traditional care-giving responsibilities of mother and home maker."[17]

Because occupational roles influence educational and career planning, the current employment status of the two sexes is quite relevant to discussions about equality of opportunity for the men and women. What a twelve- or fourteen-year-old girl sees is available for her is bound to influence her appreciation about the place in society of her sex; it is also bound to affect her planning.

Unfortunately, she is taught about her "place" at a much earlier age. In an article called "Running in Place," in which psychologist Virginia Valian explains, "After thirty years on the fast track, women are still hobbled by the cumulative effects of sexual stereotyping," Valian shows that the stereotyping begins at birth.[18] Even the very greeting cards congratulating parents on the newborn are different. Those for boys tend to convey the sense of male physical activity whereas those for girls present them as passive and decorative. For example, lace, ribbons, flowers, and hearts appear more on cards for girls than boys. Asked to rate their newborns, who objectively were no different in length and weight, parents gave their sons higher ratings for size, and fathers rated their sons higher in coordination, alertness, strength, and hardiness.

"Knowing a child's sex," Keating says, "skews perceptions."[19] From the beginning, children learn from their parents' subtle and overt indications of what each gender represents. They develop their own concepts of gender. They become what is expected of them, at least until they, themselves, become aware of societal limitations.

Even apart from their internalization of the gender concepts, the biases will emerge in their occupational life. A study of what helped determine women's and men's salaries showed that favorable ratings on various factors (such as number of graduate degrees, years of work experience) helped men much more than women. That result, Keating points out, "is just what gender schemas [concepts] would lead one to expect: women's achievements, qualifications and professional choices are worth less than men's are."[20] Unarticulated and even disavowed as they may be, gender schemas are powerful influences in the lives of children and adults. They are also insidious in that they are not entirely conscious and can operate even in people who are genuinely egalitarian.

With all the progress toward equality that has been made, barriers of the more subtle type continue to affect the consciousness and the lives of girls in school. Keating identifies three barriers of that kind.

1. The feminization of teaching. Teaching, like the other feminized occupations, has low status and wages. Teachers, especially in elementary schools, are mostly women, with less opportunity for upward economic mobility and for professional advancement. Administrators, at all levels, are most often men. The impact on students is profound. The low-status, low-wages conditions produce other negative consequences: Through observation of role models, children learn important lessons about the respective roles and relationships of men and women. The organization of the school communicates to them that men are in leadership, policy-making positions, and women are not. They may even perceive that women are often subservient to the male leaders. From what they learn in that setting, and at home, of course, they develop their own conceptions of their respective future roles and relationships.

2. Biased materials and counsel. Students' observations of roles in the real-life setting of the school are reinforced by what they find in their educational materials. There, women continue to be assigned to stereotypic activities. Even in such unexpected places as mathematics problems they are depicted, as they might have been in Abe Lincoln's time, as if no changes had occurred in a century and a half. For here, in some schoolbooks in the twenty-first century, they are still pictured sewing and cooking, whereas males are seen in diverse activities that people of both sexes would likely find more exciting. School counselors sometimes further reinforce students' biases about gender roles as they direct females toward occupations that are most open to them. By doing so, however, they foreclose other potential opportunities in what have been largely male domains.

   Future educational and occupational roles are shaped from early in life. Differences are evident when girls play with dolls and tea sets and boys with trucks and construction materials. Studies of differential gender achievement in the sciences show that the gap between the two sexes is small in the middle school years. It widens considerably in high school, where, after a year or two, science courses are optional. By then the expectations of girls, and their own attitudes, impel them to concentrate in other courses. When they choose science courses they select life sciences because, whereas biology covers more of life, as one girl Keating quoted said, "Physics and chemistry are for boys," so she dropped them. Girls could learn those subjects, she added, but they are "boys' subjects." This girl's attitude is consistent with her gender's greater interest in the more patently human aspects of science and with its tendency to choose science-related occupations involved in helping people, other species, and the environment. These observations are supported by a study of a large national sample, in which investigators Burkham, Lee, and Smerdon made two important discoveries.[21] They found, first, that the gap between the two genders is considerable in the physical sciences, but quite narrow in the life sciences. Second, they learned that when students in high school physical sciences had hands-on laboratory experiences and when particularly the teachers showed the relationship between the course and life, the gender gap was greatly narrowed.

3. Knowledge about women. Consider, for a moment, the men and women who have peopled the books we have read and lectures we have heard in our own education: monarchs, presidents, prime ministers, popes, authors, playwrights, essayists, philosophers, poets, jurists, composers, artists, musicians, dancers, actors, scientists, explorers, mathematicians, historians, physicists, chemists, engineers, architects, social scientists, physicians, psychiatrists. What proportion of them was female? The answer is small, very small. That situation is changing as women themselves, and some men, are bringing to our awareness the large number of heretofore-unknown women who were productive in one field or another over the centuries. A publication such as *Women in the Arts* of the National Museum of Women in the Arts is but one example. The condition of obscurity is also changing as women today have come upon the national and international stages in a variety of roles. Talented women of earlier days, largely ignored in their own era and up to recent times, are testimony to the unrecognized capabilities of women. Just as oppressed minorities have come to appreciate their own worth, women, the oppressed majority, have increasingly done the same. The changes

are slow to come, so that many schoolchildren today have not incorporated the new knowledge to overcome deeply rooted attitudes about the "proper place" for girls and women.

Just how much changed during the decade of the nineties was assessed by a study commissioned by the American Association of University Women Education Foundation and researched by the American Institutes for Research. The report of this study, *Gender Gaps: Where Schools Still Fail our Children*, published in 1999, compares its findings with those reported in *The AAUW Report: How Schools Shortchange Girls*, published in 1992. Here are the major findings:

- Girls' patterns of taking courses are beginning to be more like that of boys. In terms of the numbers of courses in science and math, they are coming closer; however, in terms of the more advanced courses in those fields, a wide gap still remains between the sexes. The exceedingly high valuation of these two fields in this technology-conscious period is unfortunate because it tends to give lower status to fields in which girls have always excelled—fields of considerable personal and societal value.[22]
- Girls still earn higher grades than boys and still score lower on "high-stake tests" like the Scholastic Assessment Test (SAT) and American College Test (ACT) that weigh heavily in college admissions. They still take more Advanced Placement tests than boys, and still earn fewer scores at the cut-off point or higher for college credit. However, some steps taken to achieve equity have paid off: The addition to the SAT of a section on writing skills has narrowed the gap between boys' and girls' scores. This positive development makes an important statement that probably bears on test performance differences related to sex, ethnicity, and race: *Method* of assessment as well as *content* must be addressed if equity is to be achieved.[23]
- The standards movement—the movement toward "excellence"—seems to have neglected equity. It does not acknowledge the importance of equity or the challenges of accommodating to different needs. It has paid too little attention to differentials in the availability of resources and, perhaps worst of all, does little to train teachers to deal with equity issues.[24]

- More boys than girls are both retained in grade and drop out of school. The rates are higher, however, for both black and low-income students. As one would expect, over time the effects of poverty, physical and sexual abuse, and family dysfunction impair school performance, and the toll is greater on girls than boys, with one in five physically or sexually abused and one in four depressed. Recent efforts to aid affected students have shown positive results. For example, in 1991, 62 percent of all pregnant women were teens, whereas by 1996 that figure was reduced to 55 percent. However, even in this area, discrimination is apparent: Sex education programs focus on girls' responsibility for pregnancy, giving little if any attention to changing boys' behavior and their sense of responsibility.[25]

Comments about Equity-Based Reform: Gender

How do the biases about female roles play themselves out in the three school systems? In this, as in other matters, children in the first system are in the favored position. Their parents are more demanding and have more influence over the schools' values and practices than parents in the other systems, especially the third. Their teachers, for example in science, are more likely to relate the courses to meaningful personal and societal needs and to provide hands-on experiences. Counselors in those schools whose personal sex-linked biases lead them to foreclose educational or career opportunities because of gender are bound to hear from the parents, perhaps via a headmaster/mistress or a principal. Furthermore, the female students will be getting an education, in elementary, secondary, and post-secondary institutions, that will open the door to a variety of challenging occupations. In responsibility and remuneration, these will be well beyond the categories of child care, food services, and low-level health-care occupations to which many of the girls in the third and some in the second system will be limited.

Equity-Based Reform: Income Level

The effects of poverty on achievement are powerful. Equity-based reforms are designed to mitigate the effects of poverty on mental development and school learning. How poverty affects children in schools is the question that educational researcher Martin Orland (1994) investigated. He drew on nationally representative data about poverty, and achievement test scores and demographic data, such as mother's education. His first finding was that the longer children experience poverty, the greater the likelihood that they will be low achievers. This is intuitively valid: The longer a parent is unemployed, on welfare, or on a job paying minimum wage, trying to provide food and shelter and struggling to keep a family together, the greater the likelihood of strain and stress on the parent, of demoralization, anger, and short temper. For the children, the parent is less likely to have the time or patience to encourage reading and monitor homework, and the general tenor of family life probably is not conducive to the kinds of conversations and experiences that instill motivation for school learning. No matter how much the parent may devoutly wish to see the children well educated, to see them break out of the misery of poverty, circumstances well beyond the parent's control make fulfillment of that wish less probable. The wish does not provide nourishing food, good medical care, patient parenting, intellectual stimulation, and parental tutoring. It doesn't give them time to read to their children, take them on trips to the library, zoo, a museum, or a farm, or any trips that stir their imagination and the desire to learn more. It doesn't give them the resources to engage their children in ways that promote intellectual and linguistic development.[26]

The poverty concentration of schools is the key to Orland's second finding. In performance on standardized achievement tests, the percentage that performed poorly was "dramatically higher in schools with very high concentrations of poverty compared with other schools."[27] In such schools several different forces are operating. The students know they are poor performers. The teachers and administrators know and expect it. Because the parents are not organized to lobby in the interest of their children and are relatively powerless in their communities, their children's schools can, with impunity, be given meager resources. Also, they may have been led to believe that their children's poor performance was the result of and a reflection of their own inadequacies, genetic or otherwise, and that there was little or nothing that could be done to improve it. All in all, a sense of hopelessness and resignation enshrouds the affected schools.

Some students are in the worst possible situation, suffering both from the disadvantages of long-term poverty and of attending schools with heavy concentrations of poverty. Those most affected by the dual disadvantage are black students, rural students, and those in the southern part of the United States. For them, equity-based reforms have offered little in the way of equity.

Earlier I referred to the Early Elementary School Act of 1965 and other legislative acts that were designed to assist children of low-income families. These led to important gains such as positive outcomes resulting from the Head Start program for preschool children. Yet, the gains should not be exaggerated. Because the amount of assistance was minimal, given only in one year of preschool and in the early grades, it was not sufficient to overcome the depredations of poverty and to carry educationally deprived students through high school. In all, the gains were minimal. The astounding result was that deprived teenagers who had had a supportive one year preschool experience, usually with some parental involvement in the program, showed even a slight advantage ten or twelve years later, compared with teenagers who had not had that benefit. This result demonstrates the powerful potential of early intervention.

Comments on Equity-Based Reform: Income Level

Equity based reform directed to income level has only begun to scratch the surface. The concentration of poverty and its destructive psychological consequences make the task seem as daunting as climbing Mt. Everest, particularly if the focus is narrowly directed just to the schools.

COMMUNITY-BASED REFORM

The three types of reform already discussed are easily defined, but not this type. There is little agreement on the word "community" in the context of reform. Among researchers who are studying schools as communities, some focus on participation, some on student and/or teacher sense of belonging to the school community. Some attend to the commonality of values. Some conceptualize community in terms of student needs that must be fulfilled in a group setting, others in terms of the school's ability to meet those needs, and still others address both the individual and the school as a fulfilling community.[28]

Complications do not end with the definition of the community. Research on the benefits of this type of reform has yielded contradictory results. For example, in a study extending over a period of about fifteen years, Victor Battistich and colleagues at the Developmental Studies Center in Oakland, California, worked intensively with a small number of elementary schools to enhance the social development of their students. Over time, they came to think of their aim as that of developing the school as a caring community. This concept, they believe, serves as "a powerful framework for looking at educational practice, and for helping schools to more effectively meet the needs of teachers and students."[29] Findings show that the sense of community can be enhanced for both students and teachers and that the many positive results are especially helpful to the most disadvantaged students. Students became more engaged in schoolwork, liked coming to school, and enjoyed class. These promising outcomes can be regarded as predictors of school success; however, the study at that point was not designed to measure that result. Other studies have found positive effects of a strong school community on both attendance and community.

A very different type of study casts a shadow over that positive picture. In a complex study involving 5,600 middle school students, a majority of them African Americans, Meredith Phillips compared the benefits of what she calls "communitarian climate" with "academic climate."[30] She wanted to know their relative influences on school attendance and mathematics achievement. Communitarian climate scores were based on teachers' perceptions of shared values (for example, their answer to questions such as "How comfortable do you feel with your school's approach to parent involvement?"), and their perception of democratic governance (for example, their answer to questions such as "To what extent does the principal share real power on important decisions?"). Academic climate scores were based on three indicators: Teachers' expectations about the percentage of students in their school who will complete high school and college, students' estimates of the hours they spend on homework, and the percentage of students who enroll in algebra in eighth grade.

The results clearly favored academic over communitarian climate. Academic climate, also known as academic press, is very much related to attendance and mathematics achievement, in contrast with the communitarian. Our conclusions, however, cannot rest at that point. Phillips herself, despite her conclusions, says that communitarian climate "might be [positively related to attendance and achievement in general] when combined with academic press."[31] Another study, this by psychologist Roger Shouse, found precisely that: The results differed, depending on the socioeconomic status of the high schools in the sample.[32] For high socioeconomic schools, student achievement was positively associated with community climate, whether or not there was high academic press. On the other hand, for low and for middle class socioeconomic high schools, student achievement was highest when both community and academic climate were positive.

Comments on Community-Based Reform

How valid is this last finding? Perhaps one of the best ways to evaluate it is through one's own experience. In what settings and with what teachers did we go to class with the greatest interest and learn the most? Chances are that most people would recall teachers, at whatever level of education, who had high expectations for student achievement, did their best to help students achieve that, and did so in a climate that spelled security and comfort for all students. For a description of settings and teachers of that kind one need only read the catalogues of leading private schools, because their selling points are especially those qualities. In print, they tell parents (to use the terminology of some of the studies referred to above) that their institutions are caring communities, and that both the communitarian and academic climates will be favorable to the intellectual and all-round personal development of their children.

The four types of educational reform: standards-based, market-based, equity-based, and community-based, while presumably sharing the same objective—improved student achievement—are in fact driven by different motives. The standards-based type seeks to force the raising of standards of performance by using test results as carrot and stick to make the nation more economically competitive, and to do this at a bargain-basement cost. The market-based type fosters competition, through charter schools, the voucher system, and privatization of schools. The equity-based type assumes that the problems of the schools are a consequence of poverty, discrimination, and racism, and that improvements are impossible unless those issues are addressed. The community-based type, a not-easily defined category, seeks to establish a climate of caring in a setting where teachers share power with administrators and parents are welcome participants.

To ask a rhetorical question: Who would argue against high standards, which are presumably the goal of all four types of reform? Parents choose private schools, move to suburbs with fine public schools, select charter schools, or exercise the use of vouchers in the hope of getting the best education for their children. Most parents lack the resources to do any of the above, and even if they had the resources, where could they go? This is the dilemma, especially for parents and children associated with the third school system, but equally for policy makers committed to an equitable educational system.

School reformers, in answer to the urgent need, have introduced programs over the last two decades that set high standards and are sensitive to the needs for equity and community. These reforms, and the visions of future schooling that they provide, are the subjects of the next chapter.

NOTES

1. Barbara Kingsolver, *High Tide in Tucson: Essays from Now or Never* (New York: HarperCollins, 1995), 77.

2. John Rawls, *A Theory of Justice* (Cambridge, Mass.: Harvard University Press, 1971), 114.

3. Rawls, *A Theory of Justice,* 15.

4. John Ogbu, "Low School Performance as an Adaptation: The Case of Blacks in Stockton, California," in *Minority Status and Schooling: A Comparative Study of Immigrant and Involuntary Minorities*, ed. Margaret A. Gibson and John Ogbu (New York: Garland, 1991), 249–285.

5. Ogbu, "Low School Performance as an Adaptation," 84.

6. Christopher Peterson, Steven F. Maier, and Martin E.P. Seligman, *Learned Helplessness: A Theory for the Age of Personal Control* (New York: Oxford University Press, 1993).

7. Jean Anyon, *Ghetto Schooling: A Political Economy of Urban Educational Reform* (New York: Teachers College Press, 1997).

8. Muzafer Sherif and Hadley Cantril, *The Psychology of Ego-Involvements, Social Attitudes and Identifications* (New York: Wiley; London, Chapman and Hall, 1947).

9. Anyon, *Ghetto Schooling*, 36.

10. Carl Brigham, *A Study of American Intelligence* (Princeton: Princeton University Press, 1923).

11. Alan Wolfe, *One Nation, After All: How the Middle-Class Americans Really Think about God, Country, Family, Racism, Welfare, Immigration, Homosexuality, Work, the Right, the Left, and Each Other* (New York: Viking, 1998). David Shipler, *A Country of Strangers: Blacks and Whites in America* (New York: Knopf, 1997).

12. Bernard Weinraub, "'Beloved' Tests Racial Themes at Box Office," *New York Times*, 13 October 1998, 1(E) and 8(E).

13. Anderson J. Franklin and Nancy Boyd-Franklin, "Invisibility Syndrome: A Clinical Model of the Effects of Racism on African-American Males," *American Journal of Orthopsychiatry* 70, no.1 (January 2000): 33–42, 33.

14. Franklin and Boyd-Franklin, "Invisibility Syndrome," 33.

15. Franklin and Boyd-Franklin, "Invisibility Syndrome," 33.

16. Pamela Keating, "Striving for Sex Equity in Schools," in *Access to Knowledge: The Continuing Agenda for Our Nation's Schools*, ed. John I. Goodlad and Pamela Keating (New York: College Entrance Examination Board, 1994), 91–106.

17. Keating, "Striving for Sex Equity in Schools," 96.

18. Virginia Valian, "Running in Place," in *Why So Slow? The Advancement of Women*, ed. Virginia Valian (Cambridge, Mass.: MIT Press, 1998), 18.

19. Valian, "Running in Place," 20.

20. Keating, "Striving for Sex Equity in Schools," 36.

21. David T. Burkham, Valerie E. Lee, and Betty Smerdon, "Gender and Science Learning Early in High School: Subject Matter and Laboratory Experiences," *American Educational Research Journal* 34, no. 2 (Summer 1997): 297–331.

22. American Association of University Women, *Gender Gaps: Where Schools Still Fail Our Children* (New York: Marlowe, 1999), 11–32.

23. American Association of University Women, *Gender Gaps*, 33–56.

24. American Association of University Women, *Gender Gaps,* 57–78.

25. American Association of University Women, *Gender Gaps*, 79–93.

26. Martin Orland, "Demographics of Disadvantage: Intensity of Childhood Poverty and Its Relationship to Educational Achievement," in *Access to Knowledge: The Continuing Agenda for Our Nation's Schools*, ed. John I.

Goodlad and Pamela Keating (New York: College Entrance Examination Board, 1994), 43–58.

27. Orland, "Demographics of Disadvantage," 54.

28. Victor Battistich, Daniel Solomon, Marilyn Watson, and Eric Schaps, "Caring School Communities," *Educational Psychologist* 32, no. 3 (Summer 1997): 137–151.

29. Battistich, "Caring School Communities," 137.

30. Meredith Phillips, "What Makes Schools Effective? A Comparison of the Relationship of Community Climate and Academic Achievement and Attendance during Middle School," *American Educational Research Journal* 34, no. 4 (Winter 1997): 633–662.

31. Phillips, "What Makes Schools Effective?," 653.

32. Roger C. Shouse, "Academic Press and Sense of Community: Conflict, Congruence, and Implications for Student Achievement," *Social Psychology of Education* I, no. 20 (1996): 47–68.

10

THE SHAPE OF THE FUTURE: FIVE REFORM PROGRAMS

What kind of future do we want for the in-school and at-home education of children? Teachers and other educators have been prolific in developing innovations. For example, a collection of seventy-six evaluated school interventions by Nathalie Rathvon provides a practical guide to a variety of effective methods.[1] The book contains three categories of interventions whose aims are to:

1. Create a productive, disruption free classroom environment, for example, through active teaching of classroom rules and procedures.
2. Improve academic performance, for example, by improving student presentations during small group instruction.
3. Modify behavior and enhance social competence, for example, by using verbal instructions to reduce aggressive behavior.

While these interventions can be helpful to teachers, and a comfort to them to know they have been tested and found useful, they cannot bring about major systemic changes. By contrast, the impressive work of educational reformers points the way to changes of major proportions. This chapter examines some of the leading reform programs introduced within the last thirty years and identifies their major characteristics. Afterwards, it highlights commonalties among the programs and shows how they remedy the shortcomings of the third and second school systems and where they fall short.

THE REFORM PROGRAMS

The following reform programs are presented: Comer's School Development Program, Hirsch's Core Knowledge Movement, Levin's Accelerated Schools Project, Sizer's Coalition of Essential Schools, and Slavin's Success for All and Roots and Wings. These programs were selected because of several characteristics: They are comprehensive, widely applied, extensively reported in professional literature, and hold potential for moving toward a unitary school system.

Comer's School Development Program[2]

One pioneer reformer, James P. Comer, medical doctor and Yale professor of child psychiatry, has spent thirty years in formulating, implementing, and refining the School Development Program (SDP). When he began, he said, he and his colleagues knew it was essential "to involve parents, community members, teachers, psychologists, social workers, and non-instructional staff members (the "stakeholders") in the process of school development,"[3] but they had no idea how to do that.

Dr. Comer organized a Yale Child Study Center team in which a special education teacher, psychologist, and social worker joined him to work with a New Haven school system team. The coordinated team was to become an integral part of two elementary schools, allowing them to put their ideas into practice, learn from their experience and apply their findings in the New Haven system, and perhaps nationally.

Success did not come easily or quickly. After five years, conflict with a principal forced them to replace one school with another. It took three more years to get "good school climate" and seven years to see significant academic improvement. But these schools, with 99 percent of their students African American and 70 percent on welfare, moved from being the poorest performing ones out of 33 schools, to being "tied for the third and fourth highest levels of achievement on nationally standardized tests and had the best attendance in the city. Serious behavior problems had been eliminated."[4]

Those are substantial outcomes. They were based on the understanding, in Comer's words, that "the three most important parts in school change are relationships, relationships, relationships."[5]

The number "three" appears often in the language of the School Development Program, resulting in three threes constituting the basic nine elements. The stakeholders organize themselves into three teams: School Planning and Management, Parent, and Student and Staff Support. Working separately and collaboratively they generate three plans: the comprehensive school plan, a plan for the assessment and modification of the comprehensive plan as new needs became evident, and the teachers' plan for their own professional development. As the final set of "threes," the SDP is guided by three principles: no-fault (no finger pointing); consensus in decision-making (no politicking and voting); collaboration (team members have their input, but do not paralyze the work of the principal; the principal does not ignore the views of team members). Because of these three principles, the stakeholders succeed in working cooperatively.

Over a period of about thirty years, the School Development Program has caught on, with 650 schools in 28 states now applying it in one form or another. How successful has it been? For the first two schools in the program, the success noted above took *sixteen* long years after the intervention began. According to Comer, improvement occurs for some schools now within three years:

> Our best approximation suggests that after three years about a third of the schools make significant social and academic improvements, a third show modest improvement, which is often difficult to sustain, and a third show no gain. Assessments by evaluators outside our program support our guesstimate.[6]

Note that with all the effort, after three years only one-third of the schools realized sustained "significant social and academic improvements."

Although academic gains are usually assessed by means of test scores, the SDP was not designed with test scores in mind. The focus is on creating the conditions "that promote student development, adequate teaching, and in turn adequate levels of learning."[7] This is not unlike the aim in psychotherapy, to promote the individual's self-confidence and openness to learning and changing. The paramount emphasis on positive relationships between and among all of the stakeholders is meant to create the atmosphere in which the participants can continue to develop and learn. The phrase, "All of the stakeholders," refers to students, parents, school people, community officials, and even those who are marginally connected to the schools.

This emphasis on involvement and interest in the affairs of the schools is strikingly similar to parental involvement in many private and suburban public schools as well as charter schools. In fact, Comer points out that the practices developed by SDP "are closer to those in elite private schools than in most public schools."[8] Granted, it was created to aid mostly low-income minority students. Granted, its purpose was to intervene in a situation where "students were poorly prepared for the learning process of school [they lacked the prerequisites for schooling], and the staff didn't have the training to be able to close the gap."[9] Nevertheless, the structures that were created in schools where the Comer program was well implemented, and the centrality of child development and learning through the implementation of the nine basic elements have moved those urban schools closer in kind to private schools. The threads common to both are spelled out as follows: positive school relationships; caring, responsible, predictable adults in the lives of students; a sense of belonging in constructive groups engaged in challenging learning and activities; and opportunity for students to sense direction and purpose.[10]

Those admirable qualities, sought after by the most educated and sophisticated of parents, are claimed by many a private school. However, those qualities are not easily or quickly achieved even when a new, well-endowed school, catering to a wealthy clientele, is first established. For the schools with which Comer first worked, the obstacles seem almost insurmountable. That is why even modest success is noteworthy and Comer and his colleagues deserve much credit for their accomplishments. Still, even his approach does not solve many of the problems of the third school system. For reasons related to the very nature of the third school system and its constituents—their marginality in our society, family income, health, medical services, nutrition, parental work status, qualifications of the teachers—the School Development Program's record of success leaves much to be desired for the nation as a whole. Its success was achieved only through Dr. Comer's leadership and commitment, his endless struggle to gain economic and political support, and his gritty perseverance. This sort of action by him and his colleagues moves the successful schools in the direction of first system schools, with better teachers, more instructional materials, leaders committed to the goal of excellence and, not least of all, stakeholders' involvement. Nevertheless, despite those important gains, two-thirds of the schools, as noted above, either did not experience significant improvement after three years or did not sustain it.

Recent evaluations by independent researchers of the School Development Program in elementary schools in Detroit show similar outcomes.[11] Of eleven Comer schools, three were rated as highly implemented and four each as having moderate or low implementation. Only in the highly implemented schools did the fifth graders outperform their counterparts in comparison schools. They did so to a statistically significant degree in the following: annual improvement in the staff's assessment of the respective school's social climate and higher achievement scores in reading and science. In math, the difference approached statistical significance. Only parent assessments about family-school relationships and parent-child relationships revealed no difference between the two sets of schools.

These results of the evaluation in Detroit probably understate the impact of the Comer program because, as the researchers point out, "the processes and structures of the Comer School Development Program have become the common currency of school reform. Any school that independently embarked on school reform would be expected to move closer to what our surveys identify as 'implementing Comer.'"[12] In fact, at the time that the Comer team was implementing the program, the Detroit school district began to implement Comer-like features in other schools. That, even under those circumstances, the highly implemented Comer schools fared well in the comparative studies speaks well of its potential.

During the years of establishing the SDP, and up to the present, Comer and his associates have had to struggle to obtain support for their efforts to help interested schools change themselves. In some schools, resistance and lack of support were too great to overcome. This is the old, old theme in the American drama in which, from our earliest times, those who hold the purse strings and the power are reluctant to yield more than they are compelled to surrender by well-organized, strong demonstrations of the public will.

To Dr. Comer, our future hopes rest on what he calls the "New School," an institution that fosters child development and learning after the fashion of the SDP, and on the "Good Society," a society that supports and promotes such schools because it genuinely values equality, social justice, and cooperation, and values them at least as much as it does profit. Those praiseworthy hopes will remain only hopes unless people organized to fight for them back them up. Comer himself said that "people in the helping professions needed to influence political practices,"[13] and he would apply that, I am sure, to those not in the helping professions, to people of all kinds, at all socioeconomic and educational levels.

Hirsch's Core Knowledge Movement[14]

Another program of community reform seems starkly different from the School Development Program. E. D. Hirsch Jr., a professor at the University of Virginia and critic of progressive education, has argued that American students suffer from a lack of shared knowledge. With each school district, if not each school, permitted to create virtually its own curriculum, they have little common content. That, he insists, is a serious disadvantage, both for the millions of children who, over the course of their schooling, transfer from one school district to another, and on a larger scale, for the citizenry in a democracy who do not share a common culture.

To counter this condition, Hirsch developed what has come to be known as the Core Knowledge Movement, which, he reported in 1996, had spread to "more than two hundred public schools in thirty-seven states [and] a much larger, still uncounted number of schools that are successfully using the foundation's principles and materials."[15] By 2002, the number had grown to six hundred schools in forty-seven states.[16]

The first school to apply it, and with "stunning success," was a mixed-population elementary school in Florida. The second one, in the South Bronx, drew national attention and, one might say, "put on the map" the argument that children needed a "solid, knowledge-based curriculum," preferably one that they shared with the rest of the children in the nation.[17]

According to Hirsch, the inclusion, for example, of a core curriculum that constitutes about 50 percent of the total curriculum displaces very little if anything. He bases this conclusion on the fact that district guidelines are so vague that the school hours can accommodate both those guidelines and the specified knowledge in the rigorous core curriculum. He recognizes how difficult a task it is to reach agreement on what he calls the sequence of common learnings. Yet, without it, many children are disadvantaged. "The common learnings taught in school should promote a cosmopolitan, ecumenical, hybrid public culture in which all meet on an equal footing—a culture that is as deliberately artificial and nonsectarian as our public invocations of the Divinity. This school-based culture belongs to everyone and to no one."[18]

Hirsch counterposes the Core Knowledge Movement to the Romantic Movement in education. By that, he means the educational philosophy that stresses "natural" learning, timed to each individual's developmental level. In his view, this approach neglects the substantive learning that comes from a disciplined instructional process aimed at the whole class of children. Also, the Romantic Movement de-emphasizes the content of learning by placing prime value on self-esteem, independent thinking, and creativity, achieved through the processes of instruction.

He is emphatic in claiming that he values those qualities, too, which, he believes, are best achieved through mastery of subject matter, success in accomplishment, and the possession of the "intellectual capital" that thinking and creativity require. It is difficult, he would say, to be creative in addressing problems in science, history, or literature without having a substantial bank of knowledge in those fields.

He calls for preschool education for all children, not child care. The education is to be substantive, not that geared primarily to health, nutrition, and motivation. All of those are essential, but if children are to have a fair chance when they enter school, the preschool *education* must be geared to their academic needs.

It is not enough that children be ready for kindergarten and first grade. They must be ready for *every* grade. Hence, it is the responsibility of every school to see to it that every child is evaluated periodically and given assistance to reach the level necessary to continue to progress and benefit at each grade level.

The program, too, must be evaluated, and reported assessments of Core Knowledge schools have produced impressive results. They show that when schools fully implement the program, students show significant gains in reading and learning and in active engagement in class.

In May 2000, Gracy Taylor and George Kimball of the Oklahoma Public Schools completed the first stage of an independent study of the Core
Knowledge program in Oklahoma City, where thirty-two of sixty-seven elementary schools had implemented the Core Knowledge curriculum.[19] In
particular, they wanted to know the effects of one year of Core Knowledge
on grades three, four, and five, by comparing the performance of students
with that of a group of students on the well-respected Iowa Test of Basic
Skills. They matched three hundred Core Knowledge students with three
hundred randomly selected students who had the same characteristics on
seven variables: grade level, pre-score, sex, race/ethnicity, free-lunch eligibility, Title-1 eligibility, and special-education eligibility. (Both free-lunch
eligibility and Title-1 eligibility are criteria of low income.)

The results showed that students in the Core Knowledge curriculum
made significantly greater gains following one year in the program than the
comparison students, and that those differences were apparent in reading
comprehension, vocabulary, math concepts, social studies, and science.
The greatest gains—reading, vocabulary, and social studies, but especially
the first two—are particularly noteworthy because of their importance as
building blocks for future learning and academic achievement. Vocabulary,
as the researchers point out, is the best single predictor of future academic
success and the area where the gap in test achievement between racial and
ethnic groups has been most difficult to narrow.

In a national study done at Johns Hopkins University, researchers
Samuel Stringfield and colleagues at the Center for Social Organization
of Schools, concluded a three-year assessment of Core Knowledge
schools in 1999.[20] Their findings are a validation of the program, in that
students in those schools outperformed students in comparison groups
both on norm referenced tests and criterion referenced tests of Core
Knowledge topics. That they performed at a higher level on the
Core Knowledge topics is not surprising, considering that those topics
constituted a good part of their instruction; that they performed at a
higher level on the norm referenced tests, that is, tests not keyed to their
instruction, is very supportive of the program. The study elicited other
positive outcomes. Although teachers found the extra work of obtaining
suitable study material tiring, they praised the program for enhancing
their professional lives. Parents, too, reported satisfaction with the program.

The researchers attributed the success of the curriculum to two factors. First, the nature of the curriculum itself, with its clear goals, rich content, and minimal repetitiveness appealed to students and teachers and, through its cumulative effect, led to even greater gains as students progressed through school, each year building on the prior ones. Second, with time, as schools improved their implementation of the program, student performance also improved. Experience in using the Hirsch curriculum made the teachers more effective. Its implementation in more classes in a given school seemed to add to its overall effect. Both of these, the researchers propose, contributed to the gains in student performance on the norm-referenced tests as well as the Core Knowledge tests.

At the end of their report, the Johns Hopkins researchers made an overall interpretation that may be relevant to reform programs in general. What seemed to matter most was the specificity of the curriculum, rather than the Core Knowledge content per se. This led them to conclude that the benefits they found may be applicable to other curricula that are spelled out in detail, even those developed by schools themselves. The content, as in the case of Core Knowledge, would have to be broad in scope, developed sequentially, and firmly based in theory and research, so that the material, for instance, would be age-appropriate.

With substantial validation, but even on an intuitive basis, and because of its emphasis on knowledge, the Core Knowledge program is an important contribution to the ongoing debate about the needs of America's schools. By combining the central ideas of the two major reform programs described above—Comer's School Development Program and Hirsch's Core Knowledge Movement—we pinpoint practical remedies of two basic problems in the third school system, and to a somewhat lesser degree in the second:

1. The conviction that the schools belong to the parents, teachers, and students in the school, that their interests will be recognized and protected and their views will be heard and given credence (which does not mean that they will necessarily prevail).
2. The recognition that the schools' prime objective is their students' academic and intellectual development. This is accomplished by mastering the knowledge and wisdom accumulated over the centuries and learning to apply that legacy in their lives today.

Unfortunately, Comer's and Hirsch's approaches to reform encounter resistance. The prospect that they will make a material difference and convert the third or even the second school system into the equivalent of the first is dim indeed. We have already heard from Comer on this point. As Hirsch, himself, put it, "Nothing truly effective in the way of large-scale policy change—through federal, state, or local mechanism— can be accomplished, no new power relationships can be forged, until there is a change of mind by the general public—among whom I include two and a half million teachers."[21]

He attributes the hold of the status quo to a "widespread fear of uniformity," as if a shared body of knowledge (no more than half of the curriculum, in Hirsch's model) would create cookie-cutter students, lacking in individualism and enterprise. He attributes it, also, to the laissez-faire belief that "if all schools and teachers do their own thing, then the invisible hand of nature will cause our children to be educated effectively, and thus ensure their individuality and diversity."[22]

Those concerns may well be operating, but they mask a deeper truth. To accept the essentiality of having all children ready for successful learning in first grade, ready for learning in all grades, and accountable for their *mastery* of a substantive curriculum says, in effect, that federal and state governments, and the powerful lobbies that shape their policies are prepared to provide the resources to achieve that for all children. Were it ready to do so, were it prepared to give teachers the time, training, and resources to adapt to new ways of teaching, the teachers to whom Hirsch alludes would be strong supporters of reform. Hirsch, himself, has witnessed teachers enthusiastically supportive in the implementation of Core Knowledge, just as Comer and the three educators whose programs we discuss next have seen. Teachers, like other professionals, who have been trained to function in a particular fashion, cannot by fiat suddenly transform themselves, and it is psychologically threatening to them to demand that. With understanding, support, and assistance they can and do change. Those of consequence who stonewall against change are those who shape policies, influence the media, and control the purse strings—hardly the public or the teachers. If those in power were to become influenced primarily by human values, we would witness over time the elimination of the third school system and drastic changes in the second. To this point, we have seen no evidence that such conversion is imminent.

Levin's Accelerated Schools Project[23]

In establishing the Accelerated Schools Project, Henry Levin, formerly of Stanford University, now at Teachers College, Columbia University, had his eyes on at-risk students but very decidedly not for the purpose of improving their schools' efforts at remediation. In such institutions, the at-risk students are ill equipped to benefit from the standard curriculum and only fall farther and farther behind. To the contrary, his aim was to transform such schools from remedial institutions to those that accelerated the development of the talents of all the children.

He viewed the policy of educating at-risk students as self-defeating: At a time when they needed the expectations of their teachers to be set high, they were set low. At a time when they needed a speeded up program to help them catch up, they were given a slowed-down one, and a boring form of instruction to boot. For such students, compensatory education is usually repetitive, highly structured, and a watered-down version of the standard curriculum. That approach to the deficits of the at-risk students offers little if any encouragement to be curious and imaginative or to develop one's own ideas. Whatever else it is, it slows down learning. Hence, the alternative is the *accelerated* school project.

Undergirding the accelerated school approach is the belief that all children have gifts and talents (as well as weaknesses), and the aim of the school-community is to provide opportunities for those strengths (gifts and talents) to be recognized and realized. Their strengths may derive from any and all sources, including from those of their culture, their personal experiences, and their unique knowledge.

Diverse forms of learning are used, including students tutoring students, individual and group projects, and cooperative learning. The methods that are employed are of a kind likely to *engage the students* and *capture their interest*. These methods could entail discussion, debate, investigation, hypothesis testing, and artistic expression. At one of the accelerated schools, one with mostly at-risk children, two months after the inauguration of the program, the school had developed a music conservatory for students in the afternoons and on Saturday. Music and the other art forms are regarded as valuable components of student experience.[24]

Schools don't just sign up with the Accelerated Schools program when an administrator finds the philosophy appealing. The transformation of a school-community obviously is no simple matter. Consequently, it may occur only after all those involved in the decision are well informed and 90 percent of faculty and staff and the parent representatives (at the middle school, also the student representatives) vote in favor of the project. A systematic plan for the preparation of the schools includes training of administrators, faculty, and staff, and of parents and students. Then a coach is trained to work with the school, to help it during the long process of transformation and assist it in formulating plans to evaluate progress. Levin has said that it takes about six years for the complete transformation to occur.[25] The outcomes, as reported by Levin and by others have been highly favorable: higher achievement test scores, considerable increases in parent participation in school affairs, and improved attendance both by students and teachers.

More than one thousand elementary and middle schools in forty-one states are implementing the Accelerated Schools program.[26] Evaluation has been central to the purposes of the project, both to determine its effectiveness and also to improve the Accelerated Schools model and the process of implementation. Levin and his associates claim that their own evaluations show that "Accelerated Schools consistently raise academic achievement, student attendance, and parental participation, and reduce student turnover, special education placements, students retained in grade, and teacher turnover."[27] This claim is supported by evidence from studies conducted in a variety of settings. For example, impressive test gains were found by an outside evaluator who examined the performance of the program in six schools in Missouri where it was introduced in 1988. In one school, the percentage of students who scored at or above grade level rose from 50 to almost 90. In a school in East Harlem, with 95 percent of its students in poverty, the proportion of students at grade level rose from one-third to two-thirds in four years.[28]

Studies in which the performance of Accelerated Schools students is compared with that of similar students in regular school programs also show the former to be at an advantage. In Houston, for example, a school that had slightly lower achievement scores than its comparison school showed marked gains two years after becoming an Accelerated School. Its fifth-grade students, within two years, showed gains of a year and a half in achievement beyond those of its comparison group.

An independent study of Accelerated Schools, conducted by a non-profit organization, Manpower Demonstration Research Corporation, and funded by the Ford Foundation, also found the program effective in promoting educational achievement, as measured by test results.[29] Choosing eight schools countrywide from a list of one hundred that had been using the program since the early 1990s, the researchers compared test scores of third graders during the three years prior to the program's introduction, with scores during the next five years. They were looking for increases in test performance from year to year.

They found that after students had been in the program four to five years, they showed significant gains in performance on the tests. The gains were equivalent, they said, to what one finds in teaching children in small classes.

There are reasons to believe that the evaluation understated the benefits of the program, as the researchers themselves point out. First, in their assessment they included all students in the classes, even many recent entrants to the school who had had little if any opportunity to feel the impact of the program. With those students omitted, the favorable results would probably have been greater. Second, in the program's formative years the first step was to help schools that signed on to establish more collaborative governance structures and only then, a year or two later, to work at instructional improvement. The current approach is to address both governance and instructional issues from the beginning. Had that been the case with the schools in this evaluation, the favorable results would probably have appeared a year or two earlier.

All told, the results of the various studies show that the Accelerated Schools approach is a valid one: It realizes its purpose in enabling children to accelerate their learning to a significant degree.

With its emphasis on learning experiences that engage the students, its high expectations of academic achievement, and its involvement of parents, teachers, and students in a veritable school-community, the Accelerated Schools Project is another example of an innovative program that is similar to elite private schools.

Sizer's Coalition of Essential Schools[30]

In the mid-1970s, during nine years as teacher and headmaster at Phillips Academy, an academic boarding school in Andover, Massachusetts, Theodore Sizer, now at Brown University, came to the following understanding. Despite differences between boarding schools and day schools, between private and public schools, the curricula offered by American secondary schools were remarkably similar, and similar to what had been offered in secondary schools since late in the nineteenth century: Teach subjects in unconnected ways; break the day into fifty-minute periods; assign lots of writing, but give teachers too little time to read and comment on the papers. These were the old, unchanged ways. Also unchanged was the widespread belief that high school should prepare students for college, and, in doing so, they would be preparing them for life.

Sizer saw this old way of thinking and educating as "wrongheaded" and was determined to change it. After extensive study, school visitation, and dialogue with others who were like-minded, he wrote a critique of secondary schools entitled *Horace's Compromise.* This popular book brought foundation support and led to the establishment of the Coalition of Essential Schools.[31]

They chose the word "essential" for two reasons: ". . . the work we envisioned was tellingly needed" by the secondary schools of the nation. Also, "the schools choosing to be involved would focus on the intellectual core of schooling, at the expense of 'extras,' which appeared to them and us to be weakening the ultimate work of the students."[32]

Schools that join the Coalition are given no model. There is none. Respectful of each school's uniqueness, the Coalition's view is that "excellence and vitality in schools arise from the particular people within them and the community in which that school resides. . . . We believed that each community had to find its own way. However, what we accepted in common was a set of ideas, ones that appeared to us to invest every good school we knew."[33] Sizer drafted a list of ideas in 1983, now called common principles of the Coalition, which "were meant as much to provoke thought and imagination as to give specific guidance."[34] Paraphrased below, the principles are:

1. Helping adolescents to use their minds is the focus of a Coalition school.
2. Students mastering "a limited number of essential skills and areas of knowledge" [35] is the school's goal.
3. The school's focus and goals apply to all students, although the means to achieve them are adapted to individual needs.

4. Personalized teaching and learning are the keys; consequently, no teacher is to be responsible for more than eighty students.
5. Student self-directed learning, with teachers as coaches "provoking students to learn how to learn" is the way of life in the school.
6. (a) Students who do not meet the standards of competence in language and elementary mathematics necessary for secondary education are given intensive remedial work.

    (b) A diploma is granted when students successfully demonstrate a "grasp of the central skills and knowledge of the school's program." No system of points earned or time spent in school is used.
7. The school sets values of high expectation, trust, and decency ("fairness, generosity, and tolerance"), and treats parents as "essential collaborators."[36]
8. Administrators and teachers are committed to the entire school, not just their classes, and see themselves first as generalists and second as specialists in their own fields.
9. Teachers should have loads of eighty students at most, teachers should be given time for group planning, the cost per-pupil of becoming an Essential School should not exceed that in traditional schools by more than 10 percent.

An important contrast should be noted between Levin's Accelerated School and Sizer's Essential School with regard to students whose performance does not meet grade standards. Sizer prescribes intensive remedial work for those who, upon entering secondary school, are not at an acceptable level in language arts and mathematics. Levin, with an eye on elementary education, regards the usual remedial instruction as boring and counterproductive; he places all children in the same classes, giving them accelerated rather than remedial instruction.

Already, by 1996, Sizer reported 250 schools "were beyond the exploring and planning stages and were fully engaged in their work with children." About 750 more were at earlier stages, fashioning their own designs. His view is that "[t]he overall effort has . . . hardly begun. Serious change is slow business, and a well-studied judgment about the practicality of Essential School ideas, if they have been taken seriously, will have to emerge gradually."[37]

Preliminary information was made available on the performance of some CES schools in 2002. According to an early draft of a report on student performance on state achievement tests in nineteen schools in Maine, Michigan, Massachusetts, and Ohio, CES schools show positive results.[38] The schools had chosen CES as their Comprehensive School Reform Demonstration model and had applied for and received grants.

The group was composed of eight elementary, two kindergarten to eighth grade, three middle, and six high schools. Ten of the schools began implementation in 1998 or 1999, giving them too little time to fully incorporate the program. The report, prepared by the CES research division, says, "These schools typically serve students who start out with low standardized test scores, come from diverse ethnic and racial backgrounds, and live in poverty."[39] The percentage of students passing tests of math, reading, and writing increased substantially over their performance in the initial year of testing, which occurred from two to five years earlier. Their recent scores indicate they are closing the gap between their schools and the average student performance in the respective states. On four of seventeen tests, they surpassed state averages. These signs of improvement in schools, supported in part by temporary federal funds, are encouraging. They should be seen in light of Sizer's cautionary note above, "serious change is slow business."

Slavin's Success for All and Roots and Wings[40]

Robert Slavin of Johns Hopkins University and his colleagues have been at work for about two decades to find ways to give every student a successful educational experience. Their first major efforts were in establishing a program called Success for All. They wrote: "we have shown in high-poverty schools across the United States that by combining prevention, research-based curriculum and instruction, tutoring for at-risk children, and family support, nearly every child can succeed in elementary schools."[41]

Success for All then became the basis of Roots and Wings (R&W), "the guarantee that every child will make it successfully through the elementary grades, no matter what this takes." But it is not enough, Slavin adds, for every child to be able to "read, compose, and understand math, science, history, and geography. . . . Children need to be able to creatively and flexibly solve problems, understand their own learning processes, and connect knowledge from different disciplines." On a daily basis, students are given opportunities for collaborative work in solving real and simulated problems employing their class-learned information and skills. Roots and Wings involves them in activities where they can apply "everything so that they can learn the usefulness and interconnectedness of all knowledge."[42]

Slavin, in using the phrase, "engages students in activities,"[43] is highlighting an important feature of the program. The students are *engaged* in the activities; their interests have been *captured.* They are not a captured audience, not passive recipients of information, but deeply immersed in learning. Watching young children at play with blocks, miniature cars or planes, or with dolls, one observes that they are so engrossed in what they are doing that a parent's call to dinner is an unwelcome interruption. That is the state of involvement that both the original program, Success for All, and the more advanced one, Roots and Wings, aspires to and, according to reports by Slavin, usually attains.

Roots and Wings engages students from the outset. In the early learning programs (preschool and kindergarten), R&W uses a thematic approach drawn either from science or social studies. For example, the objectives of a unit on plants are an understanding of scientific concepts about plants; learning that concepts can be drawn from readings, let us say a book about planting carrots; practicing writing skills as they record the progress of the planted carrot seeds; and enjoying the joint activity of singing "The Farmer Plants the Seed." They learn about plants, plus enhance their reading and writing abilities while they are involved in activities that *engage* them.

WorldLab, an integrated approach to science, social studies, and writing, is an innovative aspect of Roots and Wings. "In WorldLab, children take on roles as people in history, in other countries, or in various occupations. . . . The idea behind WorldLab is to make the contents of the entire elementary curriculum useful and relevant to children's daily lives by immersing them in simulations in which knowledge and skill are necessary."[44] Observers may find children involved in debate as they simulate the ongoing activities in their state legislature. This is not simply role-playing or dramatics.

In these simulations students work in small, cooperative groups to investigate topics of science and social studies. They read books and articles about their topics, write newspapers, broadsides, letters, and proposals, use mathematics skills to solve problems relating to their topics, and use the arts, music, and computer, video, and other technology to prepare multimedia reports.[45]

Another important feature is the one-on-one tutoring for the many children who need it. The tutoring is by certified teachers or paraprofessionals, some of them volunteers, who key their work to the reading going on in the child's class, focusing on the same story. Beyond that, the tutors take note of and seek to correct reading and learning problems.

Substantive learning is just as important in Slavin's programs as it is in Hirsch's. One difference is Slavin's emphasis on utilizing teaching strategies that engage the students from the outset, and continuing to do so throughout elementary school. Another difference is Slavin's use of cooperative learning—using groups of students engaged in joint activities.

Three other features reveal the character of the program.

1. The program is implemented in a school district only if at least 80 percent of the teaching staff, in secret ballot, commit themselves to it.
2. Family Support and Integrated Services, an integral part of R&W, has three goals: "(a) success for every child, (b) the empowerment of parents through partnerships, and (c) the integration of children and families."[46]
3. In this program, which makes considerable demands of the district's administrators and all staff, one of the demands is the appointment of a facilitator, to assure that all aspects of the program are implemented and all staff members are working cooperatively.

By spring 2002, Success for All was operating in 1,600 schools, 550 school districts in 48 states, as well as in a half dozen other nations.

Most of the studies evaluating the effects of Success for All and conducted by researchers at Johns Hopkins University, University of Memphis, and WestEd compared achievement of students in schools using that program with control schools.[47] The schools are matched for poverty level (for example, percentage of students eligible for free lunches), ethnicity, past achievement level, and other factors. They are also matched on standardized tests used by the district or on well-regarded tests like the Peabody Picture Vocabulary Test, given in kindergarten or first grade, and the Woodcock Word Attack scale, in first or second grade.

The overall results of numerous studies countrywide evaluating the effectiveness of Success for All in regard to reading have been decidedly positive in grades one to five. Success for All students in every district outperformed the control school students on every measure, having learned significantly more.

Researchers affiliated with the University of Tennessee, Knoxville, not associated with the Success for All movement, compared eight Success for All Schools with matched control schools in Memphis and with all schools in Memphis.[48] Before implementation of Success for All, students in those eight schools did not perform as well as either of the other two sets of schools on the Tennessee statewide tests. However, after two years of the program, their performance was significantly better than the other two in reading, language, science, and social studies. Although none of the Success for All schools had implemented MathWings, even in mathematics the Success for All students outperformed the other two sets of students but, in this case, not at a statistically significant level.

Four researchers associated with Success for All conducted the first statewide appraisal of the program.[49] They found that 111 schools in Texas were using the program, having initiated it at some point during 1994–1998. In these schools 85 percent of the students received federally subsidized lunches, compared to only 45 percent of students statewide. Despite this disadvantage, Success for All students showed significantly greater gains over the prior year than the rest of the state for every cohort in grades three to five on the reading measures of the Texas Assessment of Academic Skills. Furthermore, African American and Hispanic students in Success for All schools were closing the gap with white students at faster rates than their counterparts in regular schools.[50]

Like with Hirsch's Core Knowledge School program, Slavin and his colleagues have found that the more complete and experienced the implementation of the program, the greater the outcomes. A major study in Houston showed that schools that implemented all the components of the curriculum obtained significantly better results than schools that introduced components to only a moderate or minimal degree.[51]

Substantial evidence supports the conclusion that students who fare poorly in school benefit to a considerable degree from the Schools for All and Wings and Roots curricula. That is a significant accomplishment. It does not, however, suggest that these fortunate students are achieving at the level of the students in the elite first system schools.

The details of the program do show it to be similar in many respects to the pedagogy in an elite private school. There are exceptions, of course, especially the emphasis on tutoring children with reading problems. However, in private schools, students benefit from individual assistance, and many from individual tutoring, usually by paid tutors, and usually for assistance at a higher plane than basic reading problems.

In the remainder of this chapter, I will examine the common features as well as the differences among the reform programs and relate those common features to the three school systems.

COMMON FEATURES AND DIFFERENCES AMONG THE REFORM PROGRAMS

Chapters 8 and 9 spelled out the meaning of four categories of school reform: standards based, market based, equity based and community based. All five reform programs described above—Comer's School Development Program, Hirsch's Core Knowledge Movement, Levin's Accelerated Schools, Sizer's Coalition of Essential Schools, and Slavin's Success for All and Roots and Wings—are equity based and community based.

They are *equity based* in that they aim to give all students opportunities for optimal development and learning. They set high expectations and expect those to be achieved. They would claim that gaps between expectations and achievement represent deficiencies in what the adult world has to offer the students rather than anything inherently deficient in the students themselves.

They are *community based* in that they recognize the importance of parental participation in one or more significant roles. From the outset, Comer involves parents, community members, and teachers in the process of school development. Levin requires that parent representatives participate in the vote to determine whether there is a 90-percent mandate for adoption of the Accelerated School plan. Hirsch's Core

Knowledge schools provide parents "a detailed outline of the specific knowledge and skill goals for each grade, and we stay in constant touch with them regarding the child's progress."[52] One of the nine principles developed by Sizer, the Coalition's common principles, starts with the following: "Families should be vital members of the school community."[53] In Slavin's Roots and Wings, the district must be firmly in support of the program before it may be adopted, 80 percent of the teachers must support it by secret ballot, and parents are deemed to be members of a partnership, wherein "Family Support and Integrated Services" is one of the key components.

The five programs show their major divergence when their content is examined. The major contrast is not in grade level (Sizer's Essential Schools are mostly at the secondary level; the other four are at the elementary level). The seemingly unbridgeable chasm lies between Hirsch's Core Knowledge Movement program and the other four. Hirsch calls for a common core curriculum. Invoking the words of Thomas Jefferson and Horace Mann, who argued that a democracy required a common school, he presents data showing that in the international competition of student test scores, nations that do better have a common core curriculum.[54]

Hirsch's book, *Cultural Literacy: What Every American Needs to Know*, published in 1987, raised a storm of opposition. His position seemed to be inherently contradictory. How could a person who is a strong advocate of genuine democracy—of equality and social justice—propose a program of schooling that was so educationally conservative? The code words in educational circles in America are now—as they were when his book appeared—individualized instruction, independent learning, discovery learning, studies emanating from the child's own interests. These appear to be antithetical to a theory of education that mandates a preestablished body of information/knowledge that students are to learn. For how could they "discover" and learn "independently" and "individually" material that does not "emanate from their own interest" but has been selected by others?

On the other hand, looking at the issues from Hirsch's perspective, how could educators deny children, who first come to school impoverished in the knowledge and skills that represent the prerequisites to learning, opportunities to learn them in school? First system children and even some in the second system, enter school equipped with a body of facts and skills connected with reading, writing, counting, and story telling. How will the other children acquire them if schools do not provide them with opportunities to learn those facts and skills? Does the denial of those opportunities not widen the gap between the knowledge-haves and the knowledge-have-nots?

It is vital not to set up a false dichotomy between one's theory of education (whatever that might be), on the one hand, and dull, boring, vacuous instruction on the other, and assign all theories but our own to the latter category. Comer, Levin, Sizer, and Slavin all attest to the fact that school curricula must be related to the lives of the children, and all opt for instruction that engages the students' interests. But so does Hirsch.

Describing the meaning of "whole-class instruction," which Hirsch says is understood in the progressive tradition to imply "lockstep" and "factory-model" instruction, he adds the following:

> It is caricatured by an authoritarian teacher droning on at the head of the class, or by passive, bored students, barely conscious and slumping in their seats, or by intimidated, fearful students, sitting upright and willing only to parrot back the teacher's words. These are not accurate descriptions of what effective whole-class instruction is. It is predominantly interactive, with much interchange between students and teachers; it makes frequent use of student performances and student comments on the performances; it involves consistent informal monitoring of the students' understanding; it engages all students by dramatizing learning in various ways. . . . [I]t is useful to vary the mix with some amount of individual coaching, cooperative learning, and seatwork.[55]

All five educational reformers are intent on students' acquisition of knowledge and skills. Besides Hirsch, Comer aims for significant academic achievement. Levin wants at-risk students to experience the kind of enriched curriculum available to gifted students.[56] Sizer stresses intellectual development and "the habit of serious learning," and toward those ends he would disencumber the schools of many of the burdens a society, distraught by problems like drug abuse, teen pregnancy, and violence, has imposed on them.[57] Slavin has developed "an integrated approach to science, social studies, and writing called WorldLab," immersing them in experiences that require knowledge and skill.[58]

The underlying difference pertains to the "how" question. How do we teach so that all children learn, and all acquire knowledge and essential intellectual skills. We hope, too, that they become self-directed learners. As educational researcher Ernesto Schiefelbein wrote, "It is the motivation to choose to learn, and to act on that choice, that most distinguishes the self-directed learner. Whether or not the learning is carried out independently, cooperatively in a group, at a computer terminal or under the authority of a master teacher is not relevant."[59] "All children" means not just those who come from home all geared up for school learning. How do we teach so that students can develop their capacities for creative thinking at the same time as they are learning science and history, mathematics, and literature?

All Five Programs Promote "THINK"

Psychologist Howard Gruber, author of the award-winning book, *Darwin on Man: A Psychological Study of Scientific Creativity*, has spent much of his long career studying the processes of thinking and creative work. In 1990, he explained that innovative educators in higher education are caught "between two voices, 'learn' and 'think.' From the side of 'learn' we hear that the rapid growth of knowledge requires more discipline and more pressure on students to learn. . . . Meanwhile, from the side of 'think,' comes the recurrent refrain that our students are passive; they don't know how to learn independently, and are not taught to think critically or creatively."[60] In studies conducted both in the United States and Switzerland, he and colleagues aimed at improving thinking in university classrooms. They set up exercises for their seminars that required active participation, shared reflection, group planning, idea-production, and reflection on the ideas. The components of the course were lectures, reading assignments, and the seminars. The main conclusion was that such an approach is feasible. Students were interested and seemed to like the alternating lectures and activity seminars, in which they came to understand the process of creative thinking by *engaging* in it.

Gruber is sensitive to the factors that make change so difficult: the weight of tradition, institutional restraints, investments of teachers in their own fields, and satisfaction in teaching in a way to share their knowledge. Teachers may also feel that the traditional way is safer for their students in the real world, "a world in which employers do not always welcome individual initiative, independent moral judgment, and creative thought."[61]

It seems likely that consciously incorporating the development of thinking among the *planned* objectives is likely to be beneficial to mental development as well as learning. This belief is consistent with the theory of the Russian psychologist, Lev Vygotsky,[62] that education and mental development go hand in hand, with education preceding development. Education through experience in thinking facilitates mental development. Practice—the exercise of thinking, always, of course, thinking about something, some topic in some subject—reinforces the thinking process.

Comer, Hirsch, Levin, Sizer, and Slavin, each in his own way, have addressed the basic issues Gruber raises. No one of them proposes "think" alone, out of context with "learn," or out of context with subject matter. Hirsch by no means excludes "think." The crucial issue is not whether schools choose to have a common core, but rather whether they incorporate thinking as one of their prime educational objectives.

These programs of reform offer us hope as well as the shape of the future of public education. Yet, from the perspective of need in working toward a single school system marked by excellence, they are far from complete. They do not provide parent-teacher training. They do not—and cannot be expected to—offer parents the economic and psychological security that comes with assured employment, livable income, and health insurance; nor can they improve pre-professional teacher training. They do not have the forthright sanction and budgetary support of political leaders. These shortcomings, not at all the fault of the programs, are the subjects of the remaining chapters.

NOTES

1. Nathalie Rathvon, *Effective School Interventions* (New York: Guilford, 1999), 2.
2. James P. Comer, *Waiting for a Miracle* (New York: Dutton, 1997).
3. Comer, *Waiting for a Miracle*, 48–49.
4. Comer, *Waiting for a Miracle*, 48.
5. Comer, *Waiting for a Miracle*, 63.

6. Comer, *Waiting for a Miracle*, 72.

7. Comer, *Waiting for a Miracle*, 58.

8. Comer, *Waiting for a Miracle*, 69.

9. Comer, *Waiting for a Miracle*, 49.

10. Comer, *Waiting for a Miracle*, 72.

11. Mary Ann Millsap, Anne Chase, Dawn Obeidallah, Alina Perez-Smith, Nancy Brigham, and Karen Johnston, "Evaluation of Detroit's Comer Schools and Families Initiative," Final Report (Detroit: The Skillman Foundation, 17 April 2000).

12. Mary Ann Millsap et al., "Evaluation of Detroit's Comer Schools and Families Initiative," 7.

13. Comer, *Waiting for a Miracle*, 231.

14. E. D. Hirsch Jr., *The Schools We Need and Why We Don't Have Them* (New York: Doubleday, 1996). See also, E. D. Hirsch Jr., *Cultural Literacy: What Every American Needs to Know* (New York: Vintage Books, 1988).

15. Hirsch Jr., *The Schools We Need and Why We Don't Have Them*, 13.

16. Cyndi Wells, Director, Teacher Development, Core Knowledge Foundation, reported by e-mail, 28 February 2002.

17. Hirsch Jr., *The Schools We Need and Why We Don't Have Them*, 13.

18. Hirsch Jr., *The Schools We Need and Why We Don't Have Them*, 235.

19. Gracy Taylor, *Core Knowledge: Its Impact on Instructional Practices and Student Learning* (Ed.D. diss., Nova Southeastern University, March 2001).

20. Sam Stringfield, Amanda Datnow, Geoffrey Borman, and Laura Rachuba, *National Evaluation of Core Knowledge Sequence Implementation: Final Report* (Center for Social Organization of Schools, Johns Hopkins University, 1999). The full report is available in electronic format only. To receive one, send your e-mail address to coreknow@coreknowledge.org.

21. Hirsch Jr., *The Schools We Need and Why We Don't Have Them*, 237.

22. Hirsch Jr., *The Schools We Need and Why We Don't Have Them*, 237–238.

23. Henry M. Levin, *Building School Capacity for Effective Teacher Empowerment: Applications to Elementary Schools with At-Risk Students* (New Brunswick, N.J.: Center for Policy Research in Education, 1991). Also, Henry M. Levin, *Accelerated Schools for At-Risk Students* (New Brunswick, N.J.: Center for Policy Research in Education, 1991).

24. Henry M. Levin, "Accelerated Visions," *Teacher-to-Teacher* 5, no. 1 (1996): 1, 13.

25. Henry M. Levin, "Learning from Accelerated Schools," Stanford: Stanford University, 1993.

26. "Research Background on Accelerated Schools," *Accelerated Schools Project Research and Evaluation Bulletin,* November 2001. www.acceleratedschools.net (accessed 20 April 2002).

27. "Research Background on Accelerated Schools."

28. "Research Background on Accelerated Schools."

29. Debra Viadero, "Study Shows Test Gains in 'Accelerated Schools,'" *Education Week*, 9 January 2002.

30. Theodore R. Sizer, *Horace's School: Redesigning the American High School* (Boston: Houghton Mifflin, 1982).

31. Theodore R. Sizer, *Horace's Compromise: The Dilemma of the American High School* (Boston: Houghton Mifflin, 1984).

32. Theodore R. Sizer, *Horace's Hope: What Works for the American High School* (Boston: Houghton Mifflin, 1996), 156.

33. Sizer, *Horace's Hope:* 153.

34. Sizer, *Horace's Hope*, 153.

35. Sizer, *Horace's Hope*, 154.

36. Sizer, *Horace's Hope*, 155.

37. Sizer, *Horace's Hope*, 157.

38. "Students Thrive in Schools that Promote Intellectual Rigor and Personalize Learning," a Report on the Coalition of Essential Schools' Work with Comprehensive School Reform Demonstration (CSRD) Schools in Ohio, Maine, Massachusetts, and Michigan, preliminary draft, 25 March 2002. jpattaphongse@essentialschools.org (accessed 26 March 2002).

39. "Students Thrive in Schools that Promote Intellectual Rigor and Personalize Learning," jpattaphongse@essentialschools.org.

40. Robert E. Slavin, Nancy A. Madden, and Barbara A. Wasik, "Roots and Wings: Universal Excellence in Elementary Education," in *Bold Plans for School Restructuring* ed. Sam Stringfield, Steven Ross, and Lana Smith (Mahwah, N.J.: Erlbaum, 1996), 207–231.

41. Slavin et al., "Roots and Wings," 208.

42. Slavin et al., "Roots and Wings," 208.

43. Slavin et al., "Roots and Wings," 208.

44. Slavin et al., "Roots and Wings," 209.

45. Slavin et al., "Roots and Wings," 209.

46. Slavin et al., "Roots and Wings," 220.

47. Robert E. Slavin and Nancy A. Madden (1999). *Success for All/Roots and Wings: Summary of Research on Achievement Outcomes* (Baltimore: Johns Hopkins University, Center for Research on the Education of Students Placed At Risk, January 2002).

48. S. M. Ross, W. L. Sanders, and S. P. Wright, *An Analysis of Tennessee Value Added Assessment (TVAAS) Performance Outcomes of Roots and Wings Schools from 1995–1997* (Memphis: University of Memphis, Center for Research in Educational Policy, 1998).

49. E. A. Hurley, A. Chamberlain, Robert E. Slavin, and Nancy Madden, "Effects of Success for All on TAAS Reading: A Texas Statewide Evaluation," *Phi Delta Kappan* 82, no. 10 (June 2001): 750–756.

50. Hurley et al., "Effects of Success for All on TAAS Reading: A Texas Statewide Evaluation."

51. J. Nunnery, et al., *An Assessment of Success for All Program Component Configuration Effects on the Reading Achievement of At-Risk First Grade Students* (Baltimore: Johns Hopkins University, Center for Research on the Education of Students Placed at Risk, 1996).

52. Hirsch Jr., *The Schools We Need and Why We Don't Have Them*, 62.

53. Sizer, *Horace's Hope:* 159.

54. Hirsch Jr., *The Schools We Need and Why We Don't Have Them*, 38.

55. Hirsch Jr., *The Schools We Need and Why We Don't Have Them*, 270–271.

56. Samuel Mitchell, *Reforming Educators: Teachers, Experts, and Advocates* (Westport, Conn.: Praeger, 1998), 133.

57. Sizer, *Horace's Hope:* 159.

58. Slavin et al., "Roots and Wings," 209.

59. Ernesto Schiefelbein, "Trends in the Provision and Design of Self-Learning Models of Education," in *International Handbook of Education and Development: Preparing Students and Nations for the Twenty-First Century*, ed. William. K. Cummings and Noel F. McGuin (Oxford: Pergamon, 1997), 817.

60. Howard E. Gruber and Lucien Richard, "Active Work and Creative Thought in University Classrooms," in *Promoting Cognitive Growth over the Life Span*, ed. Milton Schwebel, Charles Maher, and Nancy Fagley (Mahwah, N.J.: Lawrence Erlbaum, 1990), 137–164.

61. Gruber and Richard, "Active Work and Creative Thought in University Classrooms," 162.

62. Lev Vygotsky, *Thought and Language* (Cambridge, Mass.: MIT Press, 1962).

11

SOCIAL STIGMA AND
DISIDENTIFICATION WITH SCHOOL

The school reformers deserve praise. Their products, implemented through the cooperative efforts of many people, show what is possible and what the future holds. At the same time, to be utterly realistic and not be deluded by modest gains in a small percentage of schools in the country, one sees that dependence on these reforms alone, with no social restructuring, will be futile.

The painful fact is that school reform, no matter how extensive the changes and how strongly supported, cannot by itself solve the nation's educational problems. These reforms are desirable and welcome. They should be encouraged and supported, but reliance on them alone is likely to lead to frustration to those who want quality education for all children. Most second and third system schools continue to be impervious to change by reform measures that are inadequate to the need, for the problem extends well beyond the reach of the schools. The educational problems are rooted in the social system at large, so that systemic changes are necessary in the communities as well as in the schools.

The remainder of the book is devoted to those systemic changes. One necessary change applies to social stigma, which leads to disaffection with the schools, the subject of this chapter. We start by examining the impact of social stigma in the 1920s and 1960s.

When E. Frederic Morrow was appointed administrative assistant to President Eisenhower in 1955, he became the first African American to serve in that position. In his autobiography, *Way Down South Up North*, published in 1973 when he was vice president of the Bank of America International, he attributed his successful career and that of his siblings to his parents. He dedicated the book as follows: "To my Mother and Father, whose unconquerable spirit and love gave their children the strength to survive man's inhumanity to man."[1]

The book's title conveys the character of his experiences, and those of his family. No matter how reputable they were as citizens, no matter how fine their character, how distinguished as students, they were still blacks "way down south" in Hackensack, New Jersey, still treated as inferiors.

Morrow's sister Nellie, trained as a teacher, succeeded in getting an assignment as a student teacher in the Hackensack schools in 1922 despite strong opposition from many parents, and largely because of the insistence and persuasive powers of her father. She did well. Later, at a stormy meeting, the board of education heard arguments concerning her application for an appointment as a teacher. Every speaker vetoed the idea of a "Negro" teacher. At last, it was the turn of the spokesperson for the black people in the community. The Morrows expected that at least they would have support from their own people. They were shocked at what he said: "[W]e believe the appointment of a Negro teacher at this time would not be in the best interest of the race or the community. We feel our children would not respond or learn under a Negro teacher. . . ."[2] His statement reflected the internalized stigma of inferiority, namely, we are not capable of teaching even our own children, and our own children know that.

The younger generation at the time, however, as hopeless as they felt about their future, did not react in this genteel and accommodating fashion. *Their* behavior is of particular relevance to this chapter on stigma and disaffection with school. Fred Morrow and his siblings' experiences with other black children and youth cast light on the school performance problems of blacks, both earlier in the twentieth century and now as well. In the elementary school they attended, many blacks were assigned to "special" classes for slow and "badly mannered" children. "There were so many Negroes in the special class, that one who wasn't stood out in bold relief. . . . To the Negro pupils, any Black who was not in class with them was 'stuck-up' and was trying to be white. This attitude was one of the great crosses of my entire school life."[3]

Some of the black children, he explained, would go to school and back in packs, as a matter of security and comfort. They shared a common attitude—disdain—toward the school, its teachers and courses, and also the community that offered them no future. So far as he himself was concerned, Morrow found those schoolmates "defiant and crude, and they hated any member of their own group who, because of performance, won a word of praise from teacher or principal. It was difficult for me to escape the wrath of these malcontents."[4]

Those "malcontents" were disaffected with the school that made them feel inferior. Everything associated with it was alien: teachers, books, homework, and tests. Such a future as they could make out for themselves, as reflected in the adults around them, had no connection with how they performed in school. School had nothing of use to offer them. Had they had the resources that backed the Morrows and known the taste of success, their attitudes would likely have been different. But very few in the ghettos of America had the benefit of those unique resources. Consequently, in ways that are understandable, if not always predictable, they turned against the institution that compelled them to attend, but could not force them to learn. Those are the costs of social stigma and disaffection.

Frederic Morrow wrote about his childhood experiences in the 1920s. How different was it in the sixties and seventies when the ideas of Martin Luther King Jr. were a force in American life, and the black liberation movement was at its height? Morrow offered his answer to that question in the early 1970s. Despite his many achievements, and those of his brother John who served as an American ambassador and later as university professor and department chairman, Morrow's depressing assessment in the early 1970s was that African Americans had made virtually no progress.

The experiences of another man during the 1960s and afterward are also depressing. Dr. Benjamin Solomon Carson is an expert on the brain, especially the brains of children. Professor of neurosurgery and director of pediatric neurosurgery at the Johns Hopkins Hospital, he is internationally known for his work in attending to difficult pediatric neurosurgical problems, like separating Siamese (conjoined) twins. Yet, in the 1960s, an observer of this African American boy, who knew no father, would hardly have predicted his glowing career. Fortunately, his mother, a domestic worker, "pushed young Benjamin to read books and eventually turn his grades around."[5] Dr. Carson, as if harking back to the earlier discussion in this book about the crucial role of self-regard and self-expectations, and the current one on social stigma, had this to say:

> When I thought I was stupid, I acted like a stupid person. And when I thought I was smart, I acted like a smart person and achieved like a smart person. I was fortunate, in that I had a mother who believed in me and kept telling me I was smart. You know, even as late as my first year in medical school, my faculty adviser advised me to drop out. He said I wasn't medical-school material.[6]

Even after Yale offered him scholarships and after the Medical School at the University of Michigan admitted him, a faculty adviser was nonetheless telling him his expectations were too high. Fortunately for Dr. Carson, his mother had done her work well. Between her efforts and his own accomplishments, she had succeeded in shielding him from confidence-shattering experiences, prompted by social stigma, that many children, especially minority and working-class children, endure on a daily basis.

What about today? An appraisal today is also depressing. In the last half century the surface conditions for minorities have changed as a middle class has emerged, but the stigma of being black remains deeply rooted in large segments of the population, and the effects continue to be costly to individuals and to society at large.

THE CONCEPT OF SOCIAL STIGMA

Researchers have found the concept of "social stigma" useful in explaining why African Americans, in respect to general school ability, and women, in respect to math-related fields, tend as groups to do poorly compared with whites and males, respectively. Psychologists Jennifer Crocker, Brenda Major, and Claude Steele, who reviewed the literature on these topics and contributed their own studies, believe that their analysis of the relationship between social stigma and performance also applies to Native Americans, some Hispanic groups, and to those in lower socioeconomic classes.[7]

They point out that African Americans have endured negative stereotypes about their mental abilities for a long time. They explain that these stereotypes may have been adopted, in part, to justify the institution of slavery and the inequities to which blacks have been subjected ever since. Their analysis is a penetrating one, going deeply into the consciousness of victims of stereotypes. What they offer has considerable relevance to education in the United States at all levels, and special relevance to the third school system.

Crocker and her coauthors recognize that inadequate schooling may contribute to the relatively low academic performance of blacks. They show, however, that deficits in instruction, due to disadvantages, by themselves alone cannot explain the gaps between blacks and whites across the board in academic subjects. And, they add, poor instruction for females in mathematics and math-involved sciences cannot explain the gaps between them and males in those subjects. Something more than deficits in teaching and learning are at work.

The theory they put forth claims that widely held negative stereotypes about a group's intellectual abilities can have an undermining effect on the readiness of members of the group to *identify with school or to value school achievement.* When children or teenagers, or for that matter college students, feel they are devalued because of their group membership they may take refuge in *disidentification* with the school or college. The devaluation may occur through overt actions or expressions of biased individuals; they may be verbally or nonverbally, consciously or unconsciously communicated. As an example of a conscious, verbal expression of bias, a teacher makes generalizations like "You people behave like animals" or "Your kind are good in sports but not in learning" or "You girls can read just fine, but you're no good with numbers." More likely, in these more enlightened times, the devaluation occurs in subtler forms and even from people of good will who are unaware of their own prejudices. This occurs because stereotypes, which are shared "mental representations,"[8] are so widely disseminated in a society and, once learned, they can unconsciously come into play, affecting feelings, thoughts, and behavior. Their subtle influence on human thought is so powerful that even individuals otherwise low in prejudice and members of the stereotyped groups will respond as if the stereotypes were valid.

The subtlety of stereotyping even at a low level of consciousness is suggested in the following study. Social psychologists Bargh, Chen, and

Burrows exposed white subjects to pictures of blacks in a subliminal computer presentation in order to prime—bring to mind—concepts related to race. Afterward, the computer presumably broke down. The result of the frustration precipitated by the presumed breakdown was that those subjects who had been primed with pictures of blacks expressed more hostility than the controls, who had been primed in neutral pictures. The African American primes apparently activated stereotypes related to aggression and hostility and affected the behavior of the subjects.[9]

The researchers point out how self-fulfilling prophecies can come into play under these circumstances:

> When Whites interact with Blacks, stereotypical conceptions of Blacks as aggressive or hostile may be activated. Activation of these concepts may increase the expression of aggression and hostility in the Whites' behavior, which may, in turn, elicit hostility in the Black interaction partner. These processes may operate totally outside of the awareness of the White interaction partner, and hence the hostile response of the Black interaction partner may be seen as confirmation of the stereotype.[10]

Adding to the extensive literature on social stigma and its effects, Bargh and colleagues summarize the process of stereotyping and its consequences this way:

> Thus, stereotypes—through their broad dissemination and their capacity to influence us beneath awareness—have the cumulative power to shape and coordinate our relations with the stereotyped, even our institutional responses to them, and thus to form around them a coordinated disposition of prejudice and devaluation that goes beyond the impact of particularly prejudiced individuals. [11]

A major point here, one with enormous consequence, is the impact on what might be called the collective, or unconscious, mind of the larger population. The stereotypes are so insidious they infect the thoughts and attitudes even of people who insistently deny any prejudice.

Those who are stigmatized, finding that the important figures in school devalue them, are less likely to use school achievement as a criterion in evaluating themselves. Blacks, Hispanics, Native Americans, lower-social class children and females (at least so far as mathematics is concerned), having "learned" that their respective group is inherently inferior in performance and destined to fail, can hardly be expected to give much if any role to school achievement in determining their self-esteem. How many students, when informed they are too lightweight for a sport, are going to include performance in that sport *in determining their self-worth?*

The theory of disidentification and its benefits for those who employ it have been validated by the findings of several studies. For example, when black and white students in desegregated schools in Illinois were compared, researchers found that black students did not perform as well academically as white students. Yet, their levels of self-esteem were comparable. Further analysis showed that whites had higher school and home self-esteem, but blacks were higher on peer group self-esteem. The whites felt good about themselves in relation to school and home; the blacks felt good about themselves in relation to their peers. In other words, the self-esteem of the blacks seemed to be impervious to poor academic performance and for a very sound reason: School performance did not enter into their self-evaluation. Psychologically, they had exited from competition in school. Under the condition of persistent devaluation as learners, their disidentification with school is a rational choice. By that action they become impervious to the effects of others' evaluations of their school achievement and, as a result, are able to protect their self-esteem.

THE INTELLIGENCE QUOTIENT (IQ) AND SOCIAL STIGMA

Some groups, especially African Americans, but also Native Americans and many immigrant groups over a long period in American history, have been stigmatized for supposed intellectual inferiority. One can say categorically that the inferior performance of students in the second and third school systems is not due to inferior intelligence of the students. For improving the education of children at home and in school, IQ is simply irrelevant. However, the subject of the IQ casts such a broad and dark shadow that it cannot be exorcised from discussions about schooling simply by declaring it irrelevant. In the minds of too many people who are important in the lives of children, the concept of an immutable genetic attribute (i.e., intelligence) holds sway and unavoidably influences policy decisions. These people believe that the natural endowment of many children at birth fates them to limited achievement and that little can be done to transcend those limitations. That belief also influences the attitudes and behavior of some teachers. The result in interactions with their students is to convey that little is expected of them, leaving the students with a sense of futility.

The belief that intelligence is predetermined and largely immutable is still widespread almost a century after a leading psychologist denounced it. Alfred Binet, the pioneer in the development of mental testing, condemned the "deplorable verdict that the intelligence of an individual is a fixed quantity."[12] Yet people of influence continue to propagate that "deplorable verdict."

Almost ninety years later, Robert Sternberg (1998), an expert on the subject and editor of the two-volume *Encyclopedia of Human Intelligence*, argued against "the traditional fixed-abilities model. The developing-expertise model sees the growing problems in our society as deriving, in part, from the traditional model of relatively fixed individual differences in abilities. . . . In other words, the traditional model may be a cause of rather than a potential answer to educational problems, in particular, and societal problems, in general. The traditional model is part of the problem, not a basis for solution."[13]

Sternberg puts forth a model in which abilities are a form of developing expertise. The IQ is one test of developing expertise, so are achievement tests, and so are teacher-made tests. All tests of these kinds tell us how far individuals have come on what we might call the ladder of developing expertise. None of them can tell us how far up that ladder an individual can eventually go, if there is such a final outcome, because the level of expertise achieved depends upon the opportunities afforded, the motivation of the individual, and the social and physical contexts within which he or she functions.

One review of studies on IQ and achievement tests, by Wendy Williams and Stephen Ceci, carried the suggestive title: "Are Americans Becoming More and More Alike?"[14] An examination of scores of blacks and whites showed a marked narrowing of the gap over a fifteen-year period. This progress was seen precisely during the period in which African American organizations pressed for equality and, with the sup-

port of other people, persuaded the U.S. government to back equal opportunity through programs of affirmative action and of supportive preschool and elementary education. Black children and parents, perhaps
for the first time, could feel that their government was working on their
behalf, a novel but welcome relationship. Presumably, the activity involved in winning those gains plus the material and psychological benefits of the changes led to the improved performance on tests. The slight
regression and then halt in gains occurred during the midst of the Reagan, and later the Bush, administrations. This was a time of political con-
servatism and a reaction, known as "white backlash," to the advances
made by blacks. It seems reasonable to propose that the changed social
and political atmosphere in the nation was involved in the halt to further
narrowing the gap.

To probe the educational problem further, we wonder why some children fare poorly, even under conditions more favorable, when the government is reaching out to improve the education of the poor. One answer to that question may be found in another review of studies on
children's achievement. Examining the causes of diminished cognitive
functioning in children, it found the following.[15] Poverty, especially persistent poverty, means higher rates of perinatal complications, which are
sometimes associated with organic damage to the fetus. When those
complications are combined with insufficient health care to buffer their
effects, they are all the more likely to lead to permanent damage. Besides that, children of poverty are more subject to lead poisoning. Also,
the parent or parents of these children are less likely to provide home-
based cognitive stimulation and their teachers are more likely to have
low expectations of them. All in all, for so many of the children, poverty
spells "no future."

But children do not have to suffer that fate. Given the opportunity,
humans have a great capacity to overcome handicaps and develop their
mental and physical functioning. That is one of the lessons learned from
the work of James Flynn of the University of Otago in New Zealand.[16] In
1987, based on data from fourteen nations, he found massive IQ gains
achieved in a single generation. These gains ranged from five to twenty-
five points. Further, these gains persist into maturity. Flynn explains that
these are gains in the ability to do abstract problem solving. IQ tests, he
insists, are not really tests of intelligence. We do not know, he argues, the

meaning of "intelligence" which has been defined by so many psychologists in so many different ways. We do know, however, that they test abstract problem solving. Differences between groups that exist are not in intelligence but in abstract problem-solving ability.

What is the impact of schooling on intelligence, or to use Flynn's term, on "abstract problem solving"? Another study shows that intelligence and schooling have a bi-directional relationship. In other words, each increase in school attendance is associated with increases in test scores, and an increase in scores is associated with an increase in school attendance.[17]

Taken together these studies say the following: IQ test scores do change. Poverty is the enemy of such changes. School attendance facilitates IQ increases. The closing gap between black and white people during one historical era strongly suggests the likelihood that differences of that kind, between racial groups and between social classes, will diminish or disappear when the society genuinely wishes them to, and takes the necessary actions to move toward equality.

The developing-expertise model in no way asserts, suggests, or implies that there are no differences in abilities or expertise among individuals. That model *does say* to all people associated with the development and education of children and adolescents that their energies should be on *facilitating development and enhancing ability and expertise*, not on using tests for the purpose of determining children's limitations and then stigmatizing certain students as a result.

The developing-expertise model is not limited to children. Recently, it has gotten a boost from evidence that brain cells are created throughout life. The prevailing view had been that humans are born with all the brain cells they will ever possess. Now come the welcome findings that "In fact, from birth through late adolescence, the brain appears to add billions of new cells, literally constructing its circuits out of freshly made neurons as children and teenagers *interact with their environments*" [emphasis added].[18] Although the process of adding new cells slows down in adulthood, it continues into old age. Through stimulating interaction with the social environment and the environment of knowledge (math and science, the humanities and social studies, the varied arts and athletics), humans can continue to develop their minds. A well-educated life-long-learning citizenry is within society's grasp.

IMPLICATIONS OF DISIDENTIFICATION WITH SCHOOL

Based on what we know from research, several specific recommendations can be made to school administrators and teachers to counteract stereotypes and their effects. Unfortunately, there are limits to their effectiveness. Social psychology has shown that in mixed groups where some members are stigmatized, the application of several principles can help avoid problems in the interactions of the groups. At the early stages in the life of groups of that kind, such as classes of children or teenagers, interactions among class members should be highly structured. The roles of students and the norms of behavior should be perfectly clear. Those safeguards are necessary because in unstructured situations, in the extreme situation where there is freedom to do or say anything one wishes, uncertainties about how to behave lead members of the group to fall back on what they have learned, which means on their stereotypes.

A study of a teaching intervention model designed to promote bonding to school and improved participation and learning had positive results on academic achievement and social relations. The study grew out of the theory that "problem behavior is prevented by high levels of social bonding to pro-social groups and activities. Positive social bonding to school consists of attachment to school, commitment to educational pursuits, and belief in the fairness of school rules. . . . An individual's level of bonding to school is thought to be determined by the level of opportunity for active involvement or participation available in the school, by the skills the individual applies in participating in school, and by the recognition provided by the school for the individual's behavior." The results of the study in grades five and six were positive: The teaching strategies "contributed to more opportunities and reinforcements for pro-social involvement, and to higher levels of bonding to school. . . ."[19] They also led to higher academic achievement.

Applying what research has shown, teachers should be guided by knowledge from social psychology about group behavior when classes are composed of stigmatized and nonstigmatized group members. They should know that tight structure about role behavior is essential early in the life of a group and be aware of the importance of social bonding. Teachers should do whatever is helpful to achieve cohesion and a climate for learning. School systems should set the tolerance of differences and even an appreciation of the richness of difference as two of their major goals. These instructional objectives can lead to improvements. Yet, desirable as they are, they will not solve the problem because they do not get at the root causes of prejudice, stigmatization, and stereotyping. If the third school system is to be eliminated and the second upgraded, those root causes must themselves be eliminated.

That is no small task. The obstacles to overcoming the psychological practice of disidentification with school seem overwhelming for a number of reasons. First is the vast number of children of all groups who are potential victims of stereotyping and its effects. These include African Americans, Native Americans, Hispanics, Asians, Muslims, and recent immigrants, especially those of color, among them millions of Hispanic and Caribbean cultures, and also people whose sexual orientation is other than heterosexual, and females who are assertive and forceful.

Second is the long and arduous process of cracking the thick armor of prejudice, so much of it concealed from those who unconsciously practice ethnocentrism, racism, or sexism.

Third are the institutional barriers to change, the tangible ones such as real estate arrangements that tend to maintain de facto segregation and lead to de facto segregated schools, and the theoretical ones such as those that attribute differential intellectual performance to large genetic components.

Fourth is the political exploitation of prejudice when candidates running for office, often using code words to avoid brazen forms of bigotry, appeal to groups that benefit—or believe they benefit—from inequality.

PERSONAL AND STRUCTURAL VIOLENCE

Understanding the deeply rooted causes of disaffection can help explain why evils such as sexism, racism, poverty, and violence have persisted despite unremitting campaigns of one kind or another over the course of many years. For example, women have had the vote for about eighty years. Still, according to the Justice Department, "one woman is raped somewhere in America every ninety seconds. Approximately 1.9 million women are subjected to physical assaults of one kind or another every year. That works out to an attack on a woman every fifteen seconds."[20]

Alongside this "noisy" kind of discrimination is the "quiet" type, such as discrepancies between the sexes in salaries and promotions, in workloads at home, in opportunities for leadership. What is the explanation for the persistence of discrimination?

A useful explanation has come from the work of the Norwegian sociologist Johan Galtung. He contrasted two forms of violence, *personal violence* and *structural violence*. In personal violence, one person commits a violent act against another. It is direct, and it is personal. In structural violence, there "may not be any person who directly harms another person in the structure. The violence is built into the structure and shows up as unequal power and consequently as unequal life chances."[21] Rape is an example of personal violence. Insufficient and inadequate health care that leads the United States, with all its wealth, to rank twelfth in the world in maternal mortality rates, is an example of structural violence.[22] Lynching of black men is an example of personal violence. The racially "separate but equal" doctrine of education, endorsed by the U.S. Supreme Court in 1896 and widely practiced to this day, is an example of structural violence.

Most people suffering the effects of structural violence are not aware of its existence. To them, the inequalities to which they are subjected are the way life is. For the most part, women in a patriarchal society and African Americans, Native Americans, and others in a racist society are not aware that their conditions are the result of how their society is structured. Consequently, when their rage over gross inequalities and oppressive conditions boils over, they don't strike out at an abstract "society" but at persons who, often in their own groups, seem to them to be their oppressors. In this way, structural violence breeds personal violence. The circle of cause and effect is completed when the personal violence leads those in power to respond by introducing further structural limitations on the perpetrators. In the school setting, for example, disaffected students, bored and angry, get into fights with other students or with their teachers. School administrators react by imposing further restrictions, such as denying the students playground time during the school day, which further alienates the students and, in turn, precipitates personal violence.

Disaffection with schools is a byproduct of structural violence in the United States. The proposals in the final chapter of this book are directed at terminating that form of violence.

NOTES

1. E. Frederic Morrow, *Way Down South Up North* (Philadelphia: Pilgrim Press, 1973).

2. Morrow, *Way Down South Up North*, 92.

3. Morrow, *Way Down South Up North*, 13–14.

4. Morrow, *Way Down South Up North*, 16.

5. Claudia Dreifus, "A Conversation with Benjamin Carson: A Pioneer at a Frontier: The Brain of a Child," *New York Times*, 4 January 2000, 7(F).

6. Dreifus, "A Conversation with Benjamin Carson," 7(F).

7. Jennifer Crocker, Brenda Major, and Claude Steele, "Social Stigma," in *Handbook of Social Psychology*, ed. Daniel T. Gilbert, Susan T. Fiske, and Gardner Lindzey (New York: McGraw Hill, 1998), 504–553.

8. Crocker et al., "Social Stigma," 535.

9. John A. Bargh, Mark Chen, and Lara Burrows, "Automaticity of Social Behavior: Effects of Trait Construct and Stereotype Activation on Action," *Journal of Personality and Social Psychology* 71, no. 2 (August 1998): 230–244.

10. Bargh et al., "Automaticity of Social Behavior," 242.

11. Bargh et al., "Automaticity of Social Behavior," 244.

12. Alfred Binet, *Les Idees Modernes sur les Enfantes* (Paris: Flammarion, 1909). Cited in J. McVeigh Hunt, *Intelligence and Experience* (New York: Ronald Press, 1961), 13.

13. Robert Sternberg, "Abilities Are Forms of Developing Expertise," *Educational Researcher* 27, no. 3 (April 1998): 11–19.

14. Wendy M. Williams and Stephen J. Ceci, "Are Americans Becoming More and More Alike? Trends in Race, Class and Ability Differences in Intelligence, *American Psychologist* 52, no. 11 (November 1997): 1226–1235.

15. Vonnie McLoyd, "Socioeconomic Disadvantage and Child Development," *American Psychologist* 53, no. 2 (February 1998): 185–204.

16. James R. Flynn, "Massive IQ Gains in 14 Nations: What IQ Tests Really Measure," *American Psychologist* 42, no. 2. (February 1987): 171–191.

17. Stephen J. Ceci and Wendy M. Williams, "Schooling, Intelligence and Income," *American Psychologist* 52, no. 10 (October 1997): 1051–1058.

18. Sandra Blakeslee, "A Decade of Discovery Yields a Shock about the Brain," *New York Times*, 4 January 2000, 1(F).

19. Robert D. Abbott, Julie O'Donnell, J. David Hawkins, Karl G. Hill, Richard Kosterman, and Richard F. Catalano, "Changing Teaching Practices to Promote Achievement and Bonding to School," *American Journal of Orthopsychiatry* 68, no. 4 (October 1998): 542–552, 543.

20. Bob Herbert, "Violence That Won't Let Go," *New York Times*, 27 August 2001, 15(A).

21. Johan Galtung, "Violence, Peace and Peace Research," *Journal of Peace Research* 6, no. 3 (1996): 167–181, 171.

22. Dyan Mazurana and Susan McKay, "Women, Girls and Structural Violence: A Global Analysis," in *Peace, Conflict and Violence: Peace Psychology for the 21st Century*, ed. Daniel J. Christie, Richard V. Wagner, and Deborah DuNann Winter (Upper Saddle River, N.J.: Prentice Hall, 2001), 130–138.

12

HALF MEASURES DON'T WORK

To eliminate the third school system and strengthen the second, policy makers, educators, and parents must recognize that systemic changes are essential. Half measures won't work. That recognition is necessary at all levels, from the local neighborhood to the White House.

The education of humans is a highly complex process. It involves the physical, social, moral, and intellectual development of individuals, and calls many different elements into play: parents, the community, professional organizations (for example, teachers' unions and associations), government, health, and social services, libraries, recreational resources, colleges and universities, cultural centers, business and industry, and still others. What happens in Ms. Jones's class on a given day has been influenced by decisions handed down by the Supreme Court, by legislation enacted by Congress or state legislatures, actions of city councils, a policy decision of a new board of education, layoffs at the town's largest plant, marital conflict in Kevin's home, illness in Karen's home, and the state of Ms. Jones's own romantic relationship.

Besides all the above-mentioned complexities, many beyond the control of the classroom teacher, those who work for universal excellence face the vexing challenge of educating a heterogeneous population in a technologically advanced nation with a huge gap in wealth and income between the upper and lower segments. For that Herculean job, partial measures will not suffice. Two recent books give testimony to that effect: They report on studies of important changes—one in the schools, the other in the community—that were expected to elicit positive educational outcomes but came up nearly empty-handed.

NO MORE TRACKING IN HIGH SCHOOL?

For many years, those seeking equality in educational opportunity objected to the use of tracking in the public schools. Recognizing the key role of cognitive training in the educational and intellectual development of individuals and in their career potentials, critics charged that the system of tracking tended to reproduce economic and political inequality.

The procedure of tracking presumably separated students according to their ability (usually based on their IQ and achievement test scores) and gave each track a prescribed program of study. The programs differed in the content of the curriculum and the speed with which material was covered. They also differed in the demands made on the students and, consequently, in the expectations of teachers and parents. Chicago, for example, had four overarching programs, and all students were assigned to one of them: honors, regular, essential, and basic. Placement in these programs determined with whom students would likely associate during school hours, the character of their school experience, and to a large extent, the level of educational attainment.

Once assigned to a low track, the chances of movement to an upper one were minimal. In effect, the system of tracking predetermined to a considerable degree the future educational and career opportunities of the students. The system came under severe attack during the civil rights movement of the 1960s, when the key "scientific" rationale for its use, the existence of a unitary intelligence, was severely contested. During much of the history of intelligence testing, the view was widespread that intelligence was a single faculty known as "g," or general factor, and that "g" was largely inherited and not materially subject to enhancement through education. That position has been widely challenged, even in the 1930s but especially in and since the 1960s, by many scientists, for example, by Harvard psychologist Howard Gardner

who, in his 1983 book reported that years of study revealed seven intelligences: linguistic, logical-mathematical, spatial, musical, bodily-
kinesthetic, interpersonal, and intrapersonal.[1] Gardner's theory was de-
bunked by former secretary of education, William J. Bennett and his
coauthors, who characterized it as "mostly nonsense."[2] Yet, earlier in
their book, the authors wrote about the importance to school success of
effort, hard work, and perseverance, which are important aspects of an
individual's intrapersonal functioning, whether or not under the rubric
of "intrapersonal intelligence."[3] In any case, education is seen today as
a facilitator of intellectual development, and people who support tracking would be hard put to argue for it on the grounds that intelligence is
largely fixed at birth.

The arguments against tracking in those politically charged times of
the 1960s were apparently deemed reasonable enough for Judge Skelly
Wright, in the case of *Hobson v. Hansen*, in 1967, to order Washington,
D.C., to abolish tracking. This high-profile case in the context of the social and political ferment of the time probably served as a powerful incentive to school administrators and school boards to follow suit and
eliminate the procedure.

Samuel Roundfield Lucas, author of *Tracking Inequality: Stratification and Mobility in American High Schools*, elaborates in careful detail
the history and current status of tracking. He points out that urban
school systems started dismantling the procedure of tracking between
1965 and 1975, so that by 1981 the majority of high schools had given it
up.[4] He makes clear beyond a doubt, however, that the elimination of
formal procedures of tracking does not mean that students are no longer
stratified. True, the old system is gone, and that is for the better. It has
been replaced by a system of stratification within subjects—math, science, English, history, and so forth—presumably based on merit. Sadly,
it turns out that the new procedure of separating students maintains and
perpetuates inequality.

In measured terms, Lucas reports that while mobility is more possible
now, "over time most (but not all) students are moving downward. And
the likelihood of reaching advantaged positions is still greater for those
who bring advantages to the school, or who already have advantaged positions in the academic system."[5] The system that was meant to reward
merit, turns out to be unmeritocratic. Lucas refers to other studies, one

of which shows that middle-class parents, who regard elementary school-teachers as their equals or subordinates, refuse to accept teacher judgments and go around the teacher to obtain what they consider to be the best placements for their children.[6] Another investigator found that middle-class parents are much better informed about the stratification system of their school and use that knowledge to get advantaged placements for their children.[7] Through statistical analysis, Lucas himself found that high performance in math led to placement in advanced English of students who were only average in English achievement. The opposite—high achievement in English and only average achievement in math—led, though less frequently, to placement in advanced math. In both cases, average students were placed in advanced courses, contrary to the very purpose of this newer system of homogeneous grouping. This led Lucas to conclude: "The results here suggest that, despite the changes in school practice, a mismatch between achievement and reward exists in American secondary schools."[8]

Lucas's research also showed that the greater the socioeconomic diversity of the school population, the greater the divisions in the curriculum. In those schools with very heterogeneous populations, the pressure for de-tracking was considerable. To counteract that pressure, middle-class parents employed political action to maintain and expand it.

Lucas's extensive studies left him disheartened. Comparing the old system to the present one, he said: "The major difference is that the system of stratification, formerly an overt and obvious set of channels students needed to negotiate, now is submerged beneath currents that drive many students, often unknowingly, to the same disadvantageous destinations."[9]

Chapter 3 of this book delineates the history of efforts in New Jersey to realize greater equity in support of schools in urban areas. For almost thirty years, every attempt to progress in that direction was thwarted by one means or another, as self-interest on the part of those with political influence prevailed in the allocation of funds and in establishing taxes for the purpose of supporting the schools. These were self-interested, not evil, people who were responsible for the legislative and executive actions that derailed the many attempts at improving conditions in the schools in the last thirty years of the twentieth century. The same people appear in Lucas's narratives. They want the best for their children, and they know how to get it. They may well be people of good will.

Whatever their moral values, the hard fact remains that self-interest prevailed. And those facts led Lucas to conclude in this way:

> Once we consider all of these ramifications together, the ostensibly egalitarian change seems a cruel and callous ruse. Given the actual way in which the allegedly egalitarian change worked in the American context, there is good reason to question whether any structural change in schools alone can bring about equal opportunity for disadvantaged students.[10]

Although it was achieved only after much effort by dedicated researchers, educators, and parents, the elimination of overarching stratification programs can be called a "half measure." It is "a half measure" in the sense that it is far short of the totality of changes that are required. In Lucas's words, it is a half measure because equal opportunity cannot be achieved by "structural change in schools *alone*." [Emphasis added to the critical word "alone."]

IS POLITICAL CONTROL THE ANSWER?

Considering that racial minorities constitute a large proportion of the school population in America's urban centers, one might expect that having a local government headed by a member of the largest minority would make a substantial difference in equalizing educational opportunity. It doesn't.

Jeffrey Henig and three other political scientists examined the educational scene in four cities where education reform had been initiated under the leadership of African American mayors and school superintendents: Atlanta, Baltimore, Detroit, and Washington. In each case, government control had passed to black leaders. More than that, as the authors point out, "in each of these cities African Americans occupy a huge percentage of the school districts' workforce, including the top administrative positions."[11] Political control in the cities and administrative dominance in the school systems did not translate into hoped-for changes, although not for lack of reform ideas.

In their book, the political scientists attribute the failures to a complex set of causes, one of them centering in the problem of establishing workable political coalitions. These they see as necessary for a community to commit the resources required to implement a policy agenda. But there are barriers to such a commitment. One of them is economic, and racially related. Private resources in the community are still controlled by whites while public resources, beyond the city level, come from state and local governments whose purse strings are controlled largely by whites. Another barrier is that within the communities, divisions among African Americans themselves did not make for a united effort at following a policy line consistently.

This scholarly work, using documentary evidence and interviews with influential people, community-based representatives, and education specialists, exposes the hard core of the problem of changing the way we educate children in the third, and even the second school system. The power of the political-economic system remains unchanged. Whether white or black, politicians, school administrators, and teachers persist in the understandable practice of protecting their turf. Patronage and the corruption associated with it seem endemic to the system. Perhaps above all else is that cruel and unspoken recognition that students in the third school system—so many of them in urban centers like these four—are redundant. That is, the economy, as it is organized now, does not need them well educated. Also, there is little, if any, political pressure for higher expenditures for schools from politically potent people (those who contribute to political campaigns and those who vote). Leaders may feel that the effort required and risks of instability encountered by teachers when reforms are instituted, are unnecessarily costly.

Does race of political and educational leaders and teachers matter in issues of education? Indeed it does. Yet, as suggested in the paragraph above, the dynamics of the political-economic system operate no matter who the students, the teachers, administrators, and political leaders happen to be, no matter what their race, ethnicity, or religion.

Race, per se, is not an explanation of the success or failure of reform. The four political scientists see it, however, as a complicating factor. Black teachers and other professionals have high status in the eyes of African American students, because their principals and teachers "constitute one of the few examples of success that they (and often their parents) know."[12] Preachers also have high status in the community and their close personal ties to the school staff encourage them to "align with black teachers even when their stance seems at variance with generally accepted notions of good school policies."[13] That is, they are reluctant to attack black teachers, not only because of racial loyalty but also because the teachers serve as role models of success in communities that have so few such models. The teachers, "perhaps the most organized stakeholders in most urban school systems," also have the backing of black politicians and community leaders. At the height of the civil rights movement, African American leaders and preachers "were among the most vocal advocates for improved educational opportunity for black youth and for holding teachers and administrators accountable." They rallied black protesters to fight the white establishment. However, when the establishment became black, and the issues involved the status of teachers, it was not easy to rally black people against them.[14]

The outcomes in these four cities were disappointing. Instead of measuring successes of the schools in terms of higher performance, something else occurred. As the authors explain: "It is a sad commentary on shrinking expectations to note the benchmark of success in inner-city education policy is often framed in terms of the physical safety of students and staff rather than learning and pedagogy."[15]

Commenting on the research and theoretical literature on urban education reform, they say the conventional explanations for failures are misleading, suffering from one or more major faults.

- The first is the tendency to "overstate the importance of getting school reform on the public agenda." That, they say, is nothing at all "like half the battle" it is claimed to be. Inner city parents and officials want reform and many have tried it, sometimes, in fact, with too many reforms and too swiftly. "The problem appears to be not in initiating reform but rather in sustaining it."[16]
- The second is "a tendency to provide one-dimensional accounts of the cause of poor performance."[17] The simplistic explanations ("it's simply this") lead to simplistic solutions and then to frustration.
- The third fault is "a tendency to ignore politics—or, just as bad, to portray politics only in negative terms, as part of the problem rather than an avenue to a solution. Education reform is fundamentally a political process."[18]
- Designing reform programs, on a scale of difficulty, is the easy part compared with that of generating an ongoing coalition that mobilizes

the *political, social, economic, and psychological* resources to implement and sustain the design.

- The fourth is literature on school reform's failure "because it suc-
cumbs to the temptation to treat issues of race as if they are best
left unspoken." The challenge of reform is not fundamentally different in urban centers no matter who leads it politically, regardless
of the racial makeup of the district. Nevertheless, "attitudes, orien-
tations, and allegiances that are tinged by race make an already difficult challenge even more formidable."[19]

The studies conducted by these four investigators can easily leave one
discouraged. But they should not. Consider all of the factors discussed
earlier in the book, from pregnancy on through birth, infancy, early
childhood, and the preschool and school years that contribute to successful learning and development.[20] Consider the ability of parents as
teachers at home and the expectations of many urban children held by
their parents and teachers. Electing minority political leaders and ap-
pointing minorities to positions of superintendent and principal do not,
ipso facto, correct those serious disadvantages. The authors point to the
difficulty of making "clear-headed assessments of school performance
that take into account the known fact that it is much more difficult to
succeed when children come to school already depleted due to the socioeconomic conditions in their families and communities."[21] Rather
than discouragement, the useful reaction ought to be determination to
understand the factors that are likely to make for significant change and
to begin the difficult and long process of implementing those changes.
That is the topic of the two remaining chapters.

IS THE EDUCATION ACT THE ANSWER?

The reauthorization of the Elementary and Secondary Education Act,
signed by President Bush in January 2002, is the first major change in
the Elementary and Secondary Act of 1965. One of its major provisions
mandates states to administer annual reading and math tests in grades
three to eight, beginning in 2005, and in science a year later. States
must present results to the public in such fashion as to show those cat-

egories of students who are having academic problems. The data will be separated by gender, race, and other subgroupings, enabling parents to know how well their children's schools compare with others. Children in poorly performing schools will be eligible for transfer to better-performing public schools, with transportation provided by federal funds, or to receive tutoring or other educational services financed by taxpayer funds. Religious institutions or private companies may provide those services.

Over time, further provisions of the legislation come into play. Parents of children in schools that fail to meet standards after three years will have the right to move them to other public schools or to obtain federal funds of $500 to $1,000 for tutoring, or after-school or summer programs for their child. After four years of no progress, schools will be required to provide supplemental instruction, and after six years of no progress, schools will be restructured, and their leaders and staff replaced. The states are given twelve years to close the achievement gap between minority and nonminority students.

The federal aid to achieve these goals is an additional eight billion dollars, a paltry sum considering that federal support of public education represents only about 7 percent of the total spent on public education annually. On a per capita basis for the forty-eight million students in the United States, the eight billion dollars amount to $166 per student, although this allocation is presumably aimed at the neediest students.

"Presumably" is a necessary modifier of "aimed at the neediest students." The lead article in the *Arizona Daily Star* on 24 March 2002 is headlined as follows: "Education Tax Breaks Miss Target: The Poor." The first paragraph says: "State tax breaks aimed at helping to educate poor kids have benefited mostly middle-class and wealthy children and their parents, according to a study."[22] Of every dollar of tax credits, 81 cents was used to pay tuition for students already attending private schools, and 52 percent of the tax credits for activities fees went to the top 25 percent of the wealthiest school districts. An editorial in the *Arizona Daily Star* a few days later urges the state legislature to repeal the tax credits because they were helping neither poor children nor the public schools. "The tax credits are, however, making the comfortable even more comfortable."[23] Now, with the new federal legislation, it remains to be seen how the poor will fare in the allocation of funds.

It is illuminating to consider the assumptions that underlay this new legislation:

- Schools fail because the leadership and staff are disinterested or inept.
- If they are given some aid and if they are threatened with mass withdrawal of their students and also with termination, the leaders and staff will turn things around. This implies that they know how to improve student achievement but don't and won't do so.
- Tests will give us new information.
- Huge expenditures of funds and time on annual tests are justified by their use in pointing out failing schools.
- There are enough good-performing schools to absorb all those in poor-performing schools.
- Adding 3 percent to the total funding of public education will make a significant difference, even at a time when the states and communities are compelled to cut their school budgets.
- "Minimal competence along a narrow range of skills, with an eye toward satisfying the low end of the labor market"[24] is the government's implicit level of expectation.

Note that the burden for poor performance is placed entirely on the school administrators and staff—not poverty, not overworked parents, not economic insecurity, and not parents who are unequipped or unavailable to provide help and support.

One critic of the education bill, arguing for national, rather than state or local funding of schools in order to achieve parity, said "leaders of both parties have perfected the art of substituting symbolism for substance. The new bill includes requirements for annual school testing that will undoubtedly confirm what we already know. . . ."[25] He added that the marginal increases in funds are not nearly enough to equalize support.

Along the same lines, the former chair of the Senate Education Committee, Senator Jim Jeffords, said that the bill requires schools to make substantial improvements without providing the necessary resources. This, he added, is a repeat of a mistake made twenty-six years earlier when the Disabilities Education Act was endorsed. The education of children with disabilities is more costly than schooling for children without disabilities. Hence, Congress authorized the government to pay up to 40 percent of the added expenses of each state. Despite the need and the authorization, the United States provides a bare 15 percent. He feared that with state and local budgets already strained by cuts, this new legislation will "saddle our school systems with federal requirements they cannot afford to meet."[26] The result— a familiar one—will be that the headlines about a major new education bill to aid urban centers will raise false hopes and future disappointments.

Prior to the new education act, the most recent major legislation on schooling, Education Goals 2000, approved in 1994, was also announced with great fanfare. It, too, promised great things without the backup to achieve them. I wrote at the time that the first goal—all children in America will start school ready to learn—"requires physiological readiness unavailable to the many children whose lives are imperiled before birth. Several ominous changes occurred between 1979 and 1991: The number of women who received no prenatal care increased by 75 percent, and the prior slow decline in the percentage of low-weight children was reversed. Over 20 percent of children live below the poverty line, more than double the rate in the countries of the Organization for Economic Cooperation and Development."[27] Sick children, I added, are poor learners. Yet in the United States, the rate of immunization was less than half of that of nations in Western Europe. And Head Start, as its pioneer and early leader, Edward Ziegler, said, was being run so poorly that one-third of the 1,400 programs were doing nothing helpful for the children. I concluded as follows: "Only those who look for favors from the tooth fairy and Santa Claus can believe the promises of Goals 2000. The rest will be tempted to wonder whether Goals 2000 should be called Educational Scam 2000."[28]

The same may be said about the new law. This time, the political leaders have given the schools—and themselves—twelve years, long enough that the president, even if elected for a second term, and many of the congresspersons, will be long gone from the political scene. In the meantime, as if it were a comedy of errors, at about the time President George W. Bush was hailing a law that would "leave no child behind,"

Governor Jeb Bush, like some other governors, slashed six hundred million from the Florida budget for education.[29]

NOTES

1. Howard Gardner, *Frames of Mind: The Theory of Multiple Intelligences* (New York: Basic Books, 1983).

2. William J. Bennett, Chester E. Finn Jr., and John T. E. Cribb Jr., *The Educated Child: A Parent's Guide from Preschool through Eighth Grade* (New York: Free Press, 1999), 597.

3. Bennett et al., *The Educated Child*, 410–411.

4. Samuel Roundfield Lucas, *Tracking Inequality: Stratification and Mobility in American High Schools* (New York: Teachers College Press, 1999).

5. Lucas, *Tracking Inequality*, 144.

6. Annette Lareau, *Home Advantage: Social Class and Parental Intervention in Elementary Education* (New York, Falmer Press, 1989).

7. Elizabeth Useem, "Middle Schools and Math Groups: Parents' Involvement in Children's Placement," *Sociology of Education* 65, no. 4 (October 1992): 263–279.

8. Lucas, *Tracking Inequality*, 59.

9. Lucas, *Tracking Inequality*, 144.

10. Lucas, *Tracking Inequality*, 144.

11. Jeffrey R. Henig, Richard C. Hula, Marion Orr, and Desiree S. Pedescleaux, *The Color of School Reform: Race, Politics, and the Challenge of Urban Education* (Princeton: Princeton University Press, 1999), 118.

12. Henig et al., *The Color of School Reform*, 154.

13. Henig et al., *The Color of School Reform*, 152.

14. Henig et al., *The Color of School Reform*, 152.

15. Henig et al., *The Color of School Reform*, 274.

16. Henig et al., *The Color of School Reform*, 274.

17. Henig et al., *The Color of School Reform*, 274.

18. Henig et al., *The Color of School Reform*, 274.

19. Henig et al., *The Color of School Reform*, 275.

20. Henig et al., *The Color of School Reform*, 271.

21. Henig et al., *The Color of School Reform*, 273.

22. "Education Tax Breaks Miss Target: The Poor," *Arizona Daily Star*, 24 March 2002, 1 and 9 (A).

23. "Not Meeting the Goal," *Arizona Daily Star*, 27 March 2002, 6(B).

24. Stephen Metcalf, "Reading between the Lines: The New Education Law Is a Victory for Bush—and for His Corporate Allies," *Nation* (12 February 2000): 18–22.

25. Ted Halstead, "Rich School, Poor School," *New York Times*, 6 January 2001, www.nytimes.com/2002/01/08 (accessed 8 January 2002).

26. Jim Jeffords, "Back to School," *New York Times*, 13 December 2001, 39(A).

27. Milton Schwebel, "Educational Pie in the Sky," *Nation* 258, no. 17 (2 May 1994): 501–502.

28. Schwebel, "Educational Pie in the Sky," 502.

29. Molly Ivins, "Not Economic 'Stimulus' but 'Security,' *Arizona Daily Star*, 10 January 2002, 7(B).

MOVING TOWARD A SINGLE SCHOOL SYSTEM: WHAT MUST BE DONE

No one can guarantee that the third school system can be eliminated and the second improved on the way to becoming equivalent to the first. No one can be *sure* of a future outcome about human behavior, no matter how high the probability. However, the *likelihood* of that outcome is increased to the degree that the projection is consistent with current knowledge. To state this in different terms, if an empirically based theory supports the future projection, the likelihood may be substantial.

Regularities observed in the past form the basis for theory development. When formulating a theory as complex as that about the sum total of variables that enter into the development and education of humans from birth—even pregnancy—onward, one must start with the available raw material and fill in as best as one can. The "raw material" is the sum of established knowledge about learning, developing, parenting, and teaching, and the psychological, economic, political, and social factors connected with them.

Albert Einstein, writing about the various kinds of theories in physics, defined one kind, namely "constructive" theories: "They attempt to build up a picture of the more complex phenomena out of the materials of a relatively simple formal scheme from which they start out."[1] Each of the proposals put forth in this book represents the starting point. Together they constitute a "picture of the . . . complex phenomena" of a society's comprehensive, long-term project to provide first-class education for all. The proposals themselves are empirically based in the sense that sound evidence—not opinion, or wishful thinking—supports each of them. Achieving the objectives of the proposals, even gradually, in ever advancing gains, is likely to lead to more than the sum of the parts.

The proposals set forth here could be justified on many grounds. They are justified here *solely* on the grounds that they are critical to educational achievement. I am presenting them as goals to *work toward* by all those individuals and organizations that value a well-educated citizenry.

STRENGTHENING THE FAMILY

The state of mind of parents, their feeling of security, and their physical condition are all critically important to the educational achievement of their children. Parents must have an income that can support a family. In a review of many studies of a livable wage, the Economic Policy Institute derived an average of $30,000 per year for a family of one adult and two children.[2] That means an hourly wage of $14 an hour. This would cover rent, food, health insurance, a telephone, and childcare, but not such items as Internet access, restaurant meals, video rentals, wine, and other such minimal pleasures. Yet, in the words of Barbara Ehrenreich, "The shocking thing is that the majority of Americans, about 60 percent, earn less than $14 an hour."[3] Near the end of the boom of the 1990s, those at the lowest 20 percent of income were earning less than in 1990.[4] At the beginning of the new century, more than forty-five million Americans were without health insurance, and rising unemployment will increase that number.[5]

The renowned cardiologist, Bernard Lown, had this to say about health needs in the United States: "The World Health Organization has ranked the United States 37th in health care among 191 countries, despite health expenditures twice that of other industrialized countries and exceeding one trillion dollars annually. A substantial reason for this poor showing relates to the [millions] of uninsured Americans. This is a national badge of shame. . . ."[6]

To give American families what they need, I suggest the following three components.

- Guaranteed employment in a full-time job.
- A minimum wage or salary sufficient to provide the parents and children the necessary resources for livelihood without recourse to a second job for either parent or to child labor.
- National health insurance, providing parents and children with adequate health and hospital coverage.

Time and again, in countless studies about student learning and achievement, the damaging effects of poverty, illness, and family insecurity are painfully evident. The proposals above are intended to reduce the stress and tension that undermine morale and destabilize families. Insecurity about holding a job, the vagaries of temporary work, worries about maintaining a family on poverty-level wages, and inadequate health care, if any, sap one's inner resources in a struggle for survival. Add those concerns to overwork and fatigue, and after some months or years a parent's immune system may be lowered to the point of serious illness, which compounds the family's problems.

If implemented, my proposals open the way to a healthier family life. They offer the prospect of more quality time to devote to children and to obtain training in parenting skills. As an important by-product, the proposed changes would be likely to raise the self-esteem of countless parents for whom both school and work experience had been self-deflating. The children's probability of living in homes with more tranquillity and closer familial relationships would be considerably increased by these measures, and these factors are as important to school performance as any others.

The proposals above are not new, and they are anything but revolutionary. In his last two State of the Union Messages (1944 and 1945), President Franklin D. Roosevelt proposed what he called "a second Bill of Rights under which a new basis of security and prosperity can be established for all—regardless of station, race, or creed."[7] He added:

True individual freedom cannot exist without economic security and independence. . . . People who are hungry and out of a job are the stuff of which dictatorships are made. Among these [rights] are the right to a useful and remunerative job in the industries, or shops or farms or mines of the Nation.

In January 1945, Senator Murray of Montana introduced a bill in the Senate called the Full Employment Act, which guaranteed full employment to all Americans able to work. By the time the bill came out of committee, the teeth necessary to enforce the legislation had been removed, and the watered-down version used the term "maximum employment" rather than "full employment."[8]

Nevertheless, the nation set a precedent: It has on its books both the Employment Act of 1946, as amended in 1982, and the later-adopted Full Employment and Balanced Growth Act of 1979, otherwise known as the "Humphrey-Hawkins Act."[9]

THE SIGNIFICANCE OF WORK

If implemented, the proposed livable wage, guaranteed employment, and health insurance will allow parents to go to bed at night and have a decent night's sleep without nightmares about being penniless, homeless, or about suffering the indignities of poverty. But there is more to it than that.

Studies by psychologists and other social scientists over the last half-century have shown the benefits of employment. Work provides us with our identity, self-esteem, purpose in life, structure in daily living, and social relationships. The Harvard specialist in social policy William Julius Wilson, writing about the effects of the disappearance of work from the urban ghettos, had this to say:

> Work is not simply a way to make a living and support one's family. It also constitutes a framework for daily behavior; it imposes discipline. Regular employment determines where you are going to be and when you are going to be there. In the absence of regular employment, life, including family life, becomes less coherent. Persistent unemployment and irregular employment hinder rational planning in daily life, the necessary condition of adaptation to an industrial economy.[10]

For many people, work provides personal identity: It helps define who they are. Work also adds to a sense of community: It offers people a network of supportive relationships and a "we feeling." This sense of pride and belonging to a group helps people construct their social identity. Work can also add focus and purpose—a sense that one's life matters.[11]

The job may be boring. Still, workers get satisfaction out of the way it structures their lives and provides them with social relationships. They have coworkers to talk with during coffee breaks and lunchtime, some of whom may become friends. They may be active in their union. One way or another, they are part of a community. So it is not surprising that people who are out of work are likely to be less satisfied with life than those who are productively employed, and that is what studies on the psychological and physiological effects of unemployment revealed.

Even just a 1-percent increase in unemployment is accompanied by an almost 6-percent increase in homicides, a 4-percent increase in suicides, 2 percent more deaths from stress-related disorders, and an increase of over 4 percent for men and 2 percent for women in mental health problems.[12] In communities affected by major layoffs, significant increases were found in child abuse, parent-child conflicts, and marital disputes.[13] Marital satisfaction was found to be low in marriages where employment of the parents was unstable.[14]

Underemployment, where people are on jobs decidedly below their knowledge and skill level, also poses threats to individuals, who tend to feel impotent and as if they were victims of fate.[15] The rapid increase in the use of temporary workers in the 1990s is likely to exacerbate feelings of insecurity, undermine self-esteem, and increase stress in spousal and parental relationships, possibly encouraging drug abuse.

Children can be profoundly affected by their parents' employment status. Growing up in families experiencing the hazards of unemployment, they sense the anxiety of their parents and may develop a dim view of their own future. The parent on welfare or struggling to keep the family afloat on a temporary, minimum-wage job is not a role model that motivates children to learn. A comparison of families from two social classes highlights these effects: The comfortable middle-class family where parents have the time and energy as well as the educational knowledge and skill to help the children learn; and the job-insecure working-class family bordering on poverty, the parents demoralized, fearful of the future, and often lacking in energy to help the children. In other words, employment status cuts deeply into the heart of family and community life, with present and future consequences for good or ill, both at home and in school.[16]

Job security and a decent income have far-reaching effects on well-being. A study by medical epidemiologist Clyde Hertzman of the principal factors that led to a marked increase in life expectancy in wealthy nations in less than half a century (from fewer than fifty to more than seventy years) shows that much of it was due to socioeconomic factors. Many of those factors, like improvements in housing, nutrition, and education, are related to income.[17] Some of the important advances in health and longevity have come about as a result of a society's policy to improve the well-being of its people and to reduce income inequalities.

Finally, the proposals for guaranteed full employment, at a livable wage and with national health insurance, are also important as a matter of national pride. The United States is a leader among advanced industrial nations in a number of respects, among them the *quality of its health sciences*. This sterling quality is tragically offset by its backwardness in providing health services to a large portion of its population. It is backward, too, in the disproportionately large percentage of its population that is incarcerated, placing the United States, unenviably, far in the lead among advanced industrial nations. The proposals for guaranteed full employment, at a living wage, accompanied by universal health insurance are likely to remedy some of the nation's serious problems and reduce the imbalance between our virtues and our vices.

PRESCHOOL EDUCATION

In connection with preschool education, the views of a renowned child psychologist, Jerome Kagan, are pertinent. Commenting on the widespread belief in infant determinism—that by the age of two the child's intellectual fate is sealed—he said that, yes, the experience of the first two years sculpts to some degree the profile we see on a child's second birthday. Infants who are neglected are obviously less alert, less verbal, and less enthusiastic than those who receive predictable care, affection, and playful encounters. However, the profile observed at age ten is the result of a decade of experiences, not just those that occurred in the first two years. If two-year-old children living in less stimulating environments suddenly found themselves in growth enhancing homes, their minds would grow quickly.

It is unfair, Kagan adds, to blame uneducated mothers living in poverty for not playing with and talking to their infants as often as they should. If these mothers knew that their deficit in stimulation harmed their infant, they would alter their actions. The problem is that they do not appreciate that they can be effective agents in their child's growth; many of them have become fatalists. We will help them more by muting their fatalism than by impugning their character.[18] Many of these mothers, it should be added, are stressed to the maximum and exhausted. Kagan's views encapsulate several of the major points of this book, and particularly, of this section:

1. Parents want to do right by their children.
2. Some parents have never learned how to be "effective agents" in the development of their children.
3. In the interest of the children—and the interest of the society—these parents should be given instruction in parenting, including the role of parent as teacher.
4. No age in the life of the child is too old for effective interventions at home—and in school, although the sooner the parents are aided, the better.
5. "Impugning the character" of uneducated mothers (or fathers) is, to put it mildly, unhelpful, especially in contrast with "muting their fatalism" by training them to be effective parents.

The following proposals are geared to giving children born into the third and second school systems effective agents from the time of their birth.

- Parent-as-teacher training. Parents are taught how to facilitate their children's school learning and development. School administrators, teachers, and other school personnel are sensitized to the needs of the parents and trained in individual and group methods to perform these new roles. Counselors and psychologists, among others, teach parent education.
- Free, public preschool. Preschool, funded by the federal government, is available to all children beginning at the age of two. Administrators, teachers, and other educational personnel for these children are fully qualified to work with young children. Preschool teachers

are graduates of accredited programs. Appropriate adult/child ratios are established as one of the necessary conditions for quality.

These two, linked together both conceptually and administratively, comprise the foundation of the strictly educational aspects of structural reform. As a further benefit, the linkage between parent-as-teacher training and preschool education contributes to building close ties between school and family.

SCHOOL REFORM

Like other institutions, schools change over time, along with changes in personnel and the composition of the student body, the neighborhood, and the community at large of which they are a part. In some schools, those changes occur as a result of conscious planning, in others, they occur willy-nilly, with little if any intervention on the part of administrators or teachers. For example, middle-class parents move out of the community, lower-class families, some non-English-speaking, move in; experienced teachers transfer to other urban districts or obtain jobs in the suburbs; school buildings fall into a state of disrepair; parent-volunteers are no longer available; the PTA has lost its voice; and other similar regressions occur. Yet, with all that, the curriculum and teaching methods and all other aspects of schooling remain much the same as before, a situation that gives rise to failure and discipline problems in number and complexity not experienced before.

The alternative reaction involves straightforward recognition of those changes and conscious planning and implementation of suitable modifications of the internal operation of the school and its relationship with parents and the community.

Schools of the first system in general use the alternative approach. They remain in control, modifying themselves in response to altered internal and external conditions. Their status as first-class institutions depends upon that approach.

The alternative approach—a self-conscious response to changing conditions—is readily available to all schools. Motivated administrators and teachers supported by involved parents and the community can use it successfully.

To illustrate what needs to be done, consider this dramatic reform that occurred in an elementary school located in the heart of Harlem, in New York City—its population composed entirely of minorities. The district hired a white, former kindergarten teacher as its principal. She and her colleagues transformed this typical urban elementary school for minorities into one that engages its students and their parents and raised the performance level of the students to a significant degree. Writing about the changes both in her school and others, where parents and teachers took advantage of newly granted local power over the schools, that principal, Deborah Meier, emphasized the following: smaller schools, parental involvement, joint management by teachers and administrators, integration of the curriculum, not just fragmented courses, cooperative learning, and fewer topics in order to allow for greater depth. Instead of traditional methods of assessment, varied forms of performance plus portfolio reviews are used.[19] Meier's professional values, methods, and successes are analogous to those of the reform programs described in chapter 10. Like the reform programs, however, the successes leave a school, like that Meier headed, far from the level of quality of the first school system.

Compared with a few decades ago, schools setting out to make conscious and deliberate change have at their disposal the invaluable experience of those reform programs. The programs can be helpful in six ways.

- First, they broaden horizons about potential futures.
- Second, they are motivators, leading school people and parents to feel "Since others have done this, we can too."
- Third, they offer knowledge about process, content, evaluation, and continuing refinement.
- Fourth, they emphasize both substantive learning and thinking, in the recognition that each of these strengthens the other.
- Fifth, some of them accentuate the value of linkages among fields of study to learning, so that students understand the interconnections among their fields of study.
- Sixth, the programs are developed in such a way that all the constituencies—administrators, teachers, parents, students—can have a sense of ownership in the program and a personal interest in their success.

I propose the following to support school reform.

1. As routine practice, schools periodically evaluate their effectiveness in serving their population of students and parents. The purpose is not to punish administrators and teachers, in the manner of
   the new federal legislation and that of many states, rather it is to
   identify strengths that can be emulated and weaknesses that need
   to be corrected.

2. As part of their professional and continuing education, all educational personnel study the various programs of reform, methods
   used to evaluate them, and the outcomes of evaluation. They learn
   the political and educational intricacies of introducing and operating them, and integrating them into the system.

3. Those who have the greatest investment in the schools—especially
   administrators, teachers, and parents—have a major voice in setting its objectives, defining the methods of achieving them, and
   evaluating outcomes.

4. Schools engage in ongoing school-to-home and home-to-school
   communications about school programs and student progress—
   much more, in other words, than the periodic report card. They
   train and use family members as school volunteers. They collaborate with the community by coordinating and integrating community services and resources to strengthen and enrich students'
   learning experiences.[20]

5. The capacity to think gets a prime position among the objectives
   of public education, from the earliest years onward, because of its
   importance in facilitating learning and development, personal fulfillment, and the well-being of a democratic society.

6. Schools provide after school programs, including supervised homework settings for students in elementary and middle schools. With
   almost 80 percent of mothers of school-age children working out of
   the home, such programs provide supervision and instruction. Preliminary studies show them to be valuable both in terms of behavior (school attendance and reduced behavior problems) and in
   school performance (achievement in class and on standardized
   tests). Still, the movement to after school programs, including ideas
   about their most desirable form and content, is in its infancy.[21]

7. The cultural and physical aspects of development are attended to: art, drama, music, and physical education are integral to the curriculum.
8. Enrichment is available to children who require extra assistance either because of special needs or because they have fallen behind.
9. Adequate ancillary services are available through counselors, nurses, physicians, school psychologists, or social workers.

Participation and clear lines of communication are essential to success in working toward these goals. More particularly, they are essential to provide the conditions for students' learning and development. Participation and good communication, however, are not easily achieved because they are so contrary to established exercises of power in schools and school districts. Over the course of centuries, the respective roles of superintendent, principal, teacher, and parent have been rather clearly defined, and authentic participation has not been part of the definition. For the most part, administrators have not sought and seriously entertained the views and opinions of teachers, parents, community members, or students, nor have teachers listened to and taken seriously parental views about content and methods of teaching. This is not a reflection on their professionalism or their integrity. This simply describes the way professional people in education have been socialized and what their institutional environment expects of them.

In his thoughtful work on participatory reform, educational researcher Gary Anderson points out that many fail "because they undermine institutional spaces within which a relatively clear set of rules, norms, and identities regulate social interactions . . . without a plan for the collaborative reconstruction of a new social ground."[22] The rules, norms, and identities apply not only to relationships and communication within the school. They extend, as well, to the school district and the community at large. Without new ways of relating, councils for participation set up by reformers often lead to rubber stamping of decisions made in the old, established way, or lead to destructive contentiousness if the old ways are undermined and new ways are not established.

These conditions do not, however, make the outlook for genuine participation hopeless. Anderson and others have found that "courageous democratic leaders in schools and central offices can foster conditions in schools that open up spaces for authentic participation . . . and that teachers tend to develop patterns of social interaction that are often in direct response to principals' leadership styles."[23] Courageous leaders and teachers work toward overcoming the barriers to genuine participation, barriers that are both institutional and psychological. They reject its use as a public relations device—for example, making the school look good by a "show" of democracy—recognizing its importance to students' learning and development. As Anderson concludes, "the notion of authentic participation is perhaps more of an ideal to work toward than a reality that can be socially engineered."[24]

THE TEACHING PROFESSION

There is a curious Alice-in-Wonderland kind of contradiction at work in connection with the nation's public school teaching force. On the one hand, political leaders engage in teacher bashing while complaining about the severe shortage of teachers. Then, again, those leaders wring their hands over the lack of sufficient experienced teachers in the needy urban centers of the country, while those centers are paying lower salaries than the suburban schools, thanks in no small part to the leaders' failures to appropriate sufficient funds for substantial increases. At the very time that "education president" Bush was hailing the new education act, some public school districts had to take actions that are plainly regressive. For example, districts in Michigan were forced to cut budgets, some of them eliminating teaching positions and increasing class size.[25]

At a time when the New York City public school system is suffering teacher shortages and may, during the next five years, lose more than half the teachers to retirement, the city is paying 25 percent less than surrounding suburbs.[26] The competition for able people is not only with the suburbs. As one twenty-three-year-old teacher put it: "It's disheartening that there aren't more teachers coming in. But the fact is that people my age can earn more in the corporate world."[27]

Elite private schools are not plagued by this problem. They attract recent graduates of leading colleges and universities, many of whom are, themselves, products of the first school system. As teachers, they are comfortable in the private schools for several reasons, even if their salaries are lower than those in public schools: The environment is a familiar one. Being quite free of discipline problems, these schools enable them to spend class time in instruction. They are not required to be licensed or even to have any training in education. It should be noted, however, that their own experiences in first system schools and colleges provide them with training in "education." For sixteen years or more, their teachers made heavy demands on them for reflection and thoughtful analyses, in class work and in homework. The emphasis on think, imagine, and create that the school reform programs value is so much part of their entire educational experience that they do not come as total initiates. In those schools, too, they learned the exceptional importance of supportive teachers and of close working relationships between teachers and students. Beyond that, elite private schools conduct ongoing continuing education, often in combination with other independent schools.

Public schools in the second and third systems cannot match those conditions. They can, at least, compensate for other shortcomings by demanding that teachers be given high-quality preparation, internships under first-rate supervisors, and then offering attractive salaries and benefits, and opportunities to participate in programs that encourage their continued intellectual and professional growth. These attractions could draw candidates of the quality—meaning educational background and accomplishment—of some of those who now choose engineering, business management, computer science, health care fields, and editorial jobs in publishing.

Of course, there is no one "fix" that will eliminate the third school system and improve the second. Yet, the obvious effects of inequity in compensation and working conditions between the urban and suburban settings and in compensation between the educational and the corporate worlds cry out for correction.

I propose the following to strengthen the teaching profession.

1. Teaching is recognized as a profession, rooted in scientific knowledge accumulated over a century.
2. Recognizing that part of the across-the-board change required for the improvement of education for all children involves the status of teachers, the nation places a higher value on its teachers. It

shows this by strengthening the curriculum for future teachers and by assuring their remuneration is not lower than the median for all professions requiring equivalent years of preparation.

3. All future teachers have the advantage of a diversified education in the liberal arts and sciences and the humanities, with a major in one subject, and a minor in professional education. Their education enables them to understand how children learn and develop and how teachers, in a multicultural society, facilitate that process.

4. Formal education gives particular emphasis to bio-psycho-social development and a profound understanding both of how humans learn and think and of the skills of facilitating the development of those abilities in children.

5. Teachers learn how to interact with students and parents of diverse cultures. Their instruction goes well beyond "skills" and "interpersonal relations," into the realm of the history that reveals the United States as a multicultural nation from the moment the first explorers reached these shores. They learn, too, of the insidiousness of subconscious racism, sexism, and the like.

6. Such an educational program requires a minimum of five years of preparation, including a supervised internship and supervision during the first three years of teaching.

STIGMA, DISAFFECTION, AND RECONCILIATION

If the nation, in the interest of all its children, is to take giant strides in dealing with its past, it must face up to its denial about the deep-seated reality of racism and other forms of stereotyping. It must confront the pain and injury it inflicts every day in the lives of millions of its own people. And it must understand that some of the prime roots of the so-called school crisis emanate from that pain and injury. One of my proposals falls in the area of reparations, in part because of the need to compensate oppressed groups. There are, however, more profound reasons: For a dramatic improvement in the education of children from birth onward, something much more than economic and material considerations must be addressed. In particular, the consciousness of the people of the nation—the stigmatizers and the stigmatized—is involved, and that consciousness is the target of the proposals in this section, be they about Asian Americans, African Americans, Hispanic Americans, Native Americans or females.

One could justify these proposals on the grounds that social justice, equality, and a better-informed citizenry in a democracy call out urgently for them. But for our purposes in this book, those are not the motives. Pure and simple, the so-called crisis in American education has its roots in remediable poverty and remediable racism and sexism, which is not to say that modifications of the schools are unhelpful. The nation needs now to engage in a national discussion, turning the lens on our past and our present, and bringing to light the stereotypes that shape the attitudes and behavior of people.

- To surmount stigma and disaffection with school, the government of the United States, on behalf of its citizens, will apologize and express its deepest regret for the inhumane treatment of African Americans during the years of slavery and de facto second-class citizenship that followed for a century and more.
- For the same purpose, it will apologize for the inhumane treatment of Native Americans in driving them off their lands, killing many of them, and excluding survivors from full citizenship.
- For the same purpose, it will apologize for the subjection of women to second-class citizenship during most of its history.
- As an agent to bring to light the nature and extent of loss and suffering endured by African Americans, Native Americans, and females, and as an aid to reconciliation and full integration, the government of the United States will establish a Truth and Reconciliation Commission. This commission will be charged with the additional responsibility of determining the extent of reparations owed to these groups and the form in which compensation is to be made.

The idea of compensating blacks for what was taken from them in their many years as chattel is not a new one; it was first proposed to George Washington by Marquis de Lafayette.[28] More than two centuries later, Randall Robinson has documented the case for reparations in his book *The Debt: What America Owes to Blacks*.[29] Those who support reparations base it on what whites gained from slavery in the past, for which blacks should be recompensed.

Already the issue of reparations is in the courts. As Harvard law professor Charles Ogletree reported, lawyers, on behalf of all descendants of African American slaves, filed a class-action lawsuit in federal court seeking compensation from a number of corporations that are charged with profiting from slave labor and slave trade.[30] Other corporations and some universities found to benefit from slavery will be future defendants; and so will the government itself, whose "officials guaranteed the viability of slavery and the segregation that followed it."[31] Bringing these issues to court has the advantage of presenting facts and documentation. It will lead to the kind of conversation, as Ogletree puts it, on slavery, its legacy, its profits for some and its continued effects on black Americans today—a conversation that America has never had.

From the perspective of today's educational problems, the issue of reparations for African Americans, Native Americans, and females is secondary. The prime issue for all oppressed groups is what the actions of the past and their aftermath are inflicting on families and children *today*. In regard to blacks, some political leaders deny that the nation is still racist, perhaps pointing to affirmative action as evidence. Yet, affirmative action reached a tiny proportion of oppressed minorities. Furthermore, the nation has been retreating from affirmative action and other supports for the poor. Prisons are filled disproportionately with blacks and minorities; the student body of the third school system is disproportionately black and other minorities; the population below the poverty level is disproportionately black and other minorities; the nation's infant mortality rate is disproportionately higher for blacks and other minorities. On a daily basis, the quality of life, even of African Americans and other minorities in the middle class, and of women, is affected by stereotyping: In some states, blacks are profiled by state police as potential criminals. In many cities, they are passed up by taxi cab drivers, who then stop for white passengers.

A number of nations, such as Argentina, Chile, Germany, Japan, and El Salvador, have been faced with the question of how to cope with a haunting past. South Africa, under Nelson Mandela's leadership and the guidance of Bishop Tutu, decided that to work effectively in the present and have hope for the future South Africa must first heal its wounds, no matter how excruciatingly painful the process might be. Through its Truth and Reconciliation Commission, it chose a way "to achieve closure of a past of oppression" while simultaneously working toward national reconstruction and reconciliation.[32]

No two nations are alike, and the oppression of blacks in the United States and in South Africa took very different forms and had very different histories. Nonetheless, the South African experience and those of other nations that have taken forthright positions about truth and reconciliation can give the United States insights about how to heighten awareness of what it has meant in the past and what it means today to be a member of a stereotyped and oppressed group.

Americans must learn from history just who profited from the oppression of others and who profits now. They must learn how useful the stereotypes have been in perpetuating the status of inequality, in the past and the present. They must learn, in other words, what this nation has done to lead so many children in the third school system to devalue schooling in defense of their self-esteem.

The proposals in this chapter require ongoing discussion and debate and, finally, political action, all of which will take many years. In the meantime, efforts to improve education in the nation by whatever means possible should continue uninterrupted. The many reforms offer a rich pool of ideas for changing education in desirable directions. Simultaneously, the challenge is to initiate a long-term campaign for the enactment of the proposals and at the same time to promote ongoing changes in the education of children, from birth onward.

NOTES

1. Albert Einstein, *Essays in Science* (New York: Philosophical Library, 1934), 53–54.

2. Barbara Ehrenreich, *Nickel and Dimed: On (Not) Getting By in America* (New York: Henry Holt, 2001).

3. Ehrenreich, *Nickel and Dimed*, 213.

4. "Gore Pledges Health Plan for All Children," *New York Times*, 9 September 1999, 1 and 18(A).

5. Marcia Angell, "Insufficient Credits," *Health Letter* 17, no. 11 (November 2001): 1–3. Reprinted from *American Prospect* (September 2001).

6. Bernard Lown, "A Developing World Fellowship," *Lown Forum* (Summer 2001): 1, 6–8.

7. Arthur M. Schlesinger Jr., *The State of the Union Messages of the Presidents* (New York: Chelsea House, 1967), 2881.

8. Harry Magdoff, "Remarks on Receiving the NECLCT Tom Paine Award," *Monthly Review* 46, no. 9 (September 1995): 32–36, 33.

9. Harold S. Roberts, *Roberts' Dictionary of Industrial Relations,* 4th ed. (Washington, D.C.: Bureau of National Affairs, 1993).

10. William Julius Wilson, "Work," *New York Times Magazine*, 18 August 1996, 26–52, 30.

11. David J. Myers and Edward Diener, "Who Is Happy," *Psychological Science* 6, no. 1 (January 1995): 10–19, 15.

12. M. H. Brenner, *Estimating the Social Costs of National Economic Policy: Implications for Mental and Physical Health and Criminal Violence*, Report for the Joint Economic Committee of Congress (Washington, D.C.: U.S. Government Printing Office, 1976).

13. Maya Pines, "Recession Is Linked to Far-Reaching Psychological Harm," *New York Times*, 6 April 1982, 1–2(C).

14. Andrew Cherlin, "Work Life and Marital Satisfaction," in *Divorce and Separation,* ed. George Levinger and Oliver C. Moles (New York: Basic Books, 1979), 151–166.

15. Beverly H. Burris, *No Room at the Top: Underemployment and Alienation in the Corporation* (New York: Praeger, 1993).

16. Portions of this paragraph were drawn from Milton Schwebel, "Job Insecurity as Structural Violence: Implications for Destructive Intergroup Conflict," *Peace and Conflict: Journal of Peace Psychology* 3, no. 4 (1997), 340.

17. Clyde Hertzman, "Health and Human Society," *American Scientist* 89, no. 6 (November–December 2001): 538–545.

18. Jerome Kagan, *The Nature of the Child* (New York: Basic Books, 1994).

19. Deborah Meier, *The Power of Their Ideas: Lessons for America from a Small School in Harlem* (Boston: Beacon. 1995).

20. J. L. Epstein, "School/Family/Community Partnership: Caring for the Children We Share," *Phi Delta Kappan* 76, no. 9 (September 1995): 701–712.

21. Jodi Wilgoren, "The Bell Rings but the Students Stay, and Stay," *New York Times*, 24 January 2000, 1 and 18(A).

22. Gary L. Anderson, "Toward Authentic Participation: Deconstructing the Discourses of Participatory Reforms in Education," *American Educational Research Journal* 35, no. 4 (1998): 571–603, 592.

23. Anderson, "Toward Authentic Participation," 593.

24. Anderson, "Toward Authentic Participation," 595.

25. "Michigan: Schools Make Cuts," *New York Times*, 29 August 2001, 18(A).

26. Lynette Holloway, "Low Pay and Retirements Aggravate Teacher Shortage," *New York Times*, 5 January 2000, 8(B).

27. Holloway, "Low Pay and Retirements Aggravate Teacher Shortage," 8(B).

28. Vern Smith, "Debating the Wages of Slavery," *Newsweek*, 27 August 2001, 20–25.

29. Randall Robinson, *The Debt: What America Owes to Blacks* (New York: E. P. Dutton, 2000).

30. Charles J. Ogletree Jr., "Litigating the Legacy of Slavery," *New York Times*, 31 March 2002, 9(A).

31. Ogletree, "Litigating the Legacy of Slavery," 9(A).

32. Cheryl de la Rey and Ingrid Owens, "Perceptions of Psychological Healing and the Truth and Reconciliation Commission in South Africa," *Peace and Conflict: Journal of Peace Psychology* 4, no. 3 (1998): 257–270, 257.

⑭

INITIATING CHANGE

The key to change is the will of the people. What American adults hold to be true leads them to choose their leaders and to support or oppose legislation. The campaign for change requires a critical mass of citizens who demand more effective ways of coping with educational problems. This chapter is about winning the active support of that critical mass. To accomplish that, Americans need to understand the following:

- The path that has been followed to cope with educational problems leads only to dead ends and ensuing frustration.
- That path reflects a lack of governmental motivation for significant change.
- There are other, more comprehensive—and more reasonable—approaches.
- The goals of these other approaches are realizable.
- The long-term objective is to reach all of the goals, not just one or two of them.
- The pursuit of these goals is not a vain one for some kind of Utopia.
- These goals are realizable only through citizens' widespread commitment to pursue them actively in concert with others.
- The *process* of change is as important as the goals.

Each of these is explained at greater length below.

Dead Ends. The current approaches to educational problems lead to dead ends that are frequently revealed in accountability reports in the news media. "Accountability," which has become the code word in discourse about reform, calls for the following. Test the children, aid some of them and test them again, and reward the schools that show progress and penalize the rest. Typically, the result of testing has been that year after year newspapers give accounts of roller coaster performance with such headlines as: "Test scores are up. Test scores are down." The tests that are employed, for the most part consisting of short-answer items, do not get at the heart of what a first-class education ought to accomplish. Even with that considerable inadequacy, they reveal little that could generate any sense of optimism about lasting improvement. In its endeavors to make things better, the government seems stuck in a quagmire, as if it were coping with intractable problems. It is, in fact, refusing to recognize the multiple factors that stubbornly maintain three separate school systems in democratic America.

Lack of Government Motivation. A condition of low interest in change, which has persisted decade after decade, exists today. The facts are readily available. For example, a lead editorial in the *New York Times*, entitled "The Fight for a Sound Education," stated the case well. About a half-century after the Supreme Court declared that segregated schools denied African Americans equal opportunities in civic and professional life, "some of the same inequalities are still evident." With state courts ruling that the states must furnish students with a sound education, some responses to legal challenges "ranged from the flip to the reprehensible. . . ." The Pennsylvania state lawyers argued that the state could interpret its constitution's education clause as it wished, "up to, or including defining basic education as teaching students to tie their shoes." New York State argued "it could fulfill its constitutional duty by teaching students to read at the eighth-grade level."[1] The editorial considered these arguments morally indefensible, whatever their legality may have been. Yet, indefensible as they are, those arguments more accurately reflect the will of the politically powerful than any declarations of intent during political campaigns, or even after a candidate becomes an incumbent. Those who present themselves with a flourish as the "educational" president or governor reveal their real intent when the legislation they propose and endorse is closely scrutinized.

More Comprehensive and Reasonable Approaches. The proposals set forth in the previous chapter represent those approaches. Their purpose is not superficial "accountability" followed by a small carrot (some financial aid) and a big stick (eventually, replacing the leaders and staff), siphoning money away from public education and toward vouchers and private schools. Instead, they address the multiple factors that have been largely ignored in past legislation.

The Goals of These Other Approaches Are Realizable. These goals are very straightforward. For example, guaranteed full employment and a living wage for all workers simply require the approval of Congress and the president. Of course, economic readjustments must follow, as they did when a national minimum wage bill was approved and when unemployment insurance and Social Security were introduced. Health insurance for all Americans is not the complex problem posed by some; as one professor of health policy and history has proposed, it could be readily accomplished by making Medicare universal.[2] Some of the other proposals, like that for apology, have little precedent (President Clinton did apologize to the Japanese community for the nation's treatment of Japanese Americans after the Pearl Harbor attacks); the experiences of other nations, however, provide plenty of guidelines.

The goals are realizable. Nothing among the proposals is novel. Here are several examples. As noted earlier, President Franklin D. Roosevelt, calling it a second Bill of Rights, called for economic security and independence, for each individual's right to a useful and remunerative job. That call came more than half a century ago. Many industrially advanced countries today provide all their people with health insurance. Teachers in some nations in Western Europe are accorded status and compensation comparable to other professions requiring equivalent education. In the United States, parents are already deeply involved in school affairs in programs like those discussed in chapter 10. As a final example, some nations, with South Africa as the leader among them, have taken extreme measures to apologize and atone for their barbaric treatment of oppressed groups. These examples demonstrate that the proposals have been around for some time, and many have been implemented somewhere in the world.

The Long-Term Objective Is to Reach All of the Goals. The uniqueness resides not in the individual proposals but in the proposals as a unitary set, for the overarching proposal is that *all of these combined* constitute the goal of the nation for the education and development of its people. It is not acceptable to work only toward one or three or half a dozen, desirable as those may be. Educational excellence demands all of them.

Of course, these goals are not something we can expect to achieve overnight. Working toward them unrelentingly is what we can do. In the process, some of the goals may be achievable before others, but all must be on the national agenda, and all with equal urgency.

The Pursuit of These Goals Is not Utopian. Calling for major change is not the same as calling for Utopia. This nation has made more than one major alteration, like freeing the slaves, suffrage for working-class white men (which they did not possess during the early years of the Republic) and, much later, for women, unemployment insurance, minimum wage, Social Security, Medicare, Medicaid, and various pollution controls. Most of these were once thought to be inconceivable, and some were opposed as radical, even "un-American," ideas. None of them required a Utopia. Once unimaginable, these changes are today part of everyday life and may now serve as springboards to modifications made in the twenty-first century.

For those troubled by the seeming Utopianism of the proposals, some relevant history is in order, perhaps best approached through a series of questions.

1. How would our ancestors in the year 1900 have responded to a prediction that this new century would produce electrically illuminated homes, the radio, sound movies, television, washer-dryer and dishwasher, jet flights around the world, space exploration, and computers and the Internet?
2. How would they respond to a prediction that their worries about the consequences of unemployment and of retirement from work and old age would be greatly alleviated through unemployment insurance, Social Security, Medicare, and Medicaid, and that the physically and mentally handicapped would receive an array of benefits unheard of in their time?
3. How would they respond to a prediction that women would win the right to vote, serve on the Supreme Court, in Congress and presidential cabinets, and as state governors and ambassadors; that

the de jure right of African Americans to vote would become a de facto one through legislative and legal actions, and that they, too, would serve in high offices like those held by women? And that those rights would be won only after long campaigns, involving millions of people?

4. And how would they respond to a prediction that within the century, instead of 7 percent of their age group completing high school or its equivalent, it would be over 84 percent; or that in sixty years, college graduates would increase from under 5 percent to over 25 percent?[3] Or that the United States would become the preeminent center of science and technology, and a major, if not the major cultural influence in the world through its literature, films, theater, music, art, and dance?

Very likely, the response from most of our ancestors to all of those questions would have been a resounding: "Just Utopian dreams!" The goal of first-class education for all is no more a Utopian prediction than any of the above would have been in 1900.

These Goals Are Realizable Only through Widespread Commitment to Pursue Them Actively in Concert with Others. History documents the hard fact that the kinds of changes the proposals demand require a monumental effort and even some sacrifice. The twentieth century bore witness to the high price when the civil rights and other movements, even at the cost of some lives, led the U.S. government to grant long denied rights to minorities, women, the physically and emotionally disadvantaged, and those of different sexual orientation. "There are no free lunches."

The Process Itself Is as Important as the Goals. In all probability, future historians, looking back at the long period of striving for first-class education for all, will see the process itself, the process of striving for change, as important in its own right. "Getting there" constitutes the experience of a nation in dialogue, learning truths about its past, and seeing remediable injustices in the present. In that sense, "getting there" is a profound educational experience. Learning is not always pleasant because it involves facing up to some wrenching truths conveniently buried in national and personal memory. Denial is a powerful defense mechanism. Yet, at the end, when the heated arguments are past and personal resistance to the truth has been abandoned, individuals feel all the better and stronger for having endured the stresses of the process. They have acquired a clearer view of themselves, the groups they identify with, and more distant groups as well. It is a liberating process. Many of those who were involved in the struggles for social justice of the second half of the twentieth century in the United States can testify to the change in consciousness, and to some degree, in behavior, generated by their experiences.

COALITION FOR IMPLEMENTING
THE PROPOSALS

A broad-based coalition of people who see the proposals as essential to the well-being of the United States will be needed to convert the proposals into the laws of the land. For that purpose, strategies to gain the support of millions of voters are a first order of business. To get those millions supporting the same cause, some past differences that bitterly divided people will have to be addressed.

For example, battles for funds to enhance the schools for low-income children have typically pitted several groups against the forces promoting the interests of the urban schools. Members of taxpayers associations usually oppose increases in taxes. Parents of children in well-funded suburban or select urban schools oppose distributions of educational funds that yield their schools a reduced proportion of appropriations for education. Parents of children in private or parochial schools and elderly people with no children in school are more likely than others to oppose increases in property taxes that fund public schools.

How would these several categories of citizens respond to calls for the costly structural and educational changes represented by the proposals? In all probability, their respective stances would be the same as in the past. For that reason, activists for these proposals need to devise strategies to win their support, to reverse their past reactions and have them join the coalition supporting the long-term campaign for a unitary school system marked by excellence. Principles to guide a new strategy are as follows:

First, funding for these proposals must not come at a cost to the middle class, the elderly, or parents of children in private or parochial schools. They should not be derived from increases in property or sales taxes, or from income taxes of the middle and working classes. In other words, implementation of the proposals should not come at a cost to those groups whose self-interest would make them, under present tax practices, opponents of the proposals. Instead, to encourage these groups to become allies, the competition for funds should be directed elsewhere. One target is higher taxation of upper income groups and corporations; another is a redistribution of the federal budget's allocation to the proposed new, national commitments. The upper income groups have grown richer to such a degree that the gap between the affluent and the poor has become obscenely wide. Their taxes could be increased enormously without affecting their lifestyles. Corporate loopholes can be closed. A review of the federal budget would likely reveal sources of wasted funds, especially in the defense allocations. The promised military economies resulting from the end of the Cold War are long overdue and need not be compromised by the war on terrorism. Furthermore, the desirability of world dependence on a United Nations force rather than those of individual nations to maintain global peace justifies further reductions.

The federal budget strictly for the schools has been paltry. At present less than 7 percent of funds to the public schools come from the federal government; about 49 percent come from state governments; and the remaining 44 percent come from local or county sources.[4] Because the United States has mandated testing of all children in grades three to eight, it has declared appropriately—even if one strongly disagrees with that action—that the education of children comes very much under its jurisdiction as well as that of the states and local communities.

As a second principle, the strategy in working toward a single school system calls for major funding by the federal government, with the balance of school budgets supplied by state governments. Similarly, the U.S. government must assume responsibility for the health and well-being of its entire people, introducing legislation to initiate all of the proposals. Just as the needs of the military forces are not left hostage to the vagaries of a local property tax referendum, the needs of the people, children and adults alike, are in the hands of their own elected representatives.

A further look at budgetary needs leads to the following predictions:

1. The American people will find upon reflection, after much debate, that they value the move toward first-class education for all and the accompanying societal restructuring more than they value expenditures for other purposes.
2. They will decide that education of that quality, brought about by the multiple changes, would strengthen this nation to such a degree that cutbacks in other directions are well worth it.
3. As they understand the enormous advantages for the nation—and for themselves, at least for most Americans—they will be willing to support a policy of higher taxation as long as the burden does not fall on those who can least afford it.
4. A nation with an ever-rising educational level can be a more creative and productive society, whose increasing wealth can be dedicated to education and other crucial needs.

Third, mass support for the proposals must come from that vast portion of the population for whom only third and second school systems are now available. They will constitute the core of people who, over time, will come to support, organize, and lobby for first-class education for all.

Reading and hearing about this movement, some will independently recognize its profound importance; others will come to appreciate its value through membership in an organization or institution that has adopted first-class education as a cause of its own.

Fourth, "In unity there is strength." The coalition to carry on the democratization of the United States must include all social classes, although we should recognize some might resist, especially the very affluent who stand to lose exclusivity. As for them, it is well to keep in mind the words of an affluent person about a century ago. Andrew Carnegie, speaking to a Bible class at the Fifth Avenue Baptist Church in New York in 1899, said this: "I was born to the blessed heritage of poverty. We hear a good deal in these days about poverty—"Oh, abolish poverty!" But the saddest day that civilization ever saw will be that in which poverty doesn't win its way. The poor, thank God, we will always have with us."[5]

The coalition must include associations of parents, teacher associations and unions, other labor unions, women's organizations, health organizations, African Americans, Hispanic Americans, Native Americans, Asian Americans, other ethnic groups, ethnic and religious organizations, and parents of special needs children. Something should be said about a few more groups.

The alliance of activists should include associations of criminal justice workers of all kinds, police forces of the nation among them. There is good reason for that: The United States spends annually about six thousand dollars for the education of each child and thirty-six thousand dollars for each prisoner. American prisons are bulging with inmates, many of them, with the exception of white-collar inmates, the products of the third school system. Consider how much more economical it would be to shift the balance of expenditures.

The elderly form a large voting bloc. Once freed of threats to their economic security, elderly people, most of them with experience in seeing their children go through the public schools, are likely to become strong supporters of the coalition.

Labor unions have been staunch supporters of public schools. It is well to remember that early in the nineteenth century, worker's associations—the precursors of today's unions—spearheaded the campaign for free elementary education. Early in the twentieth century the American Federation of Labor looked to the schools to "promote the idea that the hope of workers lay in the elevation of the working class as a class."[6] They attacked the practice of instructing workers that they should be content with their lot. At the beginning of the twenty-first century, they could join with the many other institutions and associations that also have good reason to seek first-class education. Together, these groups, with many millions as members, could organize and plan for the long campaign to implement the proposals and make this nation the home of the well educated, as well as of the brave.

Other potential major blocs are the millions of teachers and other school personnel; physicians, dentists, nurses, psychologists, social workers, and allied fields that aid not only poor, dependent, and homeless children but also the millions of parents of school children suffering the effects of economic insecurity.

Nongovernmental organizations that advocate in the interest of children, families, education, and health are likely supporters, and so are

foundations with similar interests. In other words, the potential for allies and supporters in the efforts of the coalition to gain approval of substantial proposals is as broad as the nation itself. If such strength were
to be garnered, it would be bound to gain the support of political leaders. That would be a sign of progress, but still early in the process of
change. Then comes the long struggle to get legislators to propose bills
that implement the proposals.

As a fifth principle, from the outset of its activities the coalition is
mindful of the key role of elections. Close scrutiny of candidates must
come early in a political campaign, even before candidates are nomi-
nated for office. Better than that, citizens who seek to implement the
proposals need to be involved in putting forth their own candidates,
people fully committed to the required changes. That is one of the most
important justifications for a coalition.

Finally, the coalition should not be a hierarchical structure; rather it
should be a loosely organized set of associations that share the same objectives and maintain close liaison. They seek legislation or other appropriate actions to implement the proposals. In the strictly educational
realm, they support policies and actions to bring about programs for
parent training, improved teacher education, and first-class schooling
for children.

The nation's campaign for change will not start from scratch. Many
organizations have been working to improve the conditions necessary
for effective schooling. Here are a few examples.

- The Public Education Network (PEN). PEN believes that quality
  education for all children requires an informed citizenry, one that
  understands that school quality and quality of community life are
  interrelated. Parents, citizens, in fact, whole communities are responsible for improving the schools. PEN's role, for more than ten
  years, has been to establish a network of local education funds
  (LEFs). In turn, the role of LEFs is to engage citizen support for
  quality public education.[7]

  PEN's sixty-six member LEFs in twenty-eight states and the District of Columbia serve over six million children in more than 6,600
  schools in 310 school districts. Six million represents nearly one in
  every ten children in public schools in the United States. A major-

ity of the students qualify for free or reduced-price lunches, compared with only 35 percent nationally.

PEN provides seed money and know-how to aid the LEFs in building funds and stimulating community support and involvement. In the past five years, the LEFs have raised about five hundred million dollars, some of which has gone to its initiatives to encourage reading, enhance teacher quality, and conduct community forums on educational issues, including those of education and race. These accomplishments have come about in large part because of involvement of committed citizens. In the view of the president of PEN, Wendy Puriefoy, many people feel isolated from decisions about the schools. Some citizens vote in school board elections, or buy candy to support school projects. "It is time we raised the bar and let the public know that we need them to play a much more critical role than this. LEFs have been working diligently to help send this message and engage the public."[8]

- Education Law Center (ELC). As I reported in chapter 3, the long struggle for equity in public education in New Jersey was spearheaded in the last thirty years by the Education Law Center. Established in 1973 as the voice for public school children, it has been their advocate for equal education under state and federal laws. It works to improve educational opportunities for low-income students, and students with disabilities, through public education, policy initiatives, research, communications, and when necessary, legal action. The belief underlying ELC's efforts is that all children, if given the chance, can meet high academic standards.[9]

ELC currently operates the Student Rights Project, to protect the educational rights of all students, including students with disabilities. It also operates the Abbott Schools Initiative (Abbott being the appellant in the string of lawsuits that led to a decision highly favorable to the poor children of the state), to assure the full, effective, and timely implementation of the programs and reforms ordered by the New Jersey Supreme Court in *Abbott v. Burke*.

Three lawyers have played major roles in the relentless struggle for the educational welfare of poor children in New Jersey: Paul Tractenberg, law professor at Rutgers University, was the founder and guiding spirit over the years; Marilyn Moreheuser, former nun, later a student of Tractenberg's, who in the 1980s and until her death in 1995, as executive director of ELC, doggedly pursued the case; and David Sciarra, former civil rights lawyer and New Jersey Public Advocate for ten years, who succeeded Moreheuser. They were the leaders, but they would point to the fact that the victory for the children came as a result of a powerful coalition that was built up over the years. The coalition included organizations representing ethnic and racial groups, parents, women, clergy, educators, and associations concerned with particular aspects of schooling such as early childhood education, or that for children with disabilities. Indeed, one of the important outcomes of the long struggle has been the formation of a formidable group of campaigners for quality and change. The Early Care and Education Coalition is one example. Composed of forty organizations as well as many individual members, its purpose is "to ensure that New Jersey realizes the great promise of effective early childhood education," made possible by the state's Supreme Court when it ordered the implementation of preschool programs in urban school districts.[10] As an example of cooperation within the coalition, the position paper, from which this quotation was taken, was prepared by representatives of both the Association for Children of New Jersey and the New Jersey Principals and Supervisors Association.

David Sciarra, the Education Law Center's current executive director, spelled out the promise for further advances in the future. Questioned about the effects of poverty and its accompanying social ills on children's learning and development, he conceded that the court's decisions had not attacked social ills directly. What the long years of community activism, coalition building, and the decisions did accomplish, however, was to provide the people of the state with "an engine for change."[11] In other words, resistance over the long years to giving urban children what they need has given rise to a force powerful enough to influence elections, legislation, and judicial decisions.

• The Living Wage Movement. This movement is another "engine for change," and one that has had a surprising history of growth in a brief period of time. The first living-wage ordinance, in Baltimore in 1994, affected so few workers—1,500 in all—that one would hardly have expected it to be the onset of a powerful national movement. Yet, by the summer of 2001, more than sixty municipalities had enacted living-wage laws, and campaigns were under way in seventy-two more, according to Bobbi Murray, the media director for the Los Angeles Living Wage Coalition.[12]

Most ordinances apply only to employees of companies that receive contracts or subsidies or both from a city. The result, in terms of the number of workers impacted by the ordinances, is small, for example, seven thousand in Los Angeles and thirty thousand in San Francisco. These limitations have turned out to be an advantage because they allowed for early successes, gave the campaigners experience that prepared them for more ambitious goals, to go beyond the limitation of companies that receive contracts or subsidies from their municipalities. Already, the movement has gone beyond that.

In Los Angeles, in May 2001, an alliance of twenty-nine community organizations and several unions (the Figueroa Corridor Coalition for Economic Justice) concluded an agreement with developers, including Rupert Murdoch, that in the expansion of the Staples Center, 70 percent of some 5,400 permanent jobs will pay a living wage. This will amount to $7.72 an hour with benefits or $8.97 without. The alternative could be a collective bargaining agreement.

New Orleans has been the scene of the greatest advance. There, a five-year battle led to a major victory. On 2 February 2002, a majority of voters approved a referendum to raise the city's minimum wage to one dollar over the federal level. A coalition of hotel and restaurant owners challenged the wage increase in court on the basis of a 1997 state law banning local wage standards. On 25 March, a civil court "ruled that law unconstitutional and dismissed the coalition's arguments as biased and speculative, based on no empirical study. The ruling gave weight to a study conducted by an economist working with ACORN who found that the wage increase would not adversely affect Louisiana's economy."[13] Businesses in New Orleans, the first city in the United States to raise the minimum wage for *all private employers*, are starting to raise their wages in anticipation of the effective date of the new law, May 2, 2002.

The successful campaign in New Orleans was carried out by a coalition composed of the Greater New Orleans AFL-CIO, the

Service Employees International Union Local 100 and ACORN, the nation's largest community organization of low- and moderate-income families, with over 120,000 member families organized into 600 neighborhood chapters in 45 cities across the country. Their success will benefit 50,000 workers and, of course, their families.[14]

These victories do not come easily. Members of the coalition must overcome internal divisiveness, win support of the public, gain the favorable attention of the media, and by use of political and legal methods, fend off attempts by some employer groups to side-track the campaign and undermine confidence in the coalition. Communities interested in seeking a living-wage ordinance can get advice from several organizations expert in organizing and campaigning. One resource is the Living Wage Resource Center, which was established by ACORN for the express purpose of providing that kind of help. Another resource is the Los Angeles Alliance for a New Economy, "considered by many to be one of the nation's state-of-the-art economic social justice organizations."[15]

The three examples given above—Public Education Network, Education Law Center, and the Living-Wage Movement—are mobilized to achieve the kinds of changes required to deal with the nation's educational, social, and economic problems. They are far from alone. Professional and scientific organizations like the enormous and influential American Psychological Association (APA) have taken a position on the personally and socially destructive effects of poverty.[16] In August 2000, the APA endorsed a resolution on poverty and socioeconomic status. After a lengthy and detailed documentation of the research evidence, the resolution presents APA's policy in seventeen declarations. Below are five of those most relevant to my proposals. They are preceded by the statement, "Therefore be it resolved that the American Psychological Association,"

8. Will support public policy that encourages access for all children to high-quality early childhood education and a high-quality public school education, better equipping individuals for self-sufficiency.
9. Will support public policy that ensures access to postsecondary education and training that allows working families to earn a self-sufficient wage to meet their family's needs.

10. Will support public policy and programs that ensure adequate income, access to sufficient food and nutrition, and affordable and safe housing for poor people, and all working families.
11. Will support public policy that ensures access to family-friendly jobs offering good quality health insurance, including coverage for comprehensive family planning, mental health and substance abuse services, flexible work schedules, and sufficient family and medical leave.
12. Will support public policy that ensures access to comprehensive family planning in private and public health insurance coverage.

Despite resolutions like APA's and the most reasoned arguments and scientific evidence supporting changes like those I have proposed, they will continue to encounter resistance. The next section explains in part the reasons for such resistance.

WHO MUST SURRENDER ADVANTAGES FOR THESE SYSTEMIC CHANGES?

Do these proposals add up to a policy of wealth redistribution? Indeed they do. It should be quickly added, however, that wealth redistribution is as American as apple pie; that it has been practiced in North America at least since the European explorers and settlers, mostly by force, took the land and natural resources of Native Americans. The lynching of African Americans, motivated by the desire on the part of some land-owning southerners to add to their holdings, is among the most hideous examples of redistribution.

Most redistribution has probably been legal in the sense that powerful lobbies, usually representing corporations and the affluent, succeeded in pressuring Congress and state legislatures to enact laws that favored those groups when corporate and individual income and estate taxes were under consideration. For example, the federal government bailed out investors after the savings and loan debacle not long before it decided that welfare recipients, many of them single mothers, after a specified period of time would be stricken from welfare lists and compelled to accept a job regardless of familial circumstances. After the tragic day of 11 September 2001, Congress bailed out the airline industry but not the thousands of employees fired by the airlines. In the 1990s, the states cut income taxes, to the advantage mainly of the rich, whereas sales taxes "which bear most heavily on lower and moderate-income families—by and large were never reversed" as Princeton economist Paul Krugman explained.[17]

On the other hand, some instances of wealth distribution were in the interest of the general population. The landmark legislation of the New Deal is arguably the outstanding example. President Roosevelt succeeded in getting Congress's approval because overwhelming numbers of Americans supported these measures and let that fact be known both by their votes and their own pressure groups, labor unions probably chief among them. Consider how difficult life would be for many millions of Americans without unemployment insurance and Social Security, Medicare, and Medicaid. These great advances in the interest of the mass of American people were resisted as forms of wealth redistribution by those who, over the course of American history, have been most expert in orchestrating that process on their own behalf.

The challenge, then, is the following: How to mobilize the millions in the United States who want a truly well-educated citizenry—and a more equitable society; how to join together, organize, and campaign, through every possible civil way, for the kind of coordinated, across-the-board systemic changes demanded by the proposals; and how to do that under conditions of wealth redistribution. The organizations to carry out such a process exist. They would need to adopt a unified objective and use the strength that comes from unity. From past experience, there is reason to expect that some affluent and many middle-class people will be sympathetic to the proposals. A few will be motivated by the high value they place on social justice; some will be motivated by self-interest, knowing that their children inhabit the same world as those in the third school system and cannot always be shielded from the ignorance, crime, and disease that the life circumstances of third system children breed. Still others of the middle class will join the coalition for reasons of a more painful self-interest: the shrinking of the middle class, as those in the lower ranges find themselves employed in "working-class" jobs. In reality, then, all segments of American society contain potential supporters.

WHAT TO EXPECT

The coalition sets out to achieve a first-class education for all with its eyes wide open. The goal is realizable, but only through the commitment and effort of countless people. Resistance to these changes will be powerful, and the controversy, bitter and probably vicious. We must not expect quick and easy victories. We should be prepared for a long campaign, with successes and setbacks along the way.

This goal—the proposals realized as the law of the land—is worth working toward. It's worth the time and effort, the sweat and tears that it will demand. It's worth modifying our social structure, just as it was worth doing that in the past. This may be stated in a different way. At the time when so-called welfare reform was instituted—a time when those on welfare, many of them single mothers, were told that a job would open up a better life for them—writer Barbara Ehrenreich set out to test that promise for herself. For some months she lived the life of a full-time worker on a poverty-level wage, residing in the squalid quarters she could afford from these wages and restricting herself to the limited budget her income allowed. She discovered that no matter how hard the impoverished women worked, they only sank deeper into poverty and debt. There was no way out. At the end of the book, *Nickel and Dimed: On (Not) Getting By in America,* reflecting on the fact that the poor are the nameless benefactors to everyone else, she quotes one of her coworkers at the restaurant where the two of them were waitresses: "you give and you give." In the final paragraph of the book, Ehrenreich says:

> Someday, of course—and I will make no predictions as to exactly when— they are bound to tire of getting so little in return and to demand to be paid what they're worth. There'll be a lot of anger when that day comes, and strikes and disruptions. But the sky will not fall, and we will all be better off for it in the end.[18]

Many of these women are mothers of children in the third school system. They need to be paid what they are worth, and, for the sake of their children, they need more than that: the fulfillment of all the proposals in this book.

When that objective is achieved, what a relief it will be to stop facing imaginary educational crises. Like Sisyphus, in trying one method after another to resolve the "crises," we have been rolling a huge stone up a hill trying to get to the top, only to see it roll back down every time, as one "solution to the school crisis" after another is hailed and then fails. There's no crisis. There is simply a great human need. At the very least, let us recognize and publicly acknowledge the true state of education in the country. Better yet, beyond that acknowledgment, let us begin the quest for a new and higher level of civilized life. To get there, yes, there will be strikes and strife, somewhat as in the thirties and sixties, but as Ehrenreich put it, "the sky will not fall, and we will all be better off for it in the end."[19]

ONE SCENARIO

The *American Psychologist*, the official journal of the American Psychological Association, devoted its millennial issue to "Happiness, Excellence, and Optimal Human Functioning." In the introductory article, "Positive Psychology," written by the two guest editors, one of them spoke about his personal struggle "to reconcile the twin imperatives that a science of human beings should include: to understand what *is* and what *could* be."[20] This book addressed at some length the first imperative, "what is." It then turned our attention to the second one, "what could be" in the form of proposals. Here is one version of fleshing out "what could be" in the struggle to win approval for the proposals.

What is the look of the future that "could be"? What is the look of the process of moving toward that future? The descriptions that follow in answer to those questions are suggestive, and very definitely *not prescriptive*.

There was ferment in this city and the country at large unlike anything experienced since the 1960s. This time the issue was not so much about race or gender, although these issues were part of the overarching one. Citizens in this city, like in many others in the country, were fed up. "Promises, promises—that's all we get. First during political campaigns and then in legislation that gets us nowhere, except lost years for our schoolchildren. Parents are poorly paid; many have no health insurance. All we have plenty of is worry. We demand much more than that."

Several private, nonprofit organizations, advocates for children and families, fed up with bloated political promises and repeated school failures, decided that the people had to take matters in their own hands. Working cooperatively, they shared the work of winning over mass organizations, many of them already on the verge of taking a strong position, such as labor unions, teacher associations, women's organizations of all kinds, religious, secular, ethnic, and professional associations. Slowly they made inroads, persuading citizens that foot-dragging on the part of politicians and the lobbies that prompted it was no longer acceptable. The few politicians, especially congressmen and -women, who leaned in their direction intellectually but who had been isolated in Congress, were now energized. Their voices were heard in Congress and, more important, in the media. New political leaders began to emerge from the ranks of those influenced by the new thinking about social and educational change. At every convention of labor unions and many other organizations, including now professional and scientific groups, the voices for change were prominent and influential.

Ordinary people—the men and women of America—didn't wait for conventions. They discussed the need for change, oftentimes at a high emotional pitch. The people needed, wanted, and demanded societal and educational reform. Their dissatisfaction, growing in intensity every month, reached a reluctant mass media only after the many organizations sharing the same discontent arranged public demonstrations at city hall. Not long afterward, joining with sister organizations around the state, the demonstrations were held on the steps of the state capitol.

The word was out that "enough is enough." Workers who formerly were passive about the miseries of life imposed on them had found their voice. Politicians who were favorably inclined but had formerly been cautious about expressing their views in the face of a silent working-class constituency, now began to speak out in favor of proposed changes. Not long afterward, slowly but surely, as the people let it be known that they would remain vigilant, that larger group of politicians who followed the polls joined their more liberal colleagues. A hard core group of politicians, egged on by lobbyists for particular industries in the area fearful of increased taxation, accused the coalition of trying to impose mob rule and, failing to discredit it by that aspersion, suggested that the coalition was being driven by radicals and was "un-American."

Some in the coalition were shaken by the character attacks and began to waver, but the majority stood fast. They counterattacked. With access to the press and TV—because the coalition and its objectives were too big to be ignored now—they revealed the underlying motives of the lobbyists and won more adherents.

The lobbyists used other methods to discredit the coalition. They searched records to find flaws in the character of the leaders. They quoted "anonymous sources" in efforts to divide the leadership and demoralize the supporters, but to no avail.

Over a period of years, elections brought successes to the coalition. Representatives solemnly sworn to the changes supported by the coalition were elected to city council, state legislature, and Congress. One by one, the proposals for change were introduced, and, one by one, they experienced setbacks before they were finally approved and signed into law. Then came further tests in the Supreme Court, tests that historians pointed out were reminiscent of the 1930s when New Deal legislation under President Roosevelt was threatened by a politically conservative set of justices. As in the 1930s, and with the national coalition in close watch, the president of the United States changed the tenor of the court and preserved new laws.

And so it came to pass that the nation that years earlier had enacted programs like Social Security and Medicare now established a system of guaranteed employment, with a living wage and health insurance. The days of economic and psychological insecurity, and the associated stresses and tensions in personal and family life, would in time be history. The changes were reflected both in the quality of family life, which was now so much more stable, and in the sense of well-being and self-respect experienced by individuals. Fewer parents felt like failures in life; more were quite free to walk into a school building with heads held high.

Another change in the country contributed to the positive outlook. After long and intensive national debate, the government, with the backing of most of the people, apologized to African Americans and Native Americans for the death and destruction and untold injuries to their very beings caused by the policies and practices of the country. The government apologized to women for the second-class citizenship to which they had been subjected during most of the nation's history. The debates brought to light the injustices of the present as well as the past. They also shone the light on American practices in regard to immigrants, past and present. Although the arguments brought forward seemed at times to tear the nation asunder, in the end they had a therapeutic effect and led to a healing of wounds and uniting of people unknown before. Like two spouses who have harbored hostile feelings covertly and finally opened up and shared their feelings, the dialogues that seemed to render relationships beyond repair actually had the opposite effect. They brought many people closer together. Race, for example, was no longer an unmentionable.

Had a modern day Rip Van Winkle gone to his long sleep before the coalition was formed, and wakened at the end of the process, he would not have recognized the community or the country, not because it was a Utopia—it was not that. There was still conflict, although most of it was resolved by nonviolent means. Couples still got divorced, although fewer than before. There were prisons and prisoners in them, but fewer now. Several things were strikingly new: a sense of repose that comes from feelings of fulfillment; peacefulness that comes from feelings of security; confidence that comes from self worth. The modern-day Rip, accustomed to a more frantic if not desperate pace, might at first find the new world to be less "exciting," at least until *his* values changed, too. Then he, like so many Americans, would give prime place to quality of life rather than wealth accumulation.

From the outset, the people in the community had their eyes on the schools. The local coalition, so much like the early nineteenth-century workingmen who gave equal weight to the education of their children and their own working conditions, placed educational reform high on the agenda. Changes were quick to follow. In the school district, a specialist in parenting education was appointed to head the Division of Parenting Education. The head, who reported to the superintendent of schools, was guided by an advisory board whose representatives included the head of pediatrics at the local hospital; a principal, a teacher and a parent representing each of the following levels: preschool, elementary, middle, and secondary; a librarian (expert in information retrieval and children's literature), nurse, psychologist, and social worker; and middle and high school students.

In collaboration with the head of pediatrics at the local hospital, and the school librarian, nurse, psychologist, and social worker, and with the advice of the advisory board, the head of the Division of Parenting Education, who was well versed in the literature on child development and parenting, developed a program of specialized parenting instruction for future parents. This program was prepared for pregnant women and, in two-parent families, their interested mates. The course of study places heavy emphasis on the adult role in fostering the all-round development of the infant and child, from pregnancy through all the years of schooling, with emphasis at the outset of the process of change on the early months and years. The program emphasizes the importance of social and verbal communication with the infant and child, of sensory and motor stimulation, and of reading aloud to and playing with the infant and child. The mode of instruction gives them opportunity to practice the various roles of parents as they relate to learning and development, so that they are actively involved in applying what they are learning. In brief, parents learn how children learn and develop, how they, themselves, must be actively involved in the process of development, and what criteria to use in selecting age-appropriate books, toys, and activities.

In collaboration with representatives of the school's academic departments, and with the advice of the advisory board, the head of Parenting Education developed a curriculum of studies for parents-as-teachers, covering the range of parenthood from infancy through secondary school. The content includes diverse aspects of the parental role, as it relates to learning and development. One important aspect concerns the crucial importance of reading to children on a regular basis and reading with them once they have begun to acquire reading skills. Parents are helped to develop the habits and skills of monitoring assigned studies and homework, and those who need it are taught some of the subject matter required to assist their elementary school children with their school assignments.

Active participation of parents was seen as paramount to the success of the proposed programs, and especially those parents of poorly performing children, who are most in need. Members of the coalition involved in school reform asked themselves why those parents should be expected to attend such courses, not to speak of participating actively. There were good reasons to have such doubts in the past. But what about the present?

Parents experienced a sense of security not known before among those of their social class. The changes already enumerated that helped transform the attitudes and outlook of parents—parenting education, guaranteed employment, living wage, health insurance, and, for some, the national apology—had a reciprocal effect on another important development, parental involvement in the education of their children in school. Educational policy called for more parent involvement, and parents, feeling so much more secure and assured, were quite prepared to participate. Many more parents welcomed the opportunities to help shape policy, volunteer to serve on committees, assist in class, raise money for special needs, and attend meetings in school, including those about their own children. Teachers, who had also experienced a renewal as a result of national recognition of their role and their need for adequate compensation, welcomed the new involvement as much as the parents.

Teachers and parents, along with administrators and some student representatives, became major voices in the shaping of educational policy. They undertook to become knowledgeable about the innovative programs that had been spurred by the school reform movement. Patiently, they reviewed the philosophy of each program and the empirical evidence in support of a given program's effectiveness. They selected one program and modified it, influenced both by several other reform programs and their own local needs. After careful preparation—of administrators, teachers, parents, and students—they introduced their modified program and established a system of review and assessment over the next five years.

A new outlook on schools was one of the most remarkable changes of all, in the local community as in the nation. Quality education was no longer just for the elite. In the truer democracy that was evolving, it was everyone's birthright. The modifications made in schools and universities that trained educational personnel went hand in hand with the changing consciousness. Each fueled the other in a seemingly unending process of human development.

All of this occurred and the sky did not fall.

NOTES

1. "The Fight for a Sound Education," *New York Times*, 11 September 2000, 24(A).

2. Anne-Emanuelle Birn, "Now Use Medicare for Universal Coverage," Letter to Editor, *New York Times,* 1 July 1997, 20(A).

3. www.infobeat.com (accessed 5 May 2002).

4. "Resources for Public Elementary and Secondary Schools, 1997–1998," *World Almanac 2000* (Mahwah, N.J.: World Almanac Books), 249.

5. Clyde Haberman, "100 Years Ago, a Penny Bought a World," *New York Times,* 1 January 2000, 37 (Millennium Section).

6. Merle Curti, *The Social Ideas of American Educators,* 2d ed. (Totowa, N.J.: Littlefield, Adams, 1971), 237.

7. "Public Education Network," *Connections* 8, no. 2 (Fall 2001): back cover.

8. Wendy D. Puriefoy, "President's Message," *Connections* 8, no. 1 (Winter 2001): 1–3, 2.

9. Education Law Center: "Mission and History," www.edlawcenter.org (accessed 16 April 2002).

10. Cynthia Rice and David Nash, "White Paper on Abbott and Early Childhood Program Aid Implementation," Newark: Early Care and Education Coalition, undated, 2.

11. David Sciarra, answer to a question at the Public Education Institute's Roundtable on Advocacy Groups, Rutgers University, 5 April 2002.

12. Bobbi Murray, "Living Wage Comes of Age," *Nation* 273, no. 4 (23–30 July 2001): 24–28.

13. "Living Wage and ACORN." acorn.org/acorn10/livingwage/neworleans.html (accessed 16 April 2002).

14. Murray, "Living Wage Comes of Age," 26.

15. Murray, "Living Wage Comes of Age," 24.

16. American Psychological Association, "Resolution on Poverty and Socioeconomic Status," 6 August 2000. Washington, D.C.: American Psychological Association Annual Meeting.

17. Paul Krugman, "As the States Go, So Does the Nation," *Arizona Daily Star,* 12 January 2002, 11(B).

18. Barbara Ehrenreich, *Nickel and Dimed: On (Not) Getting By in America* (New York: Holt, 2001), 221.

19. Ehrenreich, *Nickel and Dimed,* 221.

20. Martin Seligman and Mihaly Csikszenmihalyi, "Positive Psychology," *American Psychologist* 54, no. 1 (January 2000): 5–14, 7.

REFERENCES

Abbott v. Burke, 119 N.J.287 (1990), 342–343.

Abbott, Robert D., Julie O'Donnell, J. David Hawkins, Karl G. Hill, Richard Kosterman, and Richard F. Catalano. "Changing Teaching Practices to Promote Achievement and Bonding to School." *American Journal of Orthopsychiatry* 68, no. 4, (October 1998): 542–552.

American Association of University Women. *Gender Gaps: Where Schools Still Fail Our Children.* New York: Marlowe, 1999.

American Psychological Association. "Resolution on Poverty and Socioeconomic Status." 6 August 2000. Washington, D.C.: American Psychological Association Annual Meeting.

Anderson, Ariel, and Andrea B. Smith. "Community Building with Parents." *Kappa Delta Pi Record* 35, no. 4 (Summer 1999): 158–161.

Anderson, Gary L. "Toward Authentic Participation: Deconstructing the Discourses of Participatory Reforms in Education." *American Educational Research Journal* 35, no. 4 (1998): 571–603.

Anderson, Mary. Assignments for "Apple Project: A Celebration of Choice," and "The Incredible World Famous Monster Project." Fourth-grade class for gifted and talented students, Lineweaver Elementary School, Tucson, Arizona, 2002.

Angell, Marcia. "Insufficient Credits." *Health Letter* 17, no. 11 (November 2001):1–3. Reprinted from *American Prospect* (September 2001).

Anyon, Jean. *Ghetto Schooling: A Political Economy of Urban Educational Reform.* New York: Teachers College Press, 1997.

Aristotle. *Politics, 1.* In *The Great Quotations*, edited by George Seldes. New York: Lyle Stuart, 1960.

Atlas, James. "Making the Grade: Going to Private School Involves Hard Work for the Parents." *New Yorker* 73, no. 8 (April 1997): 34–39.

Ball, Eileen W. "Phonological Awareness: What's Important and to Whom?" *Reading and Writing* 5, no. 2 (June 1993): 141–159.

Bargh, John A., Mark Chen, and Lara Burrows. "Automaticity of Social Behavior: Effects of Trait Construct and Stereotype Activation on Action." *Journal of Personality and Social Psychology* 71, no. 2 (August 1998): 230–244.

Battistich, Victor, Daniel Solomon, Marilyn Watson, and Eric Schaps. "Caring School Communities," *Educational Psychologist* 32, no. 3 (Summer 1997): 137–151.

Behrman, J. R., and P. Taubman. "Birth Order, Schooling, and Earnings." *Journal of Labour Economics* 4 (1986): 121–145.

Belluck, Pam. "Gang Gunfire May Chase Chicago Children from their School." *New York Times*, 17 November 1997, 1(A), 21(A)

Bennett, William J., Chester E. Finn Jr., and John T. E. Cribb Jr. *The Educated Child: A Parent's Guide from Preschool through Eighth Grade.* New York: Free Press, 1999.

Benning, Victoris. "MSPAP, SOL Ideals as Different as Their Acronyms." *Washington Post,* 14 May 2000, 1 and 9(C).

Berliner, David C., and Bruce J. Biddle. *The Manufactured Crisis: Myths, Fraud, and the Attack on America's Public Schools.* Reading, Mass.: Perseus Books, 1995.

Binet, Alfred. *Les Idees Modernes sur les Enfantes* (Paris: Flammarion, 1909). Cited in J. McVeigh Hunt, *Intelligence and Experience.* New York: Ronald Press, 1961.

Birn, Anne-Emanuelle. "Now Use Medicare for Universal Coverage." *New York Times,* 1 July 1997, 20(A).

Blakeslee, Sandra. "A Decade of Discovery Yields a Shock about the Brain." *New York Times,* 4 January 2000, 1(F).

"Blaming the Victim." *New York Times,* 26 June 2002, 22(A).

Bracey, Gerald W. "The Third Bracey Report on the Condition of Public Education." *Phi Delta Kappan* (October 1993): 104–117.

———. "International Comparisons and the Condition of American Education." *Educational Researcher* 25, no. 1 (January–February 1996): 5–11.

———. "The TIMSS 'Final Year' Study and Report: A Critique." *Educational Researcher* 29, no. 4 (May 2000): 4–10.

Brenner, M. H. *Estimating the Societal Costs of National Economic Policy: Implications for Mental and Physical Health and Criminal Violence.* Report for the Joint Economic Committee of Congress. Washington, D.C.: U.S. Government Printing Office, 1976.

Brigham, Carl. *A Study of American Intelligence.* Princeton, N.J.: Princeton University Press, 1923.

Britannica Book of the Year, 1996. Chicago: Encyclopedia Britannica, 1996.

Brody, Nathan. *Intelligence.* San Diego: Academic Press, 1992.

Brown, Ann. "Mighty Asset: School Volunteers." *Arizona Daily Star,* 5 January 1998, 1(D).

Brunner, Borgna, ed. *Time Almanac 2002.* Boston: Information Please, 2002.

Bureau of Labor Statistics. www.bls.gov/emp/emptab4.htm (accessed 15 March 2002).

Burkham, David T., Valerie E. Lee, and Betty Smerdon, "Gender and Science Learning Early in High School: Subject Matter and Laboratory Experiences." *American Educational Research Journal* 34, no. 2 (Summer 1997): 297–331.

Burris, Beverly H. *No Room at the Top: Underemployment and Alienation in the Corporation.* New York: Praeger, 1993.

Ceci, Stephen J., and Wendy M. Williams. "Schooling, Intelligence and Income." *American Psychologist* 52, no. 10 (October 1997): 1051–1058.

Centolanza, Louis R. "The State of the Schools: Consequences of a Curricular Intervention, 1972–1980." Ed.D. diss., Rutgers University, 1986.

"Chapter 19A: Implementation of Court Decision in *Abbott v. Burke,*" Public Law 1998, c. 45, effective July 1, 1998 (Annual Appropriations Act, Fiscal year 1998–1999), New Jersey.

Cherlin, Andrew. "Work Life and Marital Satisfaction." In *Divorce and Separation,* edited by George Levinger and Oliver C. Moles. New York: Basic Books, 1979.

Christman, Jolley B., and Pat Macpherson. *The Five School Study: Restructuring Philadelphia's Comprehensive High Schools.* Philadelphia: Research for Action, 1996.

Coles, Gerald. *Reading Lessons: The Debate over Literacy.* New York: Hill and Wang, 1998.

Comer, James P. *Waiting for a Miracle.* New York: E. P. Dutton, 1997.

Crocker, Jennifer, Brenda Major, and Claude Steele. "Social Stigma." In *Handbook of Social Psychology,* edited by Daniel T. Gilbert, Susan T. Fiske, and Gardner Lindzey, 504–553. New York: McGraw Hill, 1998.

Curti, Merle. *The Social Ideas of American Educators.* 2d ed. Totowa, N.J.: Littlefield, Adams and Co. 1974.

"Dismal Grades for Schools." *Arizona Daily Star,* 10 January 1998, 12(A).

Dreifus, Claudia. "A Conversation with Benjamin Carson: A Pioneer at a Frontier: The Brain of a Child." *New York Times,* 4 January 2000, 7(F).

Education Law Center. "Mission and History." www.edlawcenter.org. (accessed 17 April 2002).

"Education Tax Breaks Miss Target: The Poor." *Arizona Daily Star,* 24 March 2002, 1 and 9(A).

Ehrenreich, Barbara. *Nickel and Dimed: On (Not) Getting By in America.* New York: Holt, 2001.

Einstein, Albert. *Essays in Science.* New York: Philosophical Library, 1934.

Eisenberg, Michael, and Robert Berkowitz. *Helping with Homework: A Parent's Guide to Information Problem-Solving.* ERIC monograph, June 1996, AN: ED418699.

Elmore, Richard F. "The Origins and Problems of Education Reform in the United States." In *Who Chooses? Who Loses? Culture, Institutions, and the Unequal Effects of School Choice,* edited by Bruce Fuller and Richard F. Elmore, with Gary Oldfield. New York: Free Press, 1996.

Epstein, J. L. "School/Family/Community Partnership: Caring for the Children We Share." *Phi Delta Kappan* 76, no. 9 (September 1995): 701–712, 155.

Erickson, Robert. "Explaining Change in Education Inequality—Economic Security and School Reforms." In *Can Education be Equalized? The Swedish Case in Comparative Perspective,* edited by Robert Erikson and Jan O. Jonsson. Boulder, Colo.: Westview Press.

Erikson, Robert, and Jan O. Jonsson. "Explaining Class Inequality in Education: The Swedish Test Case." In *Can Education be Equalized? The Swedish Case in Comparative Perspective,* edited by Robert Erikson and Jan O. Jonsson. Boulder, Colo.: Westview Press, 1996.

———. "The Swedish Context: Educational Reform and Long-Term Change in Educational Inequality." In *Can Education Be Equalized? The Swedish Case in Comparative Perspective,* edited by Robert Erikson and Jan O. Jonsson. Boulder, Colo.: Westview Press, 1996.

Erikson, Robert, and Jan O. Jonsson, eds. *Can Education be Equalized? The Swedish Case in Comparative Perspective.* Boulder, Colo.: Westview Press, 1996.

Feuerstein, Reuven. *The Dynamic Assessment of Retarded Performers.* Baltimore: University Park Press, 1979.

Feuerstein, Reuven, and Mildred B. Hoffman. "Mediating Cognitive Processes to the Retarded Performer—Rationale, Goals, and Nature of Intervention." In *Promoting Cognitive Growth over the Life Span,* edited by Milton Schwebel, Charles A. Maher, and Nancy S. Fagley. Hillsdale, N.J.: Lawrence Erlbaum Associates, 1990.

"Fight for a Sound Education." *New York Times,* 11 September 2000, 24(A).

Finders, Margaret, and Cynthia Lewis. "Why Some Parents Don't Come to School." *Educational Leadership* 51, no. 8 (May 1994): 50–54.

Firestone, William A., Margaret E. Goertz, and Gary Natriello. *The Struggle for Fiscal Reform and Educational Change in New Jersey*. New York: Teachers College Press, 1997.

Flynn, James R. "Massive IQ Gains in 14 Nations: What IQ Tests Really Measure." *American Psychologist* 42, no. 2. (February 1987): 171–191.

Franklin, Anderson J., and Nancy Boyd-Franklin. "Invisibility Syndrome: A Clinical Model of the Effects of Racism on African-American Males," *American Journal of Orthopsychiatry* 70, no.1 (January 2000), 33–42.

Franklin, Benjamin. *Memoirs of the Life & Writings of Benjamin Franklin*. London and Toronto: J. M. Dent and Sons, 1908.

Galtung, Johan. "Violence, Peace and Peace Research." *Journal of Peace Research* 6, no. 3 (August 1969), 167–191.

Gandal, Matt. *Making Standards Matter: A Fifty State Progress Report on Efforts to Raise Academic Standards*. Washington, D.C.: American Federation of Teachers, Educational Issues Department, 1995.

Gardner, Howard. *Frames of Mind: The Theory of Multiple Intelligences*. New York: Basic Books, 1983.

Goertz, Margaret E. *The Development and Implementation of the Quality Education Act of 1990*. New Brunswick, N.J.: Consortium for Policy Research in Education, Eagleton Institute of Politics, Rutgers University, 1992.

Goldhaber, Dan D. "School Choice: An Examination of the Empirical Evidence on Achievement, Parental Decision Making, and Equity." *Educational Researcher* 28, no. 8 (November 1999): 16–25.

Goodnough, Abby. "'S' is for Satisfactory, not for Satisfied on Teacher's Sentimental Journey." *New York Times*, 1 July 2001, 1 and 22 (Metro Section).

"Gore Pledges Health Plan for all Children." *New York Times*, 9 September 1999, 1 and 18(A).

Greer, Colin. *The Great School Legend*. New York: Basic Books, 1972.

Gruber, Howard E., and Lucien Richard. "Active Work and Creative Thought in University Classrooms." In *Promoting Cognitive Growth over the Life Span*, edited by Milton Schwebel, Charles Maher, and Nancy Fagley. Mahwah, N.J.: Lawrence Erlbaum, 1990.

Haberman, Clyde. "100 Years Ago, a Penny Bought a World." *New York Times*, 1 January 2000, 37 (Millennium Section).

Halstead, Ted. "Rich School, Poor School." *New York Times*, 6 January 2001, www.nytimes.com/2002/01/08 (accessed 8 January 2002).

Henig, Jeffrey R., Richard C. Hula, Marion Orr, and Desiree S. Pedescleaux. *The Color of School Reform: Race, Politics, and the Challenge of Urban Education*. Princeton: Princeton University Press, 1999.

Henry, Tamara. "Study: Arts Education Has Academic Effect." *USA Today*, 20 May 2002, 6(D).

Herbert, Bob. "Violence That Won't Let Go." *New York Times*, 27 August 2001, 15(A).

Hertzman, Clyde. "Health and Human Society." *American Scientist* 89, no. 6 (November–December 2001): 538–545.

Hewison, Jenny. "The Long-Term Effectiveness of Parental Involvement in Reading: A Follow-Up of the Haringey Project." *British Journal of Educational Psychology* 58, 1988, 184–190.

Hirsch, E. D., Jr. *Cultural Literacy: What Every American Needs to Know*. New York: Vintage Books, 1988.

———. *The Schools We Need and Why We Don't Have Them*. New York: Doubleday, 1996.

Holloway, Lynette. "Low Pay and Retirements Aggravate Teacher Shortage." *New York Times*, 5 January 2000, 8(B).

Hoover-Dempsey, Kathleen V., et al. "Parental Involvement in Homework." *Educational Psychologist* 36, no. 3 (Summer 2001): 195–209. www.infobeat.com (accessed on 10 April 2002).

Hurley, Eric A., Anne Chamberlain, Robert E. Slavin, and Nancy Madden. "Effects of Success for All on TAAS Reading: A Texas Statewide Evaluation." *Phi Delta Kappan* 82, no. 10 (June 2001): 750–756.

Ivins, Molly. "Not Economic 'Stimulus' but 'Security'." *Arizona Daily Star*, 10 January 2002, 7(B).

Jacobs, Joanne. "Even Mary Poppins Wouldn't Work for Child-Care Wages Offered in the U.S." *Arizona Daily Star*, 8 November 1997, 17(A).

Jeffords, Jim. "Back to School." *New York Times*, 13 December 2001, 39(A).

Kagan, Jerome. *The Nature of the Child*. New York: Basic Books, 1994.

Keating, Pamela. "Striving for Sex Equity in Schools." In *Access to Knowledge: The Continuing Agenda for Our Nation's Schools*, edited by John I. Goodlad and Pamela Keating. New York: College Entrance Examination Board, 1994.

Kellaghan, Thomas, et al. *The Home Environment and School Learning: Promoting Parental Involvement in the Education of Children*. San Francisco: Jossey-Bass, 1993.

Kempermann, Gerd, and Fred H. Gage. "New Nerve Cells for the Adult Brain." *Scientific American* 280, no. 5 (May 1999): 48–53.

Kingsolver, Barbara. *High Tide in Tucson: Essays from Now or Never*. New York: HarperCollins, 1995.

Kozol, Jonathan. *Savage Inequalities: Children in America's Schools*. New York: Crown Publishers, 1991.

Kremer, Barbara. *Parent Education: Abstract Bibliography*. Champaign, Ill.: ERIC Clearinghouse on Early Childhood Education, October 1971 AN: ED056782.

Krugman, Paul. "As the States Go, So Does the Nation." *Arizona Daily Star*, 12 January 2002.

Lareau, Annette. *Home Advantage: Social Class and Parental Intervention in Elementary Education*. New York: Falmer, 1989.

Levin, Henry M. *Accelerated Schools for At-Risk Students*. New Brunswick, N.J.: Center for Policy Research in Education, 1991.

———. *Building School Capacity for Effective Teacher Empowerment: Applications to Elementary Schools with At-Risk Students*. New Brunswick, N.J.: Center for Policy Research in Education, 1991.

———. "Learning from Accelerated Schools." Stanford: Stanford University, 1993.

———. "Accelerated Visions." *Teacher-To-Teacher* 5, no. 1 (1996): 1, 13.

Linn, Marcia C., Catherine Lewis, Ineko Tsuchida, and Nancy Butler Songer. "Beyond Fourth-Grade Science: Why Do U.S. and Japanese Students Diverge?" *Educational Researcher* 29, no. 3 (April 2000): 4–14.

"Living Wage and ACORN." acorn.org/acorn10/livingwage/neworleans .htm (accessed 16 April 2002).

Lopez, Geraldo, Jay D. Scribner, and Kanya Mahitivanichcha. "Redefining Parental Involvement: Lessons from High-Performing Migrant-Impacted Schools." *American Educational Research Journal* 38, no. 2 (Summer 2001): 253–288.

Lott, Bernice. "Low-Income Parents and the Public Schools." *Journal of Social Issues* 57, no. 2 (Summer 2001): 247–259.

Lown, Bernard. "A Developing World Fellowship." *Lown Forum* (Summer 2001): 1, 6–8.

Lucas, Samuel Roundfield. *Tracking Inequality: Stratification and Mobility in American High Schools*. New York: Teachers College Press, 1999.

Magdoff, Harry. "Remarks on Receiving the NECLCT Tom Paine Award." *Monthly Review* 46, no. 9 (September 1995): 32–36.

Maslow, Abraham. *Motivation and Personality*, 2d ed. New York: Harper and Row, 1987.

Massell, Diane, Michael Kirst, and Margaret Hoppe. *Persistence and Change: Standards-Based Reform in Nine States*. Philadelphia: Consortium for Policy Research in Education, University of Pennsylvania, 1997.

Mazurana, Dyan, and Susan McKay. "Women, Girls and Structural Violence: A Global Analysis," 130–138. In *Peace, Conflict and Violence: Peace*

Psychology for the 21st Century, edited by Daniel J. Christie, Richard V. Wagner, and Deborah Du Nann Winter. Upper Saddle River, N.J.: Prentice Hall, 2001.

McLoyd, Vonnie. "Socioeconomic Disadvantage and Child Development." *American Psychologist* 53, no. 2 (February 1998): 185–204.

Meier, Deborah. *The Power of Their Ideas: Lessons for America from a Small School in Harlem*. Boston: Beacon, 1995.

Mendoza, Monica. "State Schools Get a 'D': It's Unfair, Officials Say." *Arizona Daily Star*, 9 January 1998, 1 and 3(A).

Metcalf, Stephen. "Reading between the Lines: The New Education Law Is a Victory for Bush—and for His Corporate Allies." *Nation* (12 February 2000): 18–22.

"Michigan: Schools Make Cuts." *New York Times*, 29 August 2001, 18(A).

Millsap, Mary Ann, Anne Chase, Dawn Obeidallah, Alina Perez-Smith, Nancy Brigham, and Karen Johnston. "Evaluation of Detroit's Comer Schools and Families Initiative." Final Report. Detroit: The Skillman Foundation, 17 April 2000.

Mitchell, Samuel. *Reforming Educators: Teachers, Experts, and Advocates*. Westport, Conn.: Praeger, 1998.

Morrow, E. Frederic. *Way Down South Up North*. Philadelphia: Pilgrim Press, 1973.

Murray, Bobbi. "Living Wage Comes of Age." *Nation* 273, no. 4 (July 2001): 24–28.

Myers, David J., and Edward Diener. "Who Is Happy." *Psychological Science* 6, no. 1 (January 1995): 10–19.

National Education Goals Panel, *The National Education Goals Report: Building a Nation of Learners*. Washington, D.C.: National Education Goals Panel, 1994.

"Not Meeting the Goal." *Arizona Daily Star*, 27 March 2002, 6(B).

"Now, Who Speaks for Urban Children? The Supreme Court Turns Its Back on Poor Districts." *Home News Tribune*, 22 May 1998, 14(A).

Nunnery, J., et al. *An Assessment of Success for All Program Component Configuration Effects on the Reading Achievement of At-risk First Grade Students*. Baltimore: Johns Hopkins University, Center for Research on the Education of Students Placed at Risk, 1996.

"Occupations with the Largest Job Growth, 2000–2010," table 4, in "Occupational Employment Projections to 2010." *Monthly Labor Review* (November 2001) www.bls.gov/emp/emptab4.htm (accessed 15 March 2002).

Ogbu, John. "Low School Performance as an Adaptation: The Case of Blacks in Stockton, California." In *Minority Status and Schooling: A Comparative*

Study of Immigrant and Involuntary Minorities, edited by Margaret A. Gibson and John Ogbu. New York: Garland, 1991.

Ogletree, Charles J., Jr. "Litigating the Legacy of Slavery." *New York Times,* 31 March 2002, 9(A).

Olson, David R., Nancy Torrance, and Angela Hildyard, eds. *Literacy, Language, and Learning.* New York: Cambridge University Press, 1985.

Olson, Lynn. "New Study Finds Low Achievement in City Schools." *Education Week* (10 December 1997): 35–36.

Organization for Economic Cooperation and Development (OECD). *Education at a Glance: OECD Indicators.* Paris: OECD, 1998.

Orland, Martin. "Demographics of Disadvantage: Intensity of Childhood Poverty and Its Relationship to Educational Achievement." In *Access to Knowledge: The Continuing Agenda for Our Nation's Schools*, edited by John I. Goodlad and Pamela Keating, New York: College Entrance Examination Board, 1994.

Ostlund, Karen, and Kathy Fite. "Change and Children." *Science and Children* 25, no. 4 (January 1988): 20–24.

Patterson, Sharon. *Increasing Parental Involvement in Grades One, Four, and Five in a Rural Elementary School.* Ph.D. diss., Nova Southern University, 1994.

Perez-Peña, Richard. "Court Reverses Finance Ruling in City Schools," *New York Times,* 26 June 2002, 1(A), 4(B).

Peterson, Christopher, Steven F. Maier, and Martin E.P. Seligman. *Learned Helplessness: A Theory for the Age of Personal Control.* New York: Oxford University Press, 1993.

Phillips, Meredith. "What Makes Schools Effective? A Comparison of the Relationship of Community Climate and Academic Achievement and Attendance during Middle School." *American Educational Research Journal* 34, no. 4 (Winter 1997): 633–662.

Pines, Maya. "Recession Is Linked to Far-Reaching Psychological Harm." *New York Times,* 6 April 1982, 1–2 (C).

"Privatization and Failing Schools." *New York Times*, 30 June 2000, 24(A).

"Public Education Network." *Connections* 8, no. 2 (Fall 2001).

Purcell-Gates, Victoria. "Lexical and Syntactic Knowledge of Written Narrative Held by Well-Read-to Kindergartners and Second Graders." ERIC Report, 1986, AN: ED056782.

Puriefoy, Wendy D. "President's Message." *Connections* 8, no. 1 (Winter 2001).

Rathvon, Nathalie. *Effective School Interventions.* New York: Guilford, 1999.

Ravitch, Diane, ed. *Brookings Papers on Educational Policy.* Washington D.C.: Brookings Institution Press, 1998.

Rawls, John. *A Theory of Justice*. Cambridge, Mass.: Harvard University Press, 1971.

"Realistic School Standards." *New York Times*, 20 March 1999, 20(A).

"Report and Decision of Remand Court," Superior Court of New Jersey, Chancery Division-Mercer County, S. Ct. Docket No. M-622-96, 22 January 1998.

"Research Background on Accelerated Schools." *Accelerated Schools Project Research and Evaluation Bulletin*, November 2001 www.acceleratedschools .net (accessed 20 April 2002).

"Resources for Public Elementary and Secondary Schools. 1997–1998." *World Almanac 2000*. Mahwah, N.J.: World Almanac Books.

Rey, Cheryl de la, and Ingrid Owens. "Perceptions of Psychological Healing and the Truth and Reconciliation Commission in South Africa." *Peace and Conflict: Journal of Peace Psychology* 4, no. 3 (1998): 257–270.

Rice, Cynthia, and David Nash. "White Paper on Abbott and Early Childhood Program Aid Implementation." Newark: Early Care and Education Coalition, undated.

Roberts, Harold S. *Roberts' Dictionary of Industrial Relations*. 4th ed. Washington, D.C.: Bureau of National Affairs, 1993.

Robinson, Randall. *The Debt: What America Owes to Blacks*. New York: E. P. Dutton, 2000.

Robinson v. Cahill, 69 N.J. 449 (1976) 459–460.

———. 62 N.J. 473 (1973).

Romano, Jay. "Approaches to Killing Roaches." *New York Times*, 3 August 1997, 3 (Section 9).

Rosenthal, Robert, and Lenore Jacobson. *Pygmalion in the Classroom: Teacher Expectation and Pupils' Intellectual Development*. New York: Holt, Rinehart, and Winston, 1968.

Ross, S. M., W. L. Sanders, and S. P. Wright. *An Analysis of Tennessee Value Added Assessment (TVAAS) Performance Outcomes of Roots and Wings Schools from 1995–1997*. Memphis: University of Memphis, Center for Research in Educational Policy, 1998.

Rothstein, Richard. "Seeing Achievement Gains by an Attack on Poverty." *New York Times*, 7 March 2001, 9(B).

Sarason, Seymour. *Charter Schools: Another Flawed Educational Reform?* New York: Teachers College Press, 1998.

Schiefelbein, Ernesto. "Trends in the Provision and Design of Self-learning Models of Education." In *International Handbook of Education and Development: Preparing Students and Nations for the Twenty-First Century*, edited by William K. Cummings and Noel F. McGuin. Oxford: Pergamon, 1997.

Schlesinger, Arthur M., Jr. *The State of the Union Messages of the Presidents.* New York: Chelsea House, 1967.

Schwebel, Andrew, Bernice Schwebel, Carol Schwebel, and Milton Schwebel. *The Student Teacher's Handbook.* Mahwah, N.J.: Erlbaum, 1996.

Schwebel, Milton. "Educational Pie in the Sky." *Nation* 258, no. 17 (2 May 1994): 501–502.

———. "Job Insecurity as Structural Violence: Implications for Destructive Intergroup Conflict." *Peace and Conflict: Journal of Peace Psychology* 3, no. 4 (1997): 333–352.

Schwebel, Sara. Syllabus for the course, "Learning Thinking Skills in a Private School Course on Twentieth Century American Experience," 1999.

———. Personal communication, e-mail, 27 June 2001.

Sciarra, David. Answer to a question at the Public Education Institute's Roundtable on Advocacy Groups, Rutgers University, 5 April 2002.

Scribner, Sylvia, and Michael Cole. *The Psychology of Literacy.* Cambridge, Mass.: Harvard University Press, 1981.

Seligman, Martin, and Mihaly Csikszenmihalyi. "Positive Psychology: An Introduction." *American Psychologist* 54, no. 1 (January 2000): 5–14.

Sengupta, Somina. "A Traditional Career Gains New Class." *New York Times,* 3 August 1997, 48 (Section 4A).

Shankle, William R., et al. "Postnatal Doubling of Neuron Number in the Developing Human Cerebral Cortex between 15 Months and 6 Years." *Journal of Theoretical Biology* 191, no. 2 (March 1998): 115–140.

Sherif, Muzafer, and Hadley Cantril. *The Psychology of Ego-Involvements, Social Attitudes and Identifications.* New York: Wiley, 1947.

Shipler, David. *A Country of Strangers: Blacks and Whites in America.* New York: Knopf, 1997.

Shouse, Roger C. "Academic Press and Sense of Community: Conflict, Congruence, and Implications for Student Achievement." *Social Psychology of Education* I, no. 1 (1996): 47–68.

Silvestri, George T. "Occupational Employment to 2005." *Monthly Labor Review* 118, no. 11 (November 1995): 60–84, 79.

Sizer, Theodore R. *Horace's School: Redesigning the American High School.* Boston: Houghton Mifflin, 1982.

———. *Horace's Compromise: The Dilemma of the American High School.* Boston: Houghton Mifflin, 1984.

———. *Horace's Hope: What Works for the American High School.* Boston: Houghton Mifflin, 1996.

Slade, Margot. "First the Schoolhouse, Then the Home." *New York Times,* 8 March 1998, 1 and 4 (Section 11).

Slavin, Robert A., and Nancy A. Madden. *Success for All/Roots & Wings: Summary of Research on Achievement Outcomes*. Baltimore: Johns Hopkins University, Center for Research on the Education of Students Placed At Risk, January 2002.

Slavin, Robert A., Nancy A. Madden, and Barbara A. Wasik. "Roots and Wings: Universal Excellence in Elementary Education." In *Bold Plans for School Restructuring*, edited by Sam Stringfield, Steven Ross, and Lana Smith. Mahwah, N.J.: Erlbaum, 1996.

Smith, Vern. "Debating the Wages of Slavery." *Newsweek*, 27 August 2001, 20–25.

Spock, Benjamin, and Michael B. Rothenberg. *Dr. Spock's Baby and Child Care*. New York: E. P. Dutton, 1992.

Staples, Brent. "Schoolyard Brawl." *New York Times*, 4 January 1998, 49(A).

Steinberg, Laurence. "Standards Outside the Classroom." In *Brookings Papers on Educational Policy*, edited by Diane Ravitch. Washington, D.C.: Brookings Institution Press, 1998.

Steinberg, Laurence, with Bradford Brown and Sanford M. Dornbusch. *Beyond the Classroom: Why School Reform Has Failed and What Parents Need to Do*. New York: Simon and Schuster, 1996.

Sternberg, Robert. "Abilities Are Forms of Developing Expertise." *Educational Researcher* 27, no. 3 (April 1998): 11–19.

Stief, Elizabeth. *The Role of Parent Education in Achieving School Readiness*. Washington, D.C.: National Governors' Association, 1993.

Stringfield, Sam, Amanda Datnow, Geoffrey Borman, and Laura Rachuba. *National Evaluation of Core Knowledge Sequence Implementation: Final Report*. Center for Social Organization of Schools, Johns Hopkins University, 1999. The full report is available in electronic format only: coreknow@coreknowledge.org.

"Students Thrive in Schools that Promote Intellectual Rigor and Personalize Learning," A Report on the Coalition of Essential Schools' Work with Comprehensive School Reform Demonstration (CSRD) Schools in Ohio, Maine, Massachusetts, and Michigan, preliminary draft, 25 March 2002. jpattaphongse@essentialschools.org (accessed 26 March 2002).

Svensson, A. *Relative Achievement: School Performance in Relation to Intelligence, Sex and Home Environment*. Stockholm: Almquist and Wiksell, 1971.

Tapia, Sarah Tully. "Tucson Charter Schools Allow Choice." *Arizona Daily Star*, 6 January 1998, 1(C).

Taylor, Gracy. *Core Knowledge: Its Impact on Instructional Practices and Student Learning*. Ed.D. diss., Nova Southeastern University, March 2001.

Tirozzi, Gerald N., and Gabriela Uro. "Education Reform in the United States: National Policy in Support of Local Efforts for School Improvement." *American Psychologist* 52, no. 3 (March 1997): 241–249.

Traub, James, "The Test Mess." *New York Times,"* 7 April 2002, Section 6 (Magazine), 46–51, 60, 78.

United States National Commission on Excellence in Education. *A Nation at Risk: The Imperative for Educational Reform: A Report to the Nation and the Secretary of Education, United States Department of Education, by the National Commission on Excellence in Education.* Washington, D.C.: The Commission, 1983.

Useem, Elizabeth. "Middle Schools and Math Groups: Parents' Involvement in Children's Placement." *Sociology of Education* 65, no. 4 (October 1992): 263–279.

Valian, Virginia. "Running in Place." In *Why So Slow? The Advancement of Women,* edited by Virginia Valian. Cambridge, Mass.: MIT Press, 1998.

Vassar, Rena L. *Social History of American Education, Vol.1: Colonial Times to 1860.* Chicago: Rand McNally, 1965.

Viadero, Debra. "Study Shows Test Gains in 'Accelerated Schools.'" *Education Week,* 9 January 2002.

Von Praag, Henriette, Gerd Kempermann, and Fred Gage. "Running Increases Cell Proliferation." *Nature Neuroscience* 2, no. 3 (March 1999): 266–270.

Vygotsky, Lev. *Thought and Language.* Cambridge, Mass.: MIT Press, 1962.

———. *Mind in Society: The Development of Higher Psychological Processes.* Cambridge, Mass.: Harvard University Press, 1978.

Weinraub, Bernard. "'Beloved' Tests Racial Themes at Box Office." *New York Times,* 13 October 1998, 1(E), 8(E).

Wells, Cyndi. Director, Teacher Development, Core Knowledge Foundation, reported by e-mail, 28 February 2002.

Wells, Gordon. "Preschool Literacy-Related Activities and Success in School." In *Literacy, Language, and Learning,* edited by David R. Olson, Nancy Torrance, and Angela Hildyard. New York: Cambridge University Press, 1985.

Wertsch, James V. *Mind as Action.* New York: Oxford University Press, 1998.

Wilgoren, Jodi. "The Bell Rings but the Students Stay, and Stay." *New York Times,* 24 January 2000, 1 and 18(A).

Williams, Wendy M., and Stephen J. Ceci. "Are Americans Becoming More and More Alike? Trends in Race, Class and Ability Differences in Intelligence." *American Psychologist* 52, no. 11 (November 1997): 1226–1235.

Wilson, William Julius. "Work." *New York Times Magazine,* 18 August 1996, 26–52.

Wolfe, Alan. *One Nation, After All: How the Middle-Class Americans Really Think about God, Country, Family, Racism, Welfare, Immigration, Homosexuality, Work, the Right, the Left, and Each Other.* New York: Viking, 1998.

World Almanac 2000. Resources for Public Elementary and Secondary Schools, 1997–1998. Mahwah, N.J.: World Almanac Books, 2000.

World Almanac and Book of Facts 1999. Mahwah, N.J.: Primedia Reference, 1999.

World Development Indicators, 1999. World Bank, 1999, CD ROM.

Wyatt, Edward. "Investors See Room for Profit in the Demand for Education." *New York Times,* 4 November 1999, 1 and 27(A).

———. "Higher Scores Aren't Cure-All, School Run for Profit Learns." *New York Times,* 13 March 2001, 1(A) and 4(B).

Zernike, Kate. "Gap between Best and Worst Widens on U.S. Reading Test." *New York Times,* 7 April 2001, 1 and 9(A).

INDEX

ABOUT THE AUTHOR

Milton Schwebel, Ph.D., Columbia University, professor emeritus of psychology at Rutgers University, has taught children, parents, teachers, counselors, administrators, psychologists, and other school personnel. He has served as professor and associate dean at New York University's School of Education, professor and dean at Rutgers Graduate School of Education, and consultant to school districts, state and federal agencies in the United States, and ministries of education abroad. His publications include 175 articles in professional and scientific journals, book chapters, and 14 books, among them *Piaget in the Classroom, The Student Teacher's Handbook, Promoting Cognitive Growth over the Life Span, and Who Can Be Educated?* For years, he has been troubled by the incredible, if understandable, self-deception implicit in national policy that was supposed to cure the nation's educational ills, such as GOALS 2000 in the early nineties and the recent legislation by the Bush administration. This book is meant to expose that deception and open the way—and the debate—for realistic solutions.